The College Panda

ACT English

Hardcore ACT Prep

D1211068

To Henry and Albert

Thank You!

Thank you for purchasing this book. If you enjoy it, I ask that you please leave a review on amazon. It really helps support my work. I read all of them.

If you haven't already, make sure to sign up for The College Panda newsletter at http://thecollegepanda.com

You'll also receive exclusive tips and tricks, updates, college admissions advice, inspirational stories, and resources that go far beyond the useless College Board information packets. This information is not found on the blog or anywhere else.

Don't miss out on tips that could make the difference on the SAT and in college admissions. Sign up now.

Table of Contents

1   Preparing for a Perfect Score   6

2   The Art of Improvement   8

3   Test Breakdown & Test-taking Tips   14

4   Prepositional Phrases   18

5   Relative Clauses   20

6   Subject Verb Agreement   22

7   Run-ons   32

8   Modifiers   39

9   Fragments   45

10   Redundancy   49

11   Parallelism   54

12   Pronoun Reference   60

13   Tenses   67

14   Point of View   73

15   Commas   75

16   Comma Abuse   85

17   Apostrophes   91

18   Word Choice   95

19   Transitions   102

20   Transitions II   109

21   Sentence Improvement   118

22   Placement   126

23   Relevance & Purpose   150

24   Dashes & Colons   164

25   *You and Me* Errors   169

26	Idioms	171
27	Who vs. Whom	175
28	Adverbs vs. Adjectives	177
29	Comparatives vs. Superlatives	180
30	Review Cheat Sheet	182
31	Answers to the Exercises	188
32	Practice Test 1	221
33	Practice Test 2	241
34	Practice Test 3	261

1

Preparing for a Perfect Score

He who says he can and he who says he can't are both usually right. — Confucius

The SAT and the ACT are opportunities. Yes. You read that correctly. They're opportunities. The difference between a world class university and a mediocre one comes down largely to how we perform on one test. Now some critics hear that and say it's ridiculous to have that much riding on one test, but I see it as an opportunity. With one test, you have the opportunity to change everything. And not only that, you know exactly what the test is going to look like! You get to see multiple past exams and study for it all you want. In what classroom does your teacher ever allow you that much preparation? It's equivalent to the teacher saying,

Here's a stack of exams that will look exactly like my final.

Oh, and study for as long as you want, years even.

Oh, and feel free to retake the final several times.

It's an opportunity that goes to waste all too often because it isn't recognized as one. It's treated as a burden, something that must be done because colleges require it. If you start reframing the ACT as an opportunity, you're already ahead of all those students slumped in their seats.

I often wonder what separates the students who improve and those who don't, and I've come to the conclusion that it's about motivation and belief. Motivation is how bad a student wants it. Some students don't want it bad enough, and that's fair. Not everyone needs a perfect score. But if you say you want it, expect to work for it. Belief is about whether you think you can do it, and a lot of students think they can't. Belief itself takes work. You have to prove to yourself you can do it before you fully believe it. But once you reach that point, you're unstoppable.

When I was studying for the SATs, it took more than 20 practice tests and many dozens of hours reviewing those tests before I believed it, but once I did, I got a perfect score. The same applies to the ACT. I know the term "test prep" is a bit more appealing when it implies tips and tricks instead of repeatedly taking the test, but when you actually know the material, you don't need tips and tricks, which, by the way, can only take you so far. There are very few overnight successes. Sure, there are people who can just sit down with no preparation and ace the exam. A lot of them are lying, but there are definitely people like that out there. Forget about them. I'm not one of them and if you're reading this book, neither are you. But just because we aren't geniuses doesn't mean we can't get to a perfect score. There are thousands of students who improve their scores beyond what they ever expected at the start—I was one of them—and if I can do it, so can you.

How mentally tough are you?

Ok, so you're motivated and you believe it can happen. Now what? Well, scoring high on the ACT comes down to the same thing required to do well on anything else—consistent practice and review. It still boggles my mind how many students think that anything and everything else will help them improve except for honest, hard work. Flashcards, online study programs that track your progress, the new app, private tutors—all of these don't matter if you don't put in your own time. And when I say time, I mean alone time, one-on-one with the test, figuring out your mistakes before you ask somebody else for help. I often tell my students that as a teacher, I'm just an amplifier. I magnify the results of the work you put in. You put in a lot of work, you get big results. You put in no work, you get nothing. It doesn't matter that I was there.

So in addition to this book, which contains quite a bit of practice on its own, you should absolutely be doing official past exams. There are 5 in *The Real ACT, 3rd edition*, which I highly recommend. There are also 6-7 free practice tests as well as extra practice questions floating out there on the internet. Some are on the official ACT website and others might take some digging but they should be relatively easy to find (see the important note below). I highly suggest doing ALL the official past tests you can find. And if you haven't already, take a practice exam before reading this book. That way, you'll have a better context for what you'll be reading.

To quickly score yourself after taking a practice exam, check out the *ACT Score Calculator* at *thecollegepanda.com*.

For a complete understanding, this book is best read from beginning to end. That being said, each chapter was written to be independent of the others as much as possible. After all, you may already be proficient in some topics yet weak in others. If so, feel free to jump around, focusing on the chapters that are most relevant to your improvement.

Most chapters come with exercises. Do them. You won't master the material until you think through the questions yourself.

The philosophy of this book is not to sell you a bag of tricks, but to actually teach you the concepts so that all the practice and review you do is much more informed. It's my hope that after going through this book, you'll believe you can get a perfect score on the ACT.

IMPORTANT:

If you haven't already, make sure to sign up for The College Panda newsletter at http://thecollegepanda.com

You'll instantly gain access to a collection of all publicly released SAT and ACT past exams (the best preparation and practice).

You'll also receive exclusive tips and tricks, updates, college admissions advice, inspirational stories, and resources that go far beyond the useless College Board and ACT information packets. This information is not found on the blog or anywhere else.

Don't miss out on tips that could make the difference on the SAT/ACT and in college admissions. Sign up now.

2
The Art of Improvement

So you're at the point where you've taken a practice test or even a real sitting and you have a baseline score. It's not as high as you had hoped, but rarely is it ever. You want to improve. Now what?

Most of the questions I get look like this:

- *What's the study schedule I should follow if I want an 800 by the end of the summer?*

- *How should I get my score from a 500 to a 700?*

- *How long did it take you before you got an 800?*

Students always want the exact steps to X score in X months as if there was one magic formula out there. There isn't. These questions are hard to answer because everything depends on the student, but every time I get them, I can't help but reflect on the improvement process. I look back at my teaching experience and ask, *What distinguishes the students who improve a lot from the students who improve just a little? What did improvement look like for them and what was their timeline?*

Here are some of the things that I've realized:

1. Improvement is not linear

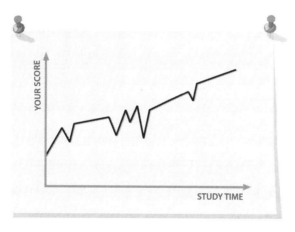

I wish I could say that if you do this and that for one month, you'll improve by 3 points. Do it for two months, and you'll improve by 6 points. Improvement doesn't work that way.

On your journey, you're going to have multiple ups and downs, breakthroughs and misconceptions that are going to set your score back temporarily until you learn to wield new knowledge to full effect.

Why is it an up-and-down process? Because as you try to apply new skills and test-taking techniques, you'll be pushed out of your comfort zone. See, most students are used to mediocrity. They're used to doing things a certain way even though it always gets them average results. The problem is that when they're introduced to a better way, it's new and uncomfortable and likely to lead to mistakes, so they resort to whatever they were doing before. The better way only starts paying off in the long term.

Think of playing a musical instrument or sport. Your teacher or coach teaches you a new technique. Chances are, you're going to feel awkward for a while. But once you get used to it, you're playing better than you did before. It's the same deal with testing. Students need time to integrate what they learn with how they were doing things before.

The biggest example of this is using your ear to answer grammar questions. Now on the easy questions, that works fine, but once you get to the harder questions, your ear will mislead you. How we talk in real life is not always grammatically correct.

So what happens is that you will do ok by using your ear. Then you'll learn a bunch of grammar rules and inevitably you'll misuse them. A lot of the questions that you were previously getting correct now don't seem so simple. In fact, you might experience even more doubt because your ear is in conflict with the rules that you've learned. The issue is not that you're getting worse, but it's that you don't have enough experience to apply the new knowledge in conjunction with what you already know.

The solution to this issue is simple: deliberate practice. Force yourself to think about what you've learned as you practice and accept that there will be an adjustment period. The mistakes you make will ultimately lead you to a more balanced way of thinking.

2. Improvement is a combination of teaching time and alone time

To learn something, obviously you have to take knowledge in from someone or something, whether it be a teacher, a video, or a book. But once you take that in, you've only become familiar with it. You haven't truly understood it. For true learning and understanding, you then have to mull it over in your head and put it to use, which is where the alone time comes in.

To score high, you'll have some lonely nights

Too often, I see students who do one but not the other. They take classes, but they rush through the homework robotically and never stop to think about what they're actually doing. Or they study by themselves, but they don't receive enough feedback or advice from outside resources. These are the students who repeatedly do practice tests to see how they score but never stop to think if they're doing them in the best way possible.

To improve fast, you need both. You must consult resources that force you to encounter new things and question the way you're currently doing them. You must also take time out for yourself to digest and apply what you're learning.

3. Improvement is a marathon, not a sprint

It is better to learn a tiny bit each and every single day than to learn a lot in one day and then stop until the next week. The very act of stopping halts progress and sets you back. Encountering material on a regular basis and making it a habit makes things stick in a way that cramming cannot.

Instead of planning one day marathon study sessions, consider daily chunks of study time that are short enough that you'll actually do it. Even if you cover less overall, it's better to do a little bit everyday than to cram it all on Sunday.

What has worked the best for me and my students is either a chapter of this book per day when learning, or one ACT English section per day when practicing. The study time does NOT have to be continuous. In fact, even if you're practicing on a section, feel free to take a break and come back to it. This leads me to my next point:

4. When you're in the learning phase, take practice tests UNTIMED.

This is one of the most important points here and paves the way for dramatic improvement. During the learning process, time pressure inhibits understanding and thinking. When you're trying to reach understanding, it's counterproductive to cut off the thinking process in order to get to the next question.

Of course, you'll need to start timing yourself at some point. Do so only once you feel you've reached a comfort level with the test and you've developed solid fundamentals in approaching the common question types.

You'll likely be at that point upon completing this book. Try taking the practice tests in this book untimed and then if you're ready, time yourself on official past exams.

5. Admitting to yourself why you really don't know something is crucial

The definition of insanity is doing the same thing over and over again and expecting different results.

— Albert Einstein

Since I've started teaching, a common pattern has been that students can't trace a mistake back to something they must learn or do—a plan of action that will prevent them from making the same mistake again. Always ask yourself, *What was it that I was missing that led to my mistake?* In other words, *If I had known X, I would have gotten this correct. What is X?*

On the reading section, for example, it can be as simple as not knowing a vocabulary word. Maybe it's not reading the tone of a paragraph correctly. Whatever it is, be completely honest with yourself. Most students get something wrong, check the right answer, and go *Eh, I should've gotten that right*, or *Whatever, that was a hard one anyway that I should've left blank.* That's the wrong approach. All too often, students just keep on making the same mistakes over and over but they never do anything about it.

So, what was it that you were missing? Every mistake tells you something, if you would only listen earnestly. Every mistake should lead to a plan of action so that when you complete that plan of action, you don't make the same mistake again.

For example, it could be knowledge based:

I got this one wrong because I wasn't aware of the ways the ACT test subject-verb agreement. I had no idea to even look for that.

OK, that's something I need to learn.

I need to read the subject-verb agreement chapter.

OR

I got this one wrong because I thought this word was a verb.

Why is this word not a verb? Anything tricky about it?

Oh, it ends in -ing. Do words that end in -ing (like running) count as verbs?

Let me look that up and review my parts of speech so that I can distinguish between nouns, verbs, adjectives, etc.

Now you might feel this sort of internal dialogue is silly, but this is exactly how top scorers think. They're adamant about figuring out why they got something wrong and how to correct it. It's an extremely self-reflective process that may be hard to do when you're first starting out. It helps to have a teacher pinpoint what you're missing, but finishing this book is definitely enough for you to start analyzing your weaknesses.

Self-reflection, not vanity, is the key to success

6. You don't know it until you've tested yourself on it

Never mistake familiarity with understanding. These are the students who read the review portion of the book but skip over the exercises because they feel they've understood everything.

We are hard wired with the psychological bias to overestimate our abilities. Testing yourself will bring you back down to earth and reveal subtleties that you couldn't see while passively absorbing the material.

7. Improvement doesn't happen if you're not leaning over the edge of your comfort zone

Scared?

So many students cry for help the moment they encounter something they haven't seen before. When a teacher or parent "carries" a student through every moment of uncertainty, it's a crutch. What happens is that students don't learn to think for themselves because they've gotten used to relying on outside help. And when they don't get that help, they just give up right away, which is a horrible habit to develop. I can't tell you how many times I've walked over to a student who asked for help only to find that he's already figured it out by himself in the few extra minutes he had to wait while I was helping someone else. It's gotten to the point where I always ask students to give a tough problem another shot before I come in for the rescue. It's amazing how many of them find a solution once they're told they can't give up right away.

On the ACT, you'll always have moments of uncertainty that you have to work through. Realize that you're not supposed to be comfortable during the improvement process. In order to get better, you're going to have to embrace the fact you'll be fumbling in the dark sometimes. Realize that if you bang your head against something long enough, you'll get to the answer more often than not. Give yourself time. Don't be a cry baby.

8. You're only done studying when you're getting your target score on practice exams

This is the only answer I give to the *How long does it take?* question. If you want a 34, review and practice until you can get a 34 on a practice exam. If you really want to ensure you get a 34, make sure you're scoring a 34 on a consistent basis. Perhaps you never get there because it's only two months until the test. If that's the case, you'll just have to do the best you can. There is no answer to the *How long should you prepare for?* question. You'll get your target score when you've gotten your target score.

Now what if you run out of practice tests? Redo them. There are a good 8-10 tests out there. By the time you finish the 10th test, you will have forgotten the first one. Trust me. You'll probably even make the same mistakes, which serves as great reinforcement for things you've already encountered but haven't truly ingrained in your mind. I speak from experience on this.

9. Keep a journal or some way to track your progress on practice tests

Successful students keep a record of what tests they've done and the mistakes they've made. Some of the biggest jumps in score come from reviewing the mistakes you made on a test you took 3 months ago and having things click when you see those old mistakes from a fresh perspective. You notice certain subtleties that you weren't able to grasp before.

Never underestimate your ability to forget. Simply looking back reinforces the lessons you've already learned and makes it less likely you'll repeat those mistakes again.

The fact that it's so personal–they were your mistakes, not someone else's—makes you take those lessons to heart.

Yes, it takes work, but if you take these principles to heart, I don't see how there's anyway you can't get a perfect score on the ACT.

3

Test Breakdown & Test-taking Tips

The ACT English section contains 75 questions to be completed in 45 minutes—that's 36 seconds per question. Not a lot of time. Here's the recommended way to approach this section:

- Always take note of the title of each passage, which can help you make sense of the passage as well as main idea questions.

- Read the whole passage, skimming the areas with no questions and slowing down in the areas that do. Of course, pause to answer the questions as you go along. With practice, you'll find there is more than enough time to finish. If you find you're going too slow, start jumping from question to question without reading any parts of the passage in between.

- Because the ACT does not penalize you for wrong answers, NEVER leave any questions blank.

- When it comes to answering questions in context, make sure you read the sentences above and below the spot in question.

- Circle your answers in the test booklet first. Bubble them in later.

Constantly switching back and forth between the question and the answer sheet throws your mental concentration off balance. You lose momentum and focus. It's like trying to do homework while texting with a friend.

You want to transition to the next question without fumbling with papers on your tiny desk.

I recommend doing one passage at a time in your test booklet and then bubbling those answers in a batch (every ~15 questions). That way, you save time by focusing on one activity at a time. You're also less likely to bubble in the wrong answer because your concentration isn't diverted back and forth.

At the end, you'll have a record of your answers circled in your test booklet, which you can then go back to and cross check with your answer sheet if a discrepancy arises.

Furthermore, some perfectionist students are obsessive about how they fill in the answer bubble. They needlessly waste time darkening the bubble more than they need to and erasing stray marks. You might be one of them. By bubbling in many answers at once, you're at least keeping that OCD behavior to a minimum.

Here are the topics that are tested, ranked by the number of questions that test them:

Topic	# of Questions
Sentence Fragments, Commas	12–20
Relevance and Purpose	10–20
Redundancy	4–8
Word Choice	3–8
Transitions	2–6
Apostrophes	2–5
Tense errors	2–5
Placement	2–5
Run-ons	1–6
Sentence and Paragraph Transitions	1–6
Sentence Improvement	1–6
Pronoun Reference	1–5
S-V Agreement	1–4
Idioms	1–4
Dashes and Colons	1–3
Modifiers	1–2
Parallelism	0–4
Shift in Point of View	0–2
Adverbs vs. Adjectives	0–2
Comparatives vs. Superlatives	0–2
Who vs. Whom	0–1
You and Me Errors	0–1

The topics in the table correspond to the chapters in this book. Some topics have been grouped together because they are commonly tested within the same question. If you're simply reviewing or you just picked up this book and don't have a lot of time, feel free to start with the most commonly tested topics. Otherwise, I recommend going through this book in order, as some topics will help you understand certain ones covered later.

When it comes to grading the test, here is a typical curve for the English section:

Raw Score	Scaled Score
75	36
73–74	35
71–72	34
70	33
69	32
67–68	31
66	30
65	29
63–64	28
62	27
60–61	26
58–59	25
56–57	24
54–55	23
52–53	22
49–51	21
46–48	20
43–45	19
41–42	18
39–40	17
36–38	16
33–35	15
30–32	14
28–29	13
26–27	12
24–25	11

Raw score refers to the number of questions answered correctly. To get a perfect 36, you'll probably have to answer every question correctly. Not all curves are the same. Check out the *ACT Score Calculator* on *thecollegepanda.com* for percentages on each score.

Anything above a 31 is generally considered to be a good score. If you're looking to apply to Ivy League schools or other top 20 universities, aim for a 34 or above.

Here are recent ACT statistics for some of the top universities:

University	25th %tile	75th %tile
Harvard	32	35
Yale	31	35
Princeton	31	35
University of Pennsylvania	30	34
Brown University	29	34
Stanford	31	34
MIT	33	35
Cornell	30	34
Dartmouth	30	34
Columbia	31	34
UC Berkeley	27	33
UCLA	25	33
Duke	30	34
University of Chicago	32	33
Northwestern	31	34
John Hopkins	30	34
Georgetown	29	33
Washington University in St. Louis	32	34
Rice	31	34
Vanderbilt	32	34
NYU	28	32

Percentile (%tile) refers to the percentage of students who performed below a certain score. So if the 25th percentile is 30, that means 25 percent of the students scored below a 30.

Prepositional Phrases

In this chapter, you'll learn about prepositions and prepositional phrases. These are all phrases that are **not essential** to the sentence they're in. While they may supply important details, sentences can stand alone grammatically without them.

Most prepositions are direction/position words. Here's a list of common prepositions:

aboard	about	above	across	after	against	along	amid	among	around
as to	**at**	before	behind	below	beneath	beside	between	beyond	**by**
circa	despite	down	due to	during	except	**for**	**from**	**in**	**into**
like	near	**of**	off	**on**	onto	out	over	past	since
through	**to**	toward	under	until	up	upon	**with**	within	without

Now do you have to memorize these? Certainly not. Just familiarize yourself, especially with the bolded ones. Some words are prepositions in some cases and something else in others. Just remember that a preposition almost always has a noun following it. Take a look at these two sentences:

1. Throughout the living room was the scent of fatty crabs that had expired weeks ago.

2. I put my sister on the diet after it worked so well for me.

The preposition + noun combinations are underlined. These preposition and noun combinations are called **prepositional phrases**.

Prepositional Phrase	=	Preposition	+	Noun	+	Any Attached Describing Phrase
	=	*of*	+	*fatty crabs*	+	*that had expired weeks ago*

If you think a word is a preposition and there's a noun following it, chances are it's a preposition. Even if it's not, don't worry about being 100% on which words are prepositions; the ACT doesn't test you on them directly. For example, *after it* is not a prepositional phrase in the second sentence because it's part of a larger phrase - *after it worked so well*. If the sentence were *After school, I put my sister on a diet*, then *After* would act as a preposition. But again, as long as you get the general idea, you'll be fine. This just helps you later when you learn about subject verb agreement.

Exercise: Cross out all prepositional phrases in the following sentences. Answers for this chapter start on page 188.

1. Hillary got into the boat for the short trip to Haiti.

2. If you do business with me, you'll never get the better end of the deal.

3. We'll need to see the receipts for the underwear you bought on Monday.

4. I drove by my house to check if the package from Amazon had arrived.

5. The eleven robbers broke into the casino vault with their perfectly executed plan.

6. Since the hypothesis of string theory, scientists have been back at the drawing board.

7. Everything that man creates carries within it the seeds of its own destruction.

8. Kelvin snuck out the door during the school assembly.

9. Within seconds of hearing about the trip to Antarctica, Charlotte packed shorts and sunglasses.

10. We found Teddy in a broken elevator at a rundown hotel in Thailand.

5

Relative Clauses

Many chapters in this book redefine or reexplain previous grammar terms so that those jumping from chapter to chapter still get a good sense of what's going on. But to get the full value out of this book, it's best that we learn a few basic things about sentences and their structures before moving on. We start by learning to identify the non-essential parts of a sentence, the ones that aren't needed for a sentence to be complete.

Take the following sentence:

The tiger ate my aunt earlier today.

Let's add something:

The tiger <u>that was hungry</u> ate my aunt earlier today.

By adding the underlined phrase to the sentence, we've described the tiger in more detail. These phrases are called **relative clauses** because they start with a relative pronoun - *who, whom, whose, which,* or *that*. While some relative clauses can be essential to the meaning of a sentence, they are never essential to the sentence being a complete sentence. In other words, they aren't important grammatically even though the resulting sentence can sound awkward when they are removed.

Let's add some more phrases:

<u>After escaping</u>, the tiger that was hungry ate my aunt, <u>who was nice and juicy</u>, earlier today.

Now these additional phrases are called **comma phrases** because they're set off by a pair of commas. Note that the second underlined phrase is also a relative clause. Some relative clauses require commas and some don't—we'll delve into those rules in a future chapter. Either way, comma phrases and relative clauses are not essential to the sentences they're in.

A crucial part of doing well on the ACT English section is knowing how to strip away all these secondary phrases to get back to the essence of the sentence:

The tiger ate my aunt earlier today.

None of the underlined phrases we added above can stand alone as complete sentences themselves. Yes, they add valuable details, but at the end of the day, what's left is the sentence that CAN stand alone by itself, the main idea. To trick you, the ACT will constantly throw long boring phrases at you left and right like a boxer jabbing at you with one hand to disguise the big punch he's planning with the other. Don't be fooled. Learn to strip away the unnecessary phrases and you'll get through questions more quickly and accurately. In future chapters, you'll learn to deconstruct other parts of sentences and develop a way of reading them that will help you get directly to the answer.

Exercise: Cross out all the comma phrases and relative clauses. Make sure that what's left is still a grammatically complete sentence. The first one is done for you. Answers for this chapter start on page 189.

1. ~~Although it may better mankind~~, some critics of animal testing, ~~which is sometimes harmful to the animals~~, claim it is cruel and inhumane.

2. After running the Boston marathon, Jack Kunis drank all the water that was left in his bottle and fell to his knees.

3. The lost ship and its treasure that had fallen to the bottom of the ocean were never found again.

4. Frank, in addition to his cousins, suffers from a condition known as hyperthymestic syndrome, which prevents one from ever forgetting anything.

5. Starting at the age of 10, Mrs. Smith kept a daily diary, which allowed her to recall the happy memories in life.

6. For years the chairman remained anonymous, referred to only by initials even within his inner circles.

7. Students whose grades are low will have to report to me, the principal of the school.

8. Every detail about every day since 1976, ranging from the time she got up to what she ate, has forever ingrained itself into her mind.

9. Ever since it allowed internet games, which were previously blocked, the library has been the place everybody wants to be nowadays.

10. With such sadness occupying her thoughts, Erika, a poor single mother of two, struggles to sleep at night, even when the babies themselves are fast asleep.

11. Farmers who want a good yield should use fertilizers that enrich the soil with nutrients.

12. Having worked so hard with blood, sweat, and tears, I long for the day I can finally say the ACTs are over.

13. Culture shock, in some cases, can be severe enough to trigger mental breakdowns.

14. Mastery of martial arts requires a dedication that many do not have.

15. Mrs. Daughtry, a 74-year old married housewife recently discharged from a local hospital after her first psychiatric admission, came to our facility for a second opinion, one that she hoped would be different.

6 Subject Verb Agreement

You know how you have to conjugate the verb to match the subject in foreign languages? We have the same thing in English, and it can get tricky even though the simple cases seem so natural and obvious to us:

Example 1

Wrong:	You **is** smart.
Correct:	You **are** smart.

Example 2

Wrong:	Everyday the alarm clock goes off and we **wakes** up to confront our lives.
Correct:	Everyday the alarm clock goes off and we **wake** up to confront our lives.

The subject is a noun (person, place, or thing) that is the "doer" or "main feature" in the sentence. A verb is an action word. Think about the simple sentences above and how awkward it would be to have verbs that don't agree with the subject. You don't even have to know what the subject and verb of each sentence is to know that it's awkward. Now the ACT won't make it that easy on you; they'll intentionally try to trick your ear. Let's do an example:

Investigations into the scandal (*shows/show*) a lot more than we want to know.

To pick the right verb, we must first find the subject. Let's start by applying what we learned in a previous chapter and cross out the prepositional phrases:

Investigations ~~into the scandal~~ (*shows/show*) a lot more than we want to know.

What's left is the subject—investigations! Now the second step is to ask yourself whether *investigations* is singular or plural. Well, it's plural because of the *s*, meaning there's more than one. Therefore, we need the plural verb *show*. And that's the whole process! Cross out the prepositional phrases and you'll be able to pick the subject from the nouns that are left. It's usually the remaining noun closest to the verb.

If you're ever unsure of whether a verb such as *show* is singular or plural, test it by putting *he* and *they* in front and then asking yourself which sounds more correct:

He show... OR *They show...*

Hopefully, *They show...* sounds more correct to you, which means *show* is the plural form (since *they* is obviously plural).

Let's try some more difficult ones. Note that in the following example, we can cross out both a prepositional phrase and a comma phrase.

Example 3

Question:	Films by Miyazaki and Itami, including Miyazaki's *Spirited Away*, (excites/excite) the imagination.
Step 1:	Cross out the prepositional phrases/comma phrases/relative clauses: Films ~~by Miyazaki and Itami, including Miyazaki's Spirited Away~~, (excites/excite) the imagination.
Step 2:	What is the subject? *Films*
Step 3:	Is *Films* singular or plural? Plural.
Answer:	Films by Miyazaki and Itami, including Miyazaki's *Spirited Away*, **excite** the imagination.

Example 4

Question:	Her jewelry, in addition to her pokemon cards, (was/were) stolen by the robber.
Step 1:	Cross out the prepositional phrases/comma phrases/relative clauses: Her jewelry, ~~in addition to her pokemon cards~~, (was/were) stolen ~~by the robber~~.
Step 2:	What is the subject? *Her jewelry*
Step 3:	Is *Her jewelry* singular or plural? Singular.
Answer:	Her jewelry, in addition to her pokemon cards, **was** stolen by the robber.

You might think that the verb should be plural because the sentence mentions both jewelry and cards, but because of the comma phrase, the subject is just the jewelry.

Example 5

Question:	Beside the bins, where one could smell the stench of rotten eggs, (was/were) a pack of philosophy majors gathering cans for recycling.
Step 1:	Cross out the prepositional phrases/comma phrases/relative clauses: ~~Beside the bins, where one could smell the stench of rotten eggs~~, (was/were) a pack ~~of philosophy majors gathering cans for recycling~~.
Step 2:	What is the subject? *a pack*
Step 3:	Is *a pack* singular or plural? Singular.
Answer:	Beside the bins, where one could smell the stench of rotten eggs, **was** a pack of philosophy majors gathering cans for recycling.

Again, make sure you can identify that *was* is singular whereas *were* is plural. Everyone uses the correct form in simple conversation, but some students have trouble identifying the correct form in a grammar test setting.

Example 6

Question:	Inside heaven's kingdom (*rests/rest*) Charlie and his angels.
Step 1:	Cross out the prepositional phrases/comma phrases/relative clauses: ~~Inside heaven's kingdom~~ (*rests/rest*) Charlie and his angels.
Step 2:	What is the subject? *Charlie and his angels*
Step 3:	Is *Charlie and his angels* singular or plural? Plural.
Answer:	Inside heaven's kingdom **rest** Charlie and his angels.

These last two examples show that the subject can appear after the verb, something the ACT loves to do to trip students up.

Another question variation you'll come across deals with helping verbs, which are necessary to form certain tenses. Examples of helping verbs are bolded below:

has seen
was forgotten
is watching
have been

When you see these verb forms, it is the helping verb that must agree with the subject.

Example 7

Question:	The few ideas that I've come up with last night (*has/have*) given my team enough to work with.
Step 1:	Cross out the prepositional phrases/comma phrases/relative clauses: The few ideas ~~that I've come up with last night~~ (*has/have*) given my team enough to work with.
Step 2:	What is the subject? *The few ideas*
Step 3:	Is *The few ideas* singular or plural? Plural.
Correct:	The few ideas that I've come up with last night **have** given my team enough to work with.

Example 8

Question:	The forks and knives are in the kitchen, and the jar with the thai peanut sauce (*has/have*) been sitting in the refrigerator.
Step 1:	Cross out the prepositional phrases/comma phrases/relative clauses: The forks and knives are in the kitchen, and the jar ~~with the thai peanut sauce~~ (*has/have*) been sitting in the refrigerator.
Step 2:	What is the subject? *the jar*
Step 3:	Is *the jar* singular or plural? Singular.
Answer:	The forks and knives are in the kitchen, and the jar with the thai peanut sauce **has** been sitting in the refrigerator.

Example 9

Question:	The players on our all-star tennis team (*is/are*) taken on luxury cruises every year.
Step 1:	Cross out the prepositional phrases/comma phrases/relative clauses: The players ~~on our all-star tennis team~~ (*is/are*) taken on luxury cruises every year.
Step 2:	What is the subject? *The players*
Step 3:	Is *The players* singular or plural? Plural.
Answer:	The players on our all-star tennis team **are** taken on luxury cruises every year.

Another question variation you might see is one in which the verb is in a phrase or clause you would normally cross out. For example,

I visited my aunt, who (*is/are*) a panda caretaker, earlier today.

Note that the underlined portion is a comma phrase. To find the subject if the verb is located in a phrase or clause like the one above, just ask yourself what it's describing. In this case, the phrase is obviously describing *my aunt*, which is singular. Therefore, we need the singular verb *is*.

I visited my **aunt**, who **is** a panda caretaker, earlier today.

Example 10

Question:	Where are the cookies that (*was/were*) in the cookie jar?
Answer:	Where are the cookies that **were** in the cookie jar?

In Example 10, we have a relative clause that describes *cookies*, which is plural.

Example 11

Question:	I have no interest in luxury products, which (*caters/cater*) only to the wealthy.
Answer:	I have no interest in luxury products, which **cater** only to the wealthy.

Now let's walk through a really tricky example that combines everything we've learned so far in this chapter:

> Mastery of magic tricks that truly (*surprises/surprise*) the audience (*requires/require*) lots of time.

Here, we have to figure out the subjects for two verbs. Cross out the prepositional phrases and relative clause:

> Mastery ~~of magic tricks that truly (*surprises/surprise*) the audience~~ (*requires/require*) lots ~~of time~~.

Now it's easy to see that *mastery* is the main subject of the sentence. *Mastery* is singular so we need the singular verb *requires*. After all, it's the *mastery* that *requires* a lot of time. But let's get back to the first verb, which is crossed out within the relative clause, and ask ourselves what that relative clause is describing. What is truly surprising the audience? Magic tricks! *Magic tricks* is plural so we need the plural verb *surprise*.

> Mastery of magic tricks that truly **surprise** the audience **requires** lots of time.

Now, a few more rules you should know:

Example 12

Question:	*The Simpsons* (*is/are*) the longest running American sitcom.
Answer:	*The Simpsons* **is** the longest running American sitcom.
Rule:	Names of books, TV shows, bands, and movies are all singular.

Example 13

Question:	Charles and Kate (*was/were*) at the ball last night.
Answer:	Charles and Kate **were** at the ball last night.
Rule:	Subjects joined by *and* are always plural.

Example 14

Question:	Everybody (*loves/love*) Raymond.
Answer:	Everybody **loves** Raymond.
Rule:	*Everybody, everything, every, anybody, anyone, no one* are all singular subjects.

Example 15

Questions:	Each of the candidates (*has/have*) two minutes to respond. Neither of the candidates (*wants/want*) to respond.
Answers:	Each of the candidates **has** two minutes to respond. Neither of the candidates **wants** to respond.
Rule:	*Each, neither,* and *either* are all singular subjects.

Before we go to the exercises, you probably have quite a few grammar rules swirling around in your head. Let's go over a few common errors that students make when they start thinking about subjects and verbs. Take a look at the following sentence:

He likes to sway to R&B music instead of rocking to AC/DC.

On the ACT, you must be able to identify which words are verbs before you can check for their subjects. Some students mistakenly think that *to sway* and *rocking* are verbs in that sentence. However, *to sway* is called an **infinitive** (*to be, to hate, to run,...*) and *rocking* is called a **gerund** (*running, cooking, exploding,...*). You've probably heard of infinitives in French or Spanish class, where it's the root form of a verb before you conjugate it. It's the same in English. Infinitives and gerunds are **not verbs so there's no need to check for subject-verb agreement**. The only actual verb in this example is *likes*. Again, gerunds and infinitives are **never verbs**. Don't waste time checking for their subjects.

Lastly, the ACT loves to throw in more than one verb in the same sentence. That way, one of the verbs can be buried deeper into the sentence to fool your ear. In these questions, split the sentence into two and make sure both verbs agree.

Example 16

Wrong:	John and Harry studied computer science and was recruited by Google to develop new services.
Sentence 1:	John and Harry studied computer science. *Correct.*
Sentence 2:	John and Harry was recruited by Google to develop new services. *Wrong.*
Correct:	John and Harry studied computer science and **were** recruited by Google to develop new services.

Example 17

Wrong:	Poisonous traps that attracts and then kills off rats are spread throughout this office.
Sentence 1:	Poisonous traps that attracts rats are spread throughout this office. *Wrong.*
Sentence 2:	Poisonous traps that then kills off rats are spread throughout this office. *Wrong.*
Correct:	Poisonous traps that **attract** and then **kill** off rats are spread throughout this office.

Example 18

Wrong:	I was walking down the street and were chatting with my friend about his day.
Sentence 1:	I was walking down the street. *Correct.*
Sentence 2:	I were chatting with my friend about his day. *Wrong.*
Correct:	I was walking down the street and **(was)** chatting with my friend about his day.

In Example 18, the second *was* is unnecessary because the first *was* serves as a helping verb for both *walking* and *chatting*. If we stripped out all the details of the sentence, it would read, *I was walking and chatting...*, which is a grammatically fine sentence.

Exercise 1: As a basic warm-up, fill in the right singular and plural verb forms for each of the following verbs. Answers for this chapter start on page 190.

		To Be	To Go	To Have	To Win	To Kiss
Present Tense	He					
	They					
Past Tense	He					
	They					

Exercise 2: Choose the correct verb. Answers for this chapter start on page 190.

1. Participants in the charity organization (*was/were*) angry when no one donated.

2. The habit of hugging your pillow while sleeping (*indicates/indicate*) that you miss someone.

3. Elderly criminals in Florida sometimes (*leads/lead*) the police on chases at speeds of 10 to 15 mph.

4. Bonnie and her boyfriend Clyde (*likes/like*) to jump into ponds to avoid the cops, often forgetting that they can't swim.

5. Every Bentley, Lamborghini, and Porsche (*is/are*) owned by Volkswagen.

6. Propaganda that's played off as the truth (*has/have*) been used throughout history to persuade the masses.

7. Forcing yourself to forget the pain someone else has caused you only (*hurts/hurt*) you more.

8. One of the skills I would like to learn (*is/are*) the ability to talk while inhaling through the nose.

9. Some of the superpowers I dream of having (*includes/include*) summoning jack o' lanterns on people's lawns during Halloween and making people burst into the Gangnam style dance.

10. Each iPhone 5 (*costs/cost*) Apple $168 and (*costs/cost*) us $699.

11. Each of the three little pigs (*was/were*) afraid of the big bad wolf.

12. According to the phonebook, the number of Americans named Herp Derp (*is/are*) four.

13. A good cook rinses the dishes and (*repeats/repeat*) the same recipes to perfection.

14. Please let me know if the group (*stumbles/stumble*) upon or (*manages/manage*) to find the train station.

15. A number of people (*has/have*) hyperthymesia, a condition that (*allows/allow*) them to remember every detail of their lives.

16. There (*was/were*) an awkward silence when Mike's date told him she hadn't showered in a month.

17. A flock of birds and a bear (*has/have*) been captured in the field.

18. There (*is/are*) three types of people in this world: those who can count and those who can't.

19. There (*is/are*) stashed below the frigid depths of the arctic a magnificent treasure that no one has ever been able to recover.

20. There (*is/are*) in the works of Emerson an underlying tone of quiet appreciation.

21. *Snow White and the Seven Dwarves* (*was/were*) purportedly based on cocaine; the seven dwarves were each side effects of the drug.

22. Harry, along with Ron and Hermione, (*attends/attend*) Hogwarts School of Wizardry.

23. Frodo, as well as Merry and Pippin, (*fights/fight*) to protect the one ring of power.

24. This picture book on the art of nudity in the modern age (*is/are*) a thought-provoking read.

25. The extent of our universe and those beyond constantly (*amazes/amaze*) me.

26. We found out that his mother, as well as his friends, (*was/were*) covering for Mike's crime.

27. Aliens from another planet (*has/have*) come here to kill us all.

28. The pigs you will be dissecting in this class (*is/are*) available as take-home dinners afterwards.

29. Human brain cells, the universe, and the internet all (*has/have*) similar structures.

30. Each team made up of one girl and one boy (*has/have*) to reenact a scene from Romeo and Juliet.

31. Speaking more than one language (*makes/make*) the brain more flexible and agile.

32. Getting to stuff my face silly with delicious food (*is/are*) the best part of being an obese food critic.

33. When (*was/were*) the cowboy and the Indians last here?

34. The class bully laughs at and then (*interferes/interfere*) with those trying to get work done.

35. Brendan and Brianna are out of money and (*has/have*) used up all possible guesses.

36. Paris and Nicole grew up rich and (*was/were*) sheltered all throughout life.

37. What (*does/do*) that fact have to do with anything we just talked about?

38. He sets his alarm but, when the morning comes, (*fails/fail*) to wake up.

39. Marcie and Michael exercise everyday and, in doing so, (*improves/improve*) their stamina.

40. Alice, in addition to a scarecrow, a tin man, and a lion, (*tries/try*) to find the Wizard of Oz.

41. A jar of hearts (*is/are*) on the counter.

42. Several trucks and an oil tanker near the highway exit (*was/were*) flipped on their sides.

43. Dreams within a dream that (*is/are*) spliced and diced up inside another dream (*confuses/confuse*) me.

44. A herd of cows and a slow moving tortoise (*is/are*) relaxing at the beach.

45. The lines for the elevator that normally (*carries/carry*) just five passengers (*was/were*) reinstated because the crowd of fat commuters (*was/were*) too heavy for it.

46. The diner near the dorms which (*houses/house*) the students (*serves/serve*) breakfast all day.

47. The widely recognized red coloring of stop signs everywhere (*alerts/alert*) people who can't even read them to stop.

Exercise 3: Answers for this chapter start on page 190.

The Writer's Life

On every author's bookshelf (*is/are*) dusty and
___
1
worn out reference books. In every desk drawer
(*sits/sit*) a stack of papers waiting to be edited. A
___
2
large case of pens, most of which are blue, red, or
black, (*is/are*) close to falling off the desk. The life of
___
3
a writer is a lonely yet hectic existence.

The act of putting words on paper and editing them (*is/are*) mentally draining. The notion
___
4
that because words come naturally to us when
we're speaking, they should also come easily when
we're writing, (*misrepresents/misrepresent*) the strug-
___
5
gles that every author faces. Putting words together
in a logical and coherent way is different from having a conversation, which has the benefit of context.
If the reader does not understand something, the
author does not have the luxury of explaining it another way.

In addition, writers do more than just write.
Research and investigation into their subject matter (*plays/play*) a crucial role in good writing. Af-
___
6
ter all, perfect grammar and well-crafted sentences
about a vague topic written off the top of one's head

(*does/do*) not make for a good read. Relevant books
___
7
must be read and interviews must be conducted before an author feels informed enough to write something substantial.

Most writers learn their craft in school.
A strong liberal arts education that (*encom-
___
8
passes/encompass*) grammar, style, structure, and
___
8
prose (*fosters/foster*) great writing. Upon gradua-
___
9
tion, writers must develop and apply all those skills
to the research, writing, and editing phases of any
given project. Draft after draft, they have to re-
work and tweak what they've already done. This
dedication to the craft and attention to detail that
(*rivals/rival*) that of a surgeon (*requires/require*) disci-
___   ___
10   11
pline and work ethic. Authors such as James Joyce
(*has/have*) equated writing to torture. Only when all
___
12
the pages in the book are written (*does/do*) writers
___
13
feel the true joy of writing.

Nevertheless, because many people think that
writing is subjective and that there (*is/are*) no right
___
14
or wrong answers, the belief that writers have it
easy, as well as all its underlying misconceptions,
(*persists/persist*).
___
15

Run-ons

Most students think they know what a run-on is based on their 6th grade English class. So when I ask students whether the following is a run-on sentence, almost all students say yes:

I took the ACT's, and I scored a 36, and I applied to MIT, and I got in!

Now this sentence may be long, wordy, and awkward, but the sentence is actually NOT a run-on sentence—it's grammatically correct. The reason it's correct is the use of the word *and*, which connects all the parts together.

I took the ACT's, I scored a 36, I applied to MIT, I got in!

Now this IS a run-on sentence because several **complete sentences are being mashed together with just commas**.

The basic form of a run-on is this:

> complete sentence   ,   complete sentence

A run-on also occurs when there is nothing between the two complete sentences:

> complete sentence   complete sentence

There are four main ways to fix a run-on. Let's go over them one by one with a simple example:

He was hungry, he bought a Chipotle burrito.

Two complete sentences connected only by a comma—definitely a run-on.

1. Use periods:

> complete sentence. complete sentence.
>
> He was hungry. He bought a burrito.

2. Use a conjunction

> complete sentence, *conjunction* complete sentence.
>
> He was hungry, **so** he bought a burrito.

Note that a comma, if necessary, comes **before** the conjunction (we'll learn more about commas in a future chapter). Most students have learned the acronym FANBOYS to memorize the list of conjunctions:

For   And   Nor   But   Or   Yet   So

Memorize this list because it's super important.

Now here's a really important point: if two sentences are being connected by a word that's not from the FANBOYS list, IT'S STILL A RUN-ON. This is how the ACT tricks you:

He was hungry, **therefore**, he bought a Chipotle burrito.

This sentence is wrong because *therefore* is not a conjunction—it's not a member of FANBOYS. Other words the ACT might use include *however, moreover, in addition to, nevertheless,* and *furthermore.* These words are transition words pretending to be conjunctions. The FANBOYS conjunctions are special.

3. Use the semicolon ;

> complete sentence; complete sentence.
>
> He was hungry; he bought a burrito.

Semicolons are the simplest way to edit run-ons, but in everyday speaking and writing, conjunctions are more common because they better express how the two connected sentences are related. The ACT will test you on both ways. Note that this is also correct:

He was hungry; therefore, he bought a Chipotle burrito.

But this one is INCORRECT:

He was hungry; and he bought a Chipotle burrito.

Do not use both a conjunction and a semicolon. **Semicolons require complete sentences on either side.** By putting in a conjunction, the second part is no longer a complete sentence.

4. Change the wording so that you no longer have two complete sentences

> incomplete sentence, complete sentence.
>
> Because he was hungry, he bought a burrito.

By inserting *because* in front, the first half is no longer a complete sentence, and we're no longer mashing two complete sentences together. As a result, we don't need anything more than the comma. *Because he was hungry* is called a **dependent clause—it doesn't make sense by itself.** An **independent clause** is just another term for a complete sentence or thought like *he bought a Chipotle burrito.* **It makes sense by itself.** A dependent clause with an independent clause is not a run-on and therefore does not require a conjunction or a semicolon.

On the ACT, you will have answer choices to choose from. Therefore, it's more important to be able to identify run-ons than to be able to reword them.

Example 1

Wrong:	You should memorize the list of conjunctions, it will help immensely on the ACT.
Correct:	You should memorize the list of conjunctions, for it will help immensely on the ACT.
Correct:	You should memorize the list of conjunctions; it will help immensely on the ACT.
Correct:	You should memorize the list of conjunctions because it will help immensely on the ACT.

As a side note, the conjunction *for* is rarely used in conversation.

Example 2

Wrong:	I love the game of basketball, however, I don't play it myself.
Correct:	I love the game of basketball, but I don't play it myself.
Correct:	I love the game of basketball; however, I don't play it myself.
Correct:	I love the game of basketball, even though I don't play it myself.

After reading the third correct version, you might be wondering why *even though* is correct and *however* is incorrect. What's the difference? Well, with *however*, you still have two independent clauses on either side of the comma. With *even though*, you have an independent clause with a dependent clause, which is not a run-on:

Wrong: I love the game of basketball, however, I don't play it myself.
          Independent clause   *Independent clause*

Fine: I love the game of basketball, even though I don't play it myself.
          Independent clause   *Dependent clause*

Example 3

Wrong:	Nightmares keep me awake at night; yet I oddly feel energized in the morning.
Correct:	Nightmares keep me awake at night; however, I oddly feel energized in the morning.
Correct:	Nightmares keep me awake at night, yet I oddly feel energized in the morning.
Correct:	Although nightmares keep me awake at night, I oddly feel energized in the morning.

Again, don't use semicolons and conjunctions (like *yet* in this example) together. Semicolons require two complete sentences on either side.

Example 4

Wrong:	One of my idols is Michael Jackson, he was one of the best performers of his time.
Correct:	One of my idols is Michael Jackson, who was one of the best performers of his time.
Correct:	One of my idols is Michael Jackson, one of the best performers of his time.

One of the ways you can reword a run-on (method 4) is to use relative clauses and comma phrases as in Example 4.

Example 5

Wrong:	When I try to go to sleep, nightmares keep me awake at night, after brushing my teeth, I oddly feel energized in the morning.
Correct:	When I try to go to sleep, nightmares keep me awake at night, yet after brushing my teeth, I oddly feel energized in the morning.
Correct:	When I try to go to sleep, nightmares keep me awake at night; after brushing my teeth, however, I oddly feel energized in the morning.

Despite all the clauses in example 4, we have two complete thoughts being mashed together:

1. When I try to go to sleep, nightmares keep me awake at night.
2. After brushing my teeth, I oddly feel energized in the morning.

The ACT will try to trick you in this way by putting in a lot of relative clauses and comma phrases to keep you from realizing something's a run-on. When that happens, read carefully and look for where a complete thought ends and where another one begins.

Reminder 1

If there's already a conjunction or if we're not connecting two complete sentences in the first place, then there's NO error. For example:

Although the plan was perfect, the clumsy criminals, who by now would have been millionaires, are locked in jail cells, slowly waiting out their sentences.

Looking at where the commas are, at no point are we trying to combine two complete sentences on either side, so the sentence is perfectly fine.

Reminder 2

Never use more than one way of correcting a run-on within the same sentence. Don't use a semicolon with a conjunction. Don't use a conjunction and also rephrase something to be an incomplete sentence, etc. The following examples are all incorrect:

- Jerry ran away last summer; and I haven't seen him since.
- Even though the coffee in Rome is amazing, but I still like Starbucks coffee more.
- Every year my brother visits New York City; which he considers the greatest city in the world.
- Henry tripped over the rock, and falling head first into the water.
- Running through the finish line, and Donna leaped for joy.

Exercise 1: Identify whether the sentence is a run-on (some may be correct) and if so, where it occurs. The first one is done for you. Answers for this chapter start on page 193.

1. A caller from Memorial Park reported a man beating his head against a wall, he was heading to work.
   ⇑

2. A completely naked long-haired brunette in her 20s was pumping gas into a Hummer on the corner of Beachmont, no one got a good look at the vehicle's license plate.

3. In New York, the train system is difficult to learn, however, the food is fantastic and diverse.

4. When a man became so upset with the lack of parking enforcement in his town, he reported his own parking violation, and the police showed up to subdue him with a stun gun, apparently he became combative and screamed at the officers that they weren't doing their job.

5. There's a big chance that if you're 16 or older, you've already met the person you'll marry.

6. Wanting to be sure that what he had been sold was real weed, Phillip Donahue approached two officers and asked them to test his pipe, as a result, he was arrested and charged with drug possession.

7. Jimmy hid in the dumpster when Mr. Clark, his boss, walked by, unfortunately, Mr. Clark had to throw something away and saw him crouching there, forcing Jimmy to confess that he actually lived there.

8. Zoe likes to ace her tests but resents it when her classmates ask her how much she studied, sometimes Zoe will just say that she didn't study at all when in fact she had stayed up all night.

9. At the time, discovering quantum physics looked like a waste of time and money, but it is now the foundation of all modern technology, thus, when people claim that math and science are of no relevance, it drives Dr. Tyson into a deep rage.

10. Playing them day and night, Shawn and his video games were inseparable, however, once he got a girlfriend, everything changed.

11. Despite his friends' tearful pleas for forgiveness, Jonathan maintained a deep grudge against everyone who had ever asked for a pencil and never returned it, an act he considered a crime against humanity.

12. Suddenly realizing the movie was too scary for her, Maya panicked and looked at her watch, there was still 20 minutes left, enough time to still make her uneasy about what was to come.

13. The salesman, aware that he was going to lose a sale if he didn't make something up, claimed that the laptop could not be customizable and that the only options were in the store.

14. As a young girl, Lindsay was praised as a talented and burgeoning actress, as an adult, she fell into the dark world of sex, drugs, and alcohol and would never reclaim her former glory.

15. Omega-3 fish oil provides essential fatty acids for your nutritional health, furthermore, it soothes back pain and muscle aches.

16. Last Saturday, Peter Parker was bit by a spider, after that incident, he would never be the same again.

Exercise 2: Answers for this chapter start on page 193.

Sir John Alexander Macdonald

Sir John Alexander Macdonald, the first Prime Minister of Canada, is widely praised as a great Canadian hero. <u>We didn't have</u> his determination
₁
and tenacity, our great country would not be the same as it is today.

<u>Born</u> in Scotland on January 11, 1815, John im-
₂
migrated to the New Country with his parents at a very young age. The exact year of his arrival is unknown. He soon began working under a local lawyer in <u>Kingston, his mentor</u> died before he
₃
could complete his apprenticeship. Young Macdonald was not quite old enough to take over the <u>prac-</u>
₄
<u>tice, however,</u> this didn't stop the ambitious lad. He
₄
immediately opened his own practice.

<u>He had</u> several high profile cases, John quickly
₅
became a prominent figure in legal venues. This notoriety prompted the young man to run for a legislative seat in the House of <u>Commons, he</u> won in
₆
1844.

Just like John, the country was struggling to make a mark on the <u>world, in 1877,</u> Mr. Macdonald
₇
was awarded the position of Premier of the United Province of Canada.

1. **A.** NO CHANGE
   B. Without
   C. We lacked
   D. Because

2. **A.** NO CHANGE
   B. He was born;
   C. He was born
   D. Born,

3. **A.** NO CHANGE
   B. Kingston, however, his mentor
   C. Kingston; but his mentor
   D. Kingston, but his mentor

4. **A.** NO CHANGE
   B. practice, so
   C. practice; however,
   D. practice,

5. **A.** NO CHANGE
   B. After,
   C. After
   D. He was in

6. **A.** NO CHANGE
   B. Commons,
   C. Commons; which he
   D. Commons, which he

7. **A.** NO CHANGE
   B. world. In 1877,
   C. world, however, in 1877,
   D. world, moreover, in 1877,

However, at this point Canada was far from being

united, much less a real province.
‾‾‾‾‾‾‾‾‾‾‾‾‾‾
        8

The political state was in shambles. The efforts

of the King of England to populate the country was

a dismal failure the people in the west had no in-
         ‾‾‾‾‾‾‾‾‾‾‾‾‾‾
              9

terest at all in joining what politicians were call-

ing "Canada." None of this deterred John's ambi-

tion of creating the country of his dreams. He de-

veloped the Canadian Pacific Railway and created

the Northwest Mounted Police; convincing British
                        ‾‾‾‾‾‾‾‾‾‾‾‾‾‾‾‾‾‾
                               10

Columbia, Manitoba, and Prince Edward Island to

join the confederation.

Even at the age of 60, Macdonald did not slow

down one bit, in 1885, he engineered the first Na-
     ‾‾‾‾‾‾‾‾‾‾‾‾‾‾
           11

tional Park in Alberta. Believing that he could at-

tract the attention of tourists to Canada, so he gath-
                                  ‾‾‾‾‾‾‾‾‾‾‾
                                      12

ered the country's best architects and construction

workers to design one of the world's most beautiful

destinations.

Sir John A. Macdonald served as the Prime

Minister of Canada from 1867 to 1873 and then

again from 1878 to 1891. He was given the honor of

knighthood for his dedication to crown and coun-
                                              ‾‾‾‾
                                              13

try, people today still travel on the Macdonald-
‾‾‾‾‾‾‾‾‾‾‾
    13

Cartier highway every day!

8. **A.** NO CHANGE
   B. united, and much less
   C. united; much less
   D. united, though much less

9. **A.** NO CHANGE
   B. failure. The people
   C. failure; and the people
   D. failure, the people

10. **A.** NO CHANGE
    B. Police convincing
    C. Police by convincing
    D. Police, he convinced

11. **A.** NO CHANGE
    B. one bit, therefore, in 1885,
    C. one bit; in 1885,
    D. one bit; and in 1885,

12. **A.** NO CHANGE
    B. Canada,
    C. Canada;
    D. Canada, and

13. **A.** NO CHANGE
    B. country, with people
    C. country, so people
    D. country. People

Modifiers

Try to recognize what's funny about this sentence:

> After being beaten and deflated, the baker shaped and seasoned the dough.

The sentence is ridiculous because of the comma phrase at the start—it seems like the baker is being beaten before he goes off to work on the dough. *After being beaten and deflated* is called a **modifier** because it modifies or describes someone or something in the same sentence. Here, the modifier is misplaced. Instead, it should go right next to the thing it's supposed to modify:

> After being beaten and deflated, the dough was shaped and seasoned by the baker.

A modifier is like a describing phrase. How do you know if a phrase is a modifier? Usually it comes at the beginning of the sentence and is separated off by a comma (but not always). If all you read was *After being beaten and deflated*, your natural thought would be, *"**Who** or **What** is being beaten?"* Having that thought is how you know you're dealing with a modifier. Without the rest of the sentence, it leaves you wondering what's being talked about. When correcting sentences that have this error, you want to make sure there is a sensible noun that is right next to the modifier.

Let's do a couple examples so you can see how modifiers are tested.

Example 1

Wrong:	I bought a house from the local bakery made of gingerbread.
Correct:	I bought a house made of gingerbread from the local bakery.

Modifiers don't necessarily have to be at the start of the sentence. Here, *made of gingerbread* should be placed next to the *house* it's describing. Otherwise, it seems like the local bakery is the thing that's made of gingerbread.

Example 2

Wrong:	Watching the end of the world, our lives flashed before our eyes.
Correct:	While we were watching the end of the world, our lives flashed before our eyes.

In this example, the sentence makes no sense because *our lives* don't have eyes to watch the end of the world with. The modifier *Watching the end of the world* needs to modify *we* even though that word's not even in the sentence. Therefore, the correct version puts in the subject *we* and re-words the sentence.

Note

A dependent clause is NOT a modifier. In the last example, note the difference between the wrong and correct versions. The wrong version uses a modifier whereas the correct version uses a dependent clause. Dependent clauses don't leave us wondering *who* or *what*. Reading just the first part of the corrected version, we already know the subject is *we*. With dependent clauses, we don't have to worry about modifier errors, because again, they aren't modifiers.

Rule

Keep modifiers right next to the thing they're supposed to describe.

Example 3

Wrong:	Running fiercely to the bathroom, John's pants dropped.
Correct:	Running fiercely to the bathroom, John dropped his pants.

Understanding this example is SUPER IMPORTANT. On rare occasions, the ACT will try to trick you by putting the modifier *Running fiercely to the bathroom* right next to *John*. But here, it's not *John* but *John's pants* that's actually being modified. And of course, pants can't by themselves run to the bathroom. So be extremely careful when there's an apostrophe *s*.

Example 4

Wrong:	Spotted dealing cocaine, the police arrested the drug dealers.
Correct:	The police arrested the drug dealers, who were spotted dealing cocaine.

Example 5

Wrong:	Though cooked and seasoned to perfection, the taste of ketchup-covered octopus was revolting.
Correct:	Though cooked and seasoned to perfection, the ketchup-covered octopus had a revolting taste.
Correct:	The taste of ketchup-covered octopus, though cooked and seasoned to perfection, was revolting.

Note

English is a weird language. Don't be confused by constructions like the one below:

The magician walked across the stage, dazzling the crowd with card tricks.

This sentence is grammatically correct and does not contain a modifier error—it's understood that *dazzling the crowd with card tricks* applies to the subject, *the magician*, even though it's placed next to *the stage*. Modifier errors will typically occur when the describing phrase is at the start of the sentence, as in the examples above, so don't overanalyze these types of sentences. Note that the comma is important; without it, there WOULD be a modifier error.

Exercise 1: After seeing enough of these, you should be able to instinctively spot the ridiculousness (is that a word?) of sentences that have this error. There can be multiple ways of correcting them. By correcting these on your own, you'll learn to think for yourself and more quickly identify the correct answers on the ACT, rather than relying on the answer choices to "think" for you. Answers for this chapter start on page 194.

1. Hunting for deer, Julian's rifle misfired and burst into flames.

2. Having finished the ACT, the rest of life was easy.

3. Having had no water for five days, the steak and cheese sandwich was squeezed for the grease that we could drink.

4. Active in community service and local affairs, Obama's passion for politics is what would eventually lead him to the presidency.

5. By blasting music at home, the neighbors will start to acquire your musical taste.

6. By majoring in basket weaving, a lifetime of regret and despair awaits.

7. After catching a cold, my lung surgery was the perfect cure.

8. While on air at the radio station, the microphone of the talk show host exploded.

9. As a young child growing up in Massachusetts, Mitt's father gave him airplanes as gifts.

10. Hidden far from sunlight in the caves of Mars, scientists have uncovered an E.T. colony.

11. Chris saw the march of marines looking outside the window as crowds cheered on either side.

12. Overcooked and over-seasoned, Gordon Ramsay swore at the cook and dumped the fish into the garbage.

13. Dressed in a cute outfit and filled with cotton, Tiffany loved the soft feel of her teddy bear.

14. The magician dazzled and surprised the audience members wearing a cloak and top hat.

15. Decorated with colorful ornaments and stars, we took pictures by the Christmas tree.

16. After missing an easy goal, the crowd booed the soccer player.

17. Having forgotten about the homework assignment, his comments on the book in class were general statements that could apply to any book.

18. To get the best view of the movie, our seats were reserved in the front and center.

19. Prancing joyously from field to field, the scientist followed the deer.

20. Though skinny and awkward from the outset, Conan's sense of humor made him a television success.

21. Climbing from tree to tree, the explorers avidly watched the red pandas.

Exercise 2: Answers for this chapter start on page 194.

Tennis

Since the age of 10, <u>tennis has been my daugh-</u> ¹ <u>ter Cayla's fascination.</u> <u>Having watched them play</u> ² <u>live,</u> Venus and Serena Williams became her idols and she tries to imitate their aggressive play style. <u>When other six year olds were watching cartoons,</u> ³ Cayla would be watching tennis. So, as encouraging parents, <u>lessons were</u> the next step. At the ages of ⁴ ten and eleven, the Williams sisters were enrolled at the Academy of Rick Macci to improve their game, so getting Cayla started with the game early seemed like a good idea.

A simple sport, <u>the rules of tennis have not</u> ⁵ <u>changed</u> since 1890. The main idea is to hit the ball inside the opponent's side of the court with a racquet. Made and shaped from wood, <u>players</u> ⁶ <u>found the first racquets</u> difficult to play with, but by improving the underlying technology, <u>today's rac-</u> ⁷ <u>quets are more powerful than ever before.</u> Hitting the ball, <u>a player's grip must remain</u> firm and bal- ⁸ anced.

1. **A.** NO CHANGE
   B. tennis has been the fascination of my daughter Cayla.
   C. my daughter Cayla has been fascinated with tennis.
   D. my daughter Cayla's fascination has been tennis.

2. **A.** NO CHANGE
   B. After Cayla watched them play live,
   C. After watching live,
   D. Watching them play live,

3. **A.** NO CHANGE
   B. Having watched cartoons,
   C. When watching cartoons,
   D. Cartoons being watched by other six year olds,

4. **A.** NO CHANGE
   B. lessons had to be
   C. Cayla's lessons were
   D. we decided lessons were

5. **A.** NO CHANGE
   B. tennis has not had its rules changed
   C. tennis's rules have not changed
   D. no one has changed the rules of tennis

6. **A.** NO CHANGE
   B. the game of tennis was
   C. the first racquets were
   D. the first racquets were found to be

7. **A.** NO CHANGE
   B. they are
   C. today's racquets have become
   D. today's racquet creators have made them

8. **A.** NO CHANGE
   B. the grip of the player must remain
   C. the grip must be kept
   D. a player must keep the grip

Because he thought of tennis as a serious sport, her coach was quite demanding. During one particular match, my daughter found it hard to see because of the sun. She swung and missed the tennis ball squinting at the sky. Her coach got very angry.
₉

Needless to say, we soon had to find her a new coach. Searching for one that was more patient, it
₁₀
was time we asked our friends for recommenda-
₁₀
tions. Playing tennis can be tough, but it should also be enjoyable. The new coach turned out to be great. With spin and power, she taught Cayla a better way
₁₁
to serve the ball. The first time she spun the ball in, she jumped up and down excitedly like it was Christmas morning.

Growing in confidence, her movements became
₁₂
more smooth. At one point, Cayla even challenged
₁₂
her coach to a friendly match. I can't wait to see how she evolves as a tennis player in the coming years.

9. The best placement for the underlined portion (assuming proper capitalization and punctuation) would be:
   A. where it is now.
   B. at the start of the sentence.
   C. after the word *swung*
   D. after the word *missed*

10. A. NO CHANGE
     B. we asked friends for
     C. our friends gave us
     D. our friends were asked for

11. The best placement for the underlined portion (assuming proper capitalization and punctuation) would be:
    A. where it is now.
    B. after the word *Cayla*
    C. after the word *serve*
    D. after the word *ball*

12. A. NO CHANGE
     B. her movements were smoother.
     C. she moved more smoothly.
     D. the way she moved became smoother.

Fragments

A sentence fragment is a piece or part of a sentence. It's an incomplete sentence, one that's missing a subject or a verb. For example:

Floating on the river.

Of course, that one's easy to spot. The ACT will give you sentence fragments so long that by the time you've read to the end of them, you'll have forgotten where you started. You'll commonly see fragments in which the entire sentence is a relative clause (e.g. *who, which, that, where*), a dependent clause (e.g *although, while, when*), or a gerund phrase (e.g. *being, walking, singing*). If you read a sentence out loud and it lacks a sense of completion or the whole thing just sounds weird by the end, chances are it's a sentence fragment.

Example 1

Wrong:	People who have a sense of entitlement and feel absolutely no sympathy for those less fortunate even when they take advantage of their services.
Correct:	People who have a sense of entitlement and feel absolutely no sympathy for those less fortunate even when they take advantage of their services **make me sick**.

Example 1 is a relative clause sentence fragment.

Example 2

Wrong:	Because my broken heart, which you have left hardly beating in my chest, is the reason for my endless suffering.
Correct:	**My broken heart**, which you have left hardly beating in my chest, is the reason for my endless suffering.

Example 2 is a dependent clause sentence fragment.

Example 3

Wrong:	Russell Brand, the English comedian, being one of the funniest celebrities alive.
Correct:	Russell Brand, the English comedian, **is** one of the funniest celebrities alive.

Example 3 is a gerund phrase sentence fragment.

Example 4

Wrong:	I made peanut butter cookies. And I know how much you love peanut butter.
Correct:	I made peanut butter cookies, **and** I know how much you love peanut butter.

In everything that we read, sentences that start with conjunctions are everywhere. On the ACT, however, a sentence that starts with a conjunction like *and* is considered a fragment and must be corrected, at least when it's underlined.

There is no one absolute way to fix a sentence fragment. On the ACT, the simpler ones are easy to spot and fix. Often times, the trickier ones will involve removing words like *who, which, although, because, since,* and *despite* as in Example 2.

Exercise 1: Turn the following sentence fragments into complete sentences. Answers are flexible. Answers for this chapter start on page 196.

1. Tony's toys, which were hidden in the cupboard so that nobody could get to them.

2. When I was given the opportunity to speak in front of the graduating class as if I were some celebrity or movie star.

3. Dumping him on the first date because he smelled so bad even though she knew he had just returned from a wrestling match.

4. It is very convenient that the grocery store I live next to. And the surrounding malls and restaurants are open late at night.

5. In the middle of the night, when most people are sleeping while I sneak to the kitchen to eat.

6. Like the moment you realize your cereal is soggy because you left it in the milk too long.

7. The butler who served the Wright family for several years and later became a successful businessman.

8. The tennis champion waving his racquet up towards a roaring crowd with his right hand and lifting the trophy with his left.

9. Even though Aaron fully believed that his actions, now the cause of much public controversy, were morally and ethically right, but the prosecutors would hear none of it.

10. The negative thoughts that were constantly on Floyd's mind as he got into the ring.

11. Disgusted by the lack of cleanliness in the men's bathroom yet curious about the sanitation in the ladies' room.

12. I wore the pants you bought me. And the purple tie that the saleswoman picked out.

13. As they walk down the street, check out the stores, and talk about life.

14. Although pandas are one of the most likable mammals but are one of the most rare.

Exercise 2: Answers for this chapter start on page 196.

Dining with the Kids

For centuries, eating in a restaurant <u>being</u> con-
                                        ¹
sidered a social event. Business meetings, family

gatherings, special events, and many other occa-

sions <u>celebrating</u> in restaurants. This is not neces-
        ²
sarily because serving a large crowd at home is a lot

of work, but more because the food and drinks are

served by <u>others, allowing</u> everyone in the group to
            ³
relax and socialize without worrying about empty

plates or glasses.

Some restaurants <u>that cater</u> specifically to fam-
                    ⁴
ilies and children, though they are the exception

rather than the rule. Unfortunately, eating a meal

in a restaurant with three children under the age of

ten is anything but <u>relaxing. Especially</u> for the wait-
                      ⁵
ers and waitresses who serve them. The Continen-

tal Diner in my town, which has a special section

just for <u>children so that they are</u> isolated from the
          ⁶
customers who want a nice and quiet conversation

over dinner.

1. **A.** NO CHANGE
    B. was being
    C. has been
    D. is

2. **A.** NO CHANGE
    B. are celebrating
    C. are celebrated
    D. celebrated

3. **A.** NO CHANGE
    B. others. Allowing
    C. others; allowing
    D. DELETE the underlined portion.

4. **A.** NO CHANGE
    B. catering
    C. are catering
    D. cater

5. **A.** NO CHANGE
    B. relaxing, especially
    C. relaxing;
    D. relaxing, and especially

6. **A.** NO CHANGE
    B. children to keep them
    C. children, keeps them
    D. children, keeping them

During one particular night on a weekday. We
                                                                    7
took our three kids to their classmate Kate's birth-
    7
day party. Held at a pizza place that combined
              8
bowling with the dining experience.   While the

kids had fun bowling and the parents could chat
                   9
with each other without too much interruption. Of

course, most of the parents being concerned with
                                 10
their children's behavior and kept a watchful eye

on them. Tommy and Lilly were, the siblings of
                         11
the birthday girl, entertained themselves by rolling

multiple bowling balls down the lane at the same

time.

To ensure that the kids were busy and engaged.
                                                                    12
The restaurant had many activities besides bowl-
   12
ing. One, air hockey, which involves two players
         13
with pushers and one puck. Another was arcade

basketball, my favorite game. As the clock ticks

down, players shooting basketballs as fast as they
                        14
can into the basket. When the night was over, my

three kids, who finding it difficult to leave the party
             15
behind.

---

7. **A.** NO CHANGE
    B. weekday, we took
    C. weekday, when we took
    D. weekday, having taken

8. **A.** NO CHANGE
    B. It was held
    C. Being held
    D. Having been held

9. **A.** NO CHANGE
    B. bowling, the parents
    C. bowling. The parents
    D. bowling, and the parents

10. **A.** NO CHANGE
    B. concerned
    C. were concerning
    D. were concerned

11. **A.** NO CHANGE
    B. Tommy and Lilly
    C. While Tommy and Lilly were
    D. As Tommy and Lilly

12. **A.** NO CHANGE
    B. engaged since the restaurant
    C. engaged at the restaurant,
    D. engaged, the restaurant

13. **A.** NO CHANGE
    B. One was
    C. One being
    D. One of these,

14. **A.** NO CHANGE
    B. who are shooting
    C. who shoot
    D. shoot

15. **A.** NO CHANGE
    B. kids, finding
    C. kids found
    D. kids, who found

Redundancy

Redundancy questions involve removing unnecessary words. On the ACT, you'll encounter two types of redundancy:

- Words that essentially repeat or unnecessarily define previous words
- Awkward and useless phrases that could be omitted or condensed into fewer words

Example 1

Wrong:	Our problem is that we're too self-aware of ourselves.
Correct:	Our problem is that we're too self-aware.

Self-aware already implies *ourselves*, so we don't need *of ourselves* in the sentence.

Example 2

Wrong:	I once believed and had faith in the power of love.
Correct:	I once believed in the power of love.

The phrase *had faith in* repeats the same meaning as *believed*.

Example 3

Wrong:	The reason why red pandas have ringed tails is because they are relatives of both the giant panda and the raccoon.
Correct:	Red pandas have ringed tails **because** they are relatives of both the giant panda and the raccoon.
Correct:	**The reason** red pandas have ringed tails is that they are relatives of both the giant panda and the raccoon.

This specific redundancy error is very common. It has three words that essentially mean the same thing—*reason, why,* and *because,* all of which point to the cause of something. You only need one of those words.

Example 4

Wrong:	After hearing the spy's information, the general knew that an attack was imminent in the future.
Correct:	After hearing the spy's information, the general knew that an attack was imminent.

Imminent by definition means *in the future.*

Example 5

Wrong:	It's only on the night before the test that I wish my notes had been more clearer.
Correct:	It's only on the night before the test that I wish my notes had been **more clear**.

It's unnecessary to use both *more* and the *-er* ending because they convey the same thing.

Example 6

Wrong:	The last to sing, Jason and Jesse made sure to amaze the crowd with a full range of vocals at the end of the performance.
Correct:	**The last to sing**, Jason and Jesse made sure to amaze the crowd with a full range of vocals.
Correct:	Jason and Jesse made sure to amaze the crowd with a full range of vocals **at the end of the performance**.

Example 7

Wrong:	We should evacuate the building immediately in the hypothetical event that a fire occurs.
Correct:	We should evacuate the building immediately **if a fire occurs**.

The phrase *in the hypothetical event that a fire occurs* is too wordy and awkward. How much a certain phrase can be shortened can be a matter of style. Luckily for you, the answer choices will be very clear-cut on the ACT. You'll definitely know from the answer choices when they're testing wordiness.

Example 8

Wrong:	Joey bought a super-sized hamburger due to the fact that he was really hungry.
Correct:	Joey bought a super-sized hamburger **because** he was really hungry.

Exercise 1: Correct the redundancy errors in the following sentences. Answers are somewhat flexible. Answers for this chapter start on page 197.

1. In her biography about her life, she writes about overcoming poverty and fear.

2. During high school, I sung in a trio that consisted of three people.

3. Scratching the rash made it more worse than before.

4. The reason why most people give up on New Year's resolutions is because they're too accustomed to old habits.

5. The plagiarist who copied the works of others was banned indefinitely from the journalism industry.

6. There's a good chance that an earthquake has the possibility of happening within the next week.

7. After her graduation speech, Zoe was thirsty and needed to drink something.

8. Because James was an optimist with a positive outlook on life, he faced his struggles with a smile on his face.

9. Seafood restaurants are becoming less and less expensive due to the abundance and oversupply of fish.

10. Her verbal statements in her conversation with me led me to believe that she was holding something from me.

11. The sisters reunited at the house where they grew up as siblings upon their father's death.

12. Building his own motorcycle, which would belong to him, Quentin looked forward to the day when he would be old enough to drive it.

13. My aunt is a beginner who just started learning about photography.

14. The president gave a strong message that was quite powerful to the world in his speech yesterday.

15. This year, the volcano came alive as if it were angry and the eruption lasted for days, which numbered quite a few.

16. In 1742, Christopher Columbus set sail and thereby rigged a boat and charted a course towards India.

17. Since he quit his job, his savings have suffered, decreasing the balance in his bank account quite a bit.

18. When she walked into the room, he lost his concentration and couldn't focus on the task at hand.

Exercise 2: Answers for this chapter start on page 197.

King Henry VIII's Divorce

King Henry VIII is famous for his large size and his many wives, <u>for which he is popularly known.</u>
₁
His most enduring legacy, however, was <u>his separa-</u>
₂
<u>tion and division</u> of the Church of England from the
₂
Roman Catholic Church.

Henry was never expected to be king. His older brother Arthur was <u>the heir and next in line</u>
₃
to the throne, but when Henry was 11 years old, Arthur <u>perished fatally.</u> Arthur had recently mar-
₄
ried Catherine of Aragon, the daughter of King Fer-dinand of <u>Spain, a short time ago.</u> Eager to protect
₅
diplomatic relations with Spain, Henry's father be-trothed <u>his son Henry</u> to marry Catherine when he
₆
came of age.

Henry became <u>king, ascending to the throne</u>
₇
in 1509 at the young age of 17 upon his father's death. Over the years, Catherine bore him six chil-dren <u>throughout their time together,</u> but only one
₈
survived infancy, a daughter. Henry needed a male heir to ensure a peaceful succession of the throne af-ter his death. As time passed, the absence of a son increasingly <u>worried and troubled Henry more and</u>
₉
<u>more,</u> to the point that he began to fear that
₉

1. A. NO CHANGE
    B. for which he is most known.
    C. which he is known for.
    D. OMIT the underlined portion and end the sentence with a period.

2. A. NO CHANGE
    B. his separation
    C. the separateness
    D. his splitting division

3. A. NO CHANGE
    B. the successive heir
    C. the heir
    D. the successive next in line

4. A. NO CHANGE
    B. died.
    C. fatally died.
    D. perished and died.

5. A. NO CHANGE
    B. Spain, shortly before.
    C. Spain.
    D. Spain, not long ago.

6. A. NO CHANGE
    B. his son, Henry,
    C. Henry, his son,
    D. Henry

7. A. NO CHANGE
    B. king
    C. king, on the throne
    D. king to the throne

8. A. NO CHANGE
    B. as time passed
    C. one by one
    D. OMIT the underlined portion

9. A. NO CHANGE
    B. worried Henry more and more,
    C. worried Henry,
    D. troubled Henry more and more,

God was punishing him for marrying his brother's wife.

At this time, the Catholic Church had the
<u>   </u>
                    10
sole authority to end a marriage, and even then only by declaring in an announcement that the
                        <u>   </u>
                                    11
marriage had never truly existed in God's sight. Henry sought such an annulment from the Pope. Unswayed by Henry's arguments from the biblical book of Leviticus and pressured by Catherine's nephew, King Charles V of Spain, the Pope was un-
                                                      <u>   </u>
                                                          12
convinced and refused the annulment.
<u>   </u>
           12

And so Henry took matters into his own hands to obtain the divorce he wanted on his own. Hav-
                                      <u>   </u>
                                          13
ing already begun an affair with a woman named Anne Boleyn, all he needed was a church that would marry him to Anne and that would be sufficient. He
<u>   </u>
                  14
maneuvered to get his own man appointed Archbishop of Canterbury in 1532, and then he got Parliament to declare him the Supreme Head of the Church of England after that in 1534.
                  <u>   </u>
                          15

Henry's actions opened the door for the Protestant Reformation in England, which led the way to
                        <u>   </u>
                                    16
forever altering the future of his country. Anne, however, did not bear him a son. In fact, only one of his six wives bore him a son, and this son, Edward, reigned for only a few years, six as a matter
                      <u>   </u>
                                  17
of fact.
<u>   </u>
  17

10. A. NO CHANGE
    B. only the Catholic Church
    C. the Catholic Church was the only one that
    D. it was only the Catholic Church that

11. A. NO CHANGE
    B. declaring
    C. proclaiming and declaring
    D. proclaiming under a declaration

12. A. NO CHANGE
    B. refused
    C. unconvincingly refused
    D. decided to refuse

13. A. NO CHANGE
    B. himself.
    C. by himself.
    D. OMIT the underlined portion and end the sentence with a period.

14. A. NO CHANGE
    B. Anne, which would be adequate.
    C. Anne.
    D. Anne, being enough to nullify the divorce.

15. A. NO CHANGE
    B. subsequently in 1534.
    C. in 1534.
    D. OMIT the underlined portion and end the sentence with a period.

16. A. NO CHANGE
    B. England to
    C. England, which
    D. England,

17. A. NO CHANGE
    B. six years.
    C. six years, in fact.
    D. six short years.

Parallelism

You probably know from math that parallel lines are two lines that go in the same direction. The concept is similar in English in the way we structure certain things together.

I like flying planes, riding trains, and driving automobiles.

Notice the same format for each of the things in the list: gerund (word ending in *ing*)-noun, gerund-noun, gerund-noun. It sounds nice and fluid when the sentence is put together that way. It would be awkward and incorrect to say:

I like flying planes, riding trains, and to drive automobiles.

Here's another correct version:

I like to fly planes, to ride trains, and to drive automobiles. (infinitive-noun pattern)

It's also correct to leave out the *to*'s because they're implied to carry over to all three items in the list:

I like to fly planes, ride trains, and drive automobiles.

But again, you must be consistent—it would be incorrect to write:

I like to fly planes, ride trains, and to drive automobiles.

The *to* is used again after being left out in the second item. Let's walk through some examples so you see what sentences need to be parallel on the ACT:

Example 1

| Wrong: | In chess, remember these three goals: get your pieces to the center, capture the opposing pieces, and attacking the opposing king. |
| Correct: | In chess, remember these three goals: get your pieces to the center, capture the opposing pieces, and **attack** the opposing king. |

Example 2

| Wrong: | Fans of Teresa admire her ability to sing, her passion for performance, and she has good looks. |
| Correct: | Fans of Teresa admire her ability to sing, her passion for performance, and **her good looks**. |

Example 3

| Wrong: | The baby crawled quickly, sleeps softly, and cried loudly. |
| Correct: | The baby crawled quickly, **slept** softly, and cried loudly. |

Parallelism requires the verb tenses to be the same.

Example 4

| Wrong: | The fashion designer was praised for her creative, comfortable, and her having innovative clothing. |
| Correct: | The fashion designer was praised for her creative, comfortable, and ~~her having~~ innovative clothing. |

Parallelism most often shows up in a series or a list of things as in the examples above, but it can also come up when pairing two phrases together, especially with *and* or *or*:

Example 5

| Wrong: | I respect his eloquence and that he is brave. |
| Correct: | I respect his eloquence and **his bravery**. |

Example 6

| Wrong: | Hunting under the moonlight and to howl on top of the mountains were instinctual when the full moon appeared above the werewolves. |
| Correct: | Hunting under the moonlight and **howling** on top of the mountains were instinctual when the full moon appeared above the werewolves. |

Example 7

| Wrong: | I like singing more than dance. |
| Correct: | I like singing more than **dancing**. |

Example 8

| Wrong: | To learn what it means to love someone is accepting the flaws of others. |
| Correct: | To learn what it means to love someone is **to accept** the flaws of others. |

Example 9

Wrong:	The school was designed to be a place where creativity would be celebrated and hard work was rewarded there.
Correct:	The school was designed to be a place where creativity would be celebrated and **hard work (would be) rewarded**.

Note that *would be* can be left out because it's implied to carry over.

Example 10

Wrong:	The principal planned to improve teacher training and clearer rules for student conduct should be established.
Correct:	The principal planned to improve teacher training and **(to) establish clearer rules for student conduct**.

Example 11

Wrong:	The people who ride the bus or have taken the train can't afford to drive to work.
Correct:	The people who ride the bus or **take** the train can't afford to drive to work.

Example 12

Wrong:	Traveling the world has given me the pleasure of meeting new people, to explore different ways of life.
Correct:	Traveling the world has given me the pleasure of meeting new people, **of exploring** different ways of life.

Exercise 1: Make the following sentences parallel. Answers for this chapter start on page 199.

1. That she looks beautiful and her charm help her get out of speeding tickets.

2. Visitors to my hometown in the middle of nowhere can experience rides on the bus, drinks at the tavern, and eating at the McDonald's.

3. Because of their amazing sense of smell, quick agility, and they have fierceness when protecting themselves, lions are the kings of the savannah.

4. My tasks today are to file for divorce, burn my house down, and to start all over.

5. By investing in nuclear energy, we can save the environment, jobs, and it costs us less.

6. In his free time, Wild Bill likes smoking Cuban cigars and to drink the finest red wine Martha's Vineyard has to offer.

7. Quickly and being silent, Jesse and Walt snuck by the sleeping police officers and made off with a barrel of methylamine.

8. Inspired by the hard work of his immigrant father, Jeremy wanted to pay for college, find a job, and a new house.

9. According to Apple, Samsung's directors need to admit they violated Apple's patent, pay the fines, and also needed is to recall all their products.

10. Samsung's executives responded by completely rejecting Apple's ultimatum in court and they countersued Apple back for patent infringement.

11. The 300 men trained diligently, screamed fiercely into battle, and valiantly fights.

12. At the yard sale, Jimmy found dusty writings of Einstein, containers of fossils, and Chinese opium boxes.

13. American immigrants took huge risks to leave their homelands and searching for a better life elsewhere.

14. Come to the next party prepared to eat a lot, to dance a lot, and with a thirst for drinks.

15. As soon as he graduated from high school, he packed all his belongings, rushed to the college campus, and leaves his parents behind.

Exercise 2: Answers for this chapter start on page 199.

Trip to Paris

The last year of high school was filled with optimism and <u>emotions that were nostalgic.</u> It was like
₁
standing on a bridge that must be crossed, leaving behind the carefree days of youth and <u>stepped</u> into a
₂
life of responsibilities, business meetings, and <u>pay-</u>
₃
<u>ing bills.</u> My friends and I decided to have one last
₃
trip together before heading off in our own directions.

My friends had decided to go to college on the other side of the country, <u>join</u> an environmental
₄
group to save the rainforest, or work for their parents in the family business, which was what I was doing in the same town I'd lived in all my life. Out of the three of us, I needed this vacation the most. I had never left the state, let alone <u>departing from</u>
₅
<u>the country.</u> So when Tom suggested we spend the
₅
summer in Europe, I was thrilled. After all, travel is a great way to bond with others and <u>to learn about</u>
₆
<u>the world.</u>
₆

1. **A.** NO CHANGE
   B. nostalgia.
   C. nostalgic emotions.
   D. emotions of nostalgia.

2. **A.** NO CHANGE
   B. to step
   C. stepping
   D. we stepped

3. **A.** NO CHANGE
   B. bills that have to be paid.
   C. having to pay bills.
   D. bills.

4. **A.** NO CHANGE
   B. to join
   C. joining
   D. they will join

5. **A.** NO CHANGE
   B. the country.
   C. from the country.
   D. depart from the country.

6. **A.** NO CHANGE
   B. the world can be learned about.
   C. for learning about the world.
   D. we can learn about the world.

We landed at Heathrow Airport at about 4pm, would sleep in the terminal for a few hours, and
—————
  7

took a connecting flight to Paris. We almost missed our flight because of the loud, pushy, and large size
                                                                                              —————
                                                                                                8

of the crowd. On the flight, we were reading books,
—————   ————————————
  8   9

watched movies, and listened to music. When we arrived, it finally dawned on us that we were all alone in a foreign country. As students and we were
                                                        ——————
                                                          10

clueless tourists, we walked aimlessly through the streets with giant backpacks.

We found a car rental place and chose a Volkswagen Beetle that was inexpensive to rent and easily driven. It was perfect for taking us through the
——————
  11

streets of Paris and to show us the popular tourist
                   ——————
                     12

sites. The history of Paris dates back to the third century. Today, the city is known for its coffee culture and for its fashion boutiques. It didn't take long
                    —————————————————
                           13

for us to realize there was no way we could see everything in just a few hours, so we just toured the usual tourist attractions like the Louvre, the Eiffel tower, and we went to the Arc de Triomphe. By
          ————————————————————————
                        14

having a budget and we stuck to it, we had enough
                   ——————————
                        15

money to try a three star Michelin restaurant afterwards!

7. A. NO CHANGE
    B. we slept
    C. slept
    D. sleeping

8. A. NO CHANGE
    B. large crowd.
    C. crowd that was large.
    D. having a large crowd.

9. A. NO CHANGE
    B. read books,
    C. decided to read books,
    D. had books to read,

10. A. NO CHANGE
    B. as well
    C. being
    D. as

11. A. NO CHANGE
    B. easy to drive.
    C. driven easily.
    D. was easily driven.

12. A. NO CHANGE
    B. showed us
    C. showing us
    D. the showing of

13. A. NO CHANGE
    B. having fashion boutiques.
    C. with its fashion boutiques.
    D. it has fashion boutiques.

14. A. NO CHANGE
    B. the landmark called the Arc de Triomphe.
    C. such as the Arc de Triomphe.
    D. the Arc de Triomphe.

15. A. NO CHANGE
    B. stuck to it,
    C. having it stick,
    D. sticking to it,

Pronoun Reference

Take a look at this sentence:

To avoid a ticket, Alice told the police that Alice didn't realize Alice was pressing harder on the accelerator pedal because Alice had gained 40 pounds in two months.

Hopefully, reading that shows you why we need pronouns, which are words that represent other nouns. If we didn't have pronouns, everything would sound repetitive and confusing.

Here's the better version:

To avoid a ticket, Alice told the police that **she** didn't realize **she** was pressing harder on the accelerator pedal because **she** had gained 40 pounds in two months.

Here are some examples of pronouns:

	Singular	Plural
Subject Pronouns	*He, She, It*	*They*
Object Pronouns	*Her, Him, It*	*Them*
Possessive Pronouns	*Hers, His, Its*	*Theirs*
Possessive Adj. Pronouns	*Her, His, Its*	*Their*
Relative Pronouns	*This, That, Which*	*These, Those*
Reflexive Pronouns	*Himself, Herself, Itself*	*Themselves*

Don't worry about memorizing the names or types—just familiarize yourself with the words so that you can tell whether something's a pronoun or not.

You need to know only two rules for pronouns, but they're really important:

Rule 1

A pronoun must clearly stand for ONE and ONLY ONE other NOUN.

Rule 2

A singular noun must be referred to by a singular pronoun. Likewise, a plural pronoun must be referred to by a plural pronoun.

Example 1

Wrong:	Whenever Jason and Alexander sit down at a buffet, **he** eats way more food.
Correct:	Whenever Jason and Alexander sit down at a buffet, **Jason** eats way more food.

This example violates rule 1 because we don't know who eats more. *He* could refer to either Jason or Alexander.

In conversation, we might say something like *"He eats way more food,"* and that's grammatically fine because we know from the context of our conversation who *he* is. But on the ACT, a pronoun with no clear reference is an error.

Example 2

Wrong:	Even if a student gets in early, **they** still have to maintain good grades during senior year.
Correct:	Even if a student gets in early, **he or she** still **has** to maintain good grades during senior year.

In this example, rule 2 is being violated. We know that *they* obviously refers to *student*, but *they* is a plural pronoun while *student* is a singular noun. *He or she* is the singular pronoun we must use (yes, it's singular). Again, we must use singular pronouns for singular nouns and plural pronouns for plural nouns.

Example 3

Wrong:	At the police station, **they** found a pile of cash stashed in her bra.
Correct:	At the police station, **the inspectors** found a pile of cash stashed in her bra.

Who's *they*? Here, *they* doesn't even have a reference—it doesn't represent any noun that we can see in front of us. Sure, we could assume that *they* refers to the police, but *police* is not a noun in this sentence—it's an adjective. Remember that a pronoun MUST stand for an existing noun somewhere.

Example 4

Wrong:	My teammate deleted my part of the essay. The next day, I confronted him about **this**.
Correct:	My teammate deleted my part of the essay. The next day, I confronted him about **this deletion**.
Correct:	My teammate deleted my part of the essay. The next day, I confronted him about **his reasons for doing so**.

In this example, it's not explicit what *this* stands for. The easiest way to fix reference errors involving *this, that, these,* or *those* is to either add the noun right after or replace the pronoun altogether with something else. By inserting the word *deletion* into the sentence, we essentially define what *this* is.

Think of pronouns as shortcuts or aliases for other files on your computer. The original file must exist for there to be a shortcut. Furthermore, the shortcut must match the file it represents. You wouldn't want to click on a shortcut only to open something other than what you were expecting.

Note

The pronoun *it* can be used in the following way:
- It was a dark and stormy night.
- It took 10,000 years for the star's rays to reach us.

These are completely fine sentences where you shouldn't worry at all about pronoun errors.

Here are a few more questions and answers so you get the hang of it:

Example 5

Wrong:	Drunk with beer bottles in both hands, Michael slid and dropped **it** on the rug.
Correct:	Drunk with beer bottles in both hands, Michael slid and dropped **them** on the rug.

Example 6

Wrong:	The senior class has organized **their** school trip to the Antarctic.
Correct:	The senior class has organized **its** school trip to the Antarctic.

Example 7

Wrong:	Because the restaurant was amazingly successful, **they** hired more employees to run it.
Correct:	Because the restaurant was amazingly successful, **it** hired more employees to run it.

Example 8

Wrong:	I got so much in the mail today. I've been opening all **those** since noon.
Correct:	I got so much in the mail today. I've been opening all **those letters** since noon.

Example 9

Wrong:	Everyone wished that **they** had cheaper textbooks rather than the rip-offs that were required.
Correct:	Everyone wished that **he or she** had cheaper textbooks rather than the rip-offs that were required.

Example 10

Wrong:	A good chef always takes good care of **their** equipment.
Correct:	A good chef always takes good care of **his or her** equipment.

Example 11

Wrong:	Because the blankets got torn in the wash, we must replace **it** before the customer gets back.
Correct:	Because the blankets got torn in the wash, we must replace **them** before the customer gets back.

Example 12

Wrong:	The lion and the tortoise were about to get into a fight when **it** fell down a ditch.
Correct:	The lion and the tortoise were about to get into a fight when **the tortoise** fell down a ditch.

Example 13

Wrong:	Few chairs are as comfortable as **that** made by the Herman-Miller company.
Correct:	Few chairs are as comfortable as **those** made by the Herman-Miller company.

In this last example, *those* refers to *chairs*. Because *chairs* is plural, we need *those* instead of *that*, which is singular. It's easy to remember because you would always say *that car, that jet, that book* and *those cars, those jets, those books* rather than the other way around.

Exercise 1: Fix the pronoun error in the following sentences. The pronoun you need to fix is bolded. Some of them have flexible answers and some require you to also change the verb. Answers for this chapter start on page 200.

1. When I looked up at the stars, I couldn't believe **it was** so many light-years away.

2. Although many people believe the tiger is fierce and ferocious, **they are** actually quite peaceful.

3. Anyone who misses **their** parents can just go home.

4. The toxic level of water bottles isn't apparent to most people because they assume **its** plastic content is harmless.

5. After searching the whole day for my brother's shoes, I told him I wasn't able to find **it**.

6. Birds must migrate south during the winter season because **it manages** to survive only in warmer climates.

7. Until technological advances enable **it** to consume less fuel for thrust and power, the possibility of space rockets to Mars will remain remote.

8. By the time **it** can be fixed up, cleaned, and upgraded, old cell phones will be completely irrelevant compared to newer ones.

9. The food that **they** serve at the restaurant is absolutely delicious.

10. The secretary unplugged the keyboard from the computer and cleaned **it**.

11. Joey was required to go to a meeting but **it** never stated the location.

12. Before the state university could open up a new program in astrophysics, **they** needed funding from alumni.

13. The government is so arrogant in **their** ability to solve problems that **they have** silenced the voice of the people.

14. The show *American Idol* has as **their** premiere judge a man who can't sing himself.

15. Elle told the teacher that **she** had made a mistake.

16. My iPhone fell onto the glass plate, but thankfully **it** didn't break.

17. Some spiders can inject **itself** with poison to enact revenge on their predators.

18. Anthony used to hang out all the time with Albert until **he** got the big promotion at work.

19. When a person dies, **their** sense of hearing is the last to go whereas touch and sight are the first.

20. The city of Boston, which weathered the American Revolution, regularly offers tours that honor **their** local heroes.

21. One of the unique features of the red panda, an exotic creature that lives in the eastern Himalayas, is **their** ringed tail, which is used as a blanket in the cold.

22. The health department should be able to handle the paperwork by **themselves**.

23. My mom cooked some traditional Russian dishes, but I hate eating **that**.

24. I took my old computer to the store and luckily **they** were able to fix it.

Exercise 2: Answers for this chapter start on page 200.

True Crime Writer

Like most authors, Ann Rule didn't dive into the world of writing right after college. Although she did major in creative writing, her real passion was in unraveling the mysteries of the criminal mind. They didn't have majors related to forensics
$\overline{1}$
and crime, so she took many courses related to science and psychology.

Ann began her adult life as a police officer for the Seattle Police Department, which was known across the country for their high profile cases. Even
$\overline{2}$
though she liked it more, she also wrote regularly
$\overline{3}$
for the *True Detective* magazine and volunteered at an abuse hot line.

When writing for the magazine, Ann used a fake name, Andy Stark. She also published several books under that. While many say that the writing
$\overline{4}$
style of her works is similar to that of Edward Stratemeyer, creator of the Nancy Drew series, she maintains that they aren't.
$\overline{5}$

1. **A.** NO CHANGE
    B. It
    C. Those
    D. Her college

2. **A.** NO CHANGE
    B. its
    C. these
    D. her

3. **A.** NO CHANGE
    B. them
    C. the police work
    D. that

4. **A.** NO CHANGE
    B. this.
    C. that name.
    D. them.

5. **A.** NO CHANGE
    B. it isn't.
    C. they aren't them.
    D. they don't.

Her stories' characters, who are quite eccentric, by

itself are enough to distinguish her work from oth-
___
6

ers.

Ms. Rule's first book was titled *The Stranger Be-

side Me*, which, like many of her other books, was

turned into a movie. Ann played a large part in its
___
7

making. In fact, she wrote the script for the movie
___
7

and distributed them to everyone involved. She also
___
8

worked as a consultant and even helped choose the

actors for the different roles. Ann liked to choose ac-

tors that resembled the characters that he or she was
___
9

playing.

Ann Rule loves her fan base. After the release of

each book, she makes a special point of answering

their emails and attending as many book signings
___
10

as possible even though they have caused her seri-
___
11

ous problems with her wrist. Halfway through, she

had to start using a rubber stamp instead of signing

them personally. Ann had to cancel appearances af-
___
12

ter the release of her latest book because of a broken

hip, but any reader can still get his or her favorite
___
13

book autographed by mailing it in.

6.   **A.** NO CHANGE
     B. its own
     C. their own
     D. themselves

7.   **A.** NO CHANGE
     B. their makings.
     C. those.
     D. them.

8.   **A.** NO CHANGE
     B. it
     C. this
     D. those

9.   **A.** NO CHANGE
     B. it was
     C. they were
     D. were

10. **A.** NO CHANGE
     B. these
     C. her fans'
     D. its

11. **A.** NO CHANGE
     B. it has caused
     C. this has caused
     D. this is of the cause of

12. **A.** NO CHANGE
     B. the books
     C. it
     D. those

13. **A.** NO CHANGE
     B. their
     C. them
     D. its

13 Tenses

There are a lot of different tenses but here are some of the ones you'll encounter:

Tense	Verb		
	To Hug	To Swim	To Be
Present	*He hugs…*	*He swims…*	*He is…*
Past	*He hugged…*	*He swam…*	*He was…*
Future	*He will hug…*	*He will swim…*	*He will be…*
Present Perfect	*He has hugged…*	*He has swum…*	*He has been…*
Past Perfect	*He had hugged…*	*He had swum…*	*He had been…*

The present perfect and past perfect tenses require the use of a past participle:

$$\text{Past Participle} = \text{verb} + ed$$

Past participles are always used with *to have* and *to be* verbs out in front (*has **packed**, was **kicked**, had **screamed**,…*). Some past participles, however, don't end with *ed* (*has **won**, has **made**, has **swum**, has **been**,…*). The ACT will always throw in an incorrect past participle and some of them can be tricky to spot, especially if you're rushing through. To get you familiar with them, here's a list of verbs with tricky past participles. Focus on how the third row differs from the second.

Verb	sing	go	write	eat	swim	take	drive	run	give	ride
Past Tense	*sang*	*went*	*wrote*	*ate*	*swam*	*took*	*drove*	*ran*	*gave*	*rode*
Past Participle	*sung*	*gone*	*written*	*eaten*	*swum*	*taken*	*driven*	*run*	*given*	*ridden*

Example 1

Wrong:	The student had took his phone out of his pocket before the teacher noticed.
Correct:	The student had **taken** his phone out of his pocket before the teacher noticed.

Example 2

Wrong:	By the time the whole group arrived at the wedding, the maid of honor already begun her speech.
Correct:	By the time the whole group arrived at the wedding, the maid of honor **had** already begun her speech.

The ACT will also switch *have* with *of* to trick your ear. Just remember:

might have	NOT	*might of*
would have	NOT	*would of*
should have	NOT	*should of*

Exercise 1: Fix the past participle errors. Answers for this chapter start on page 202.

1. Jay, with no care whatsoever, has repeatedly swam in the polluted East River.

2. Advocates of drug control have loudly and frequently point out the dangers to society.

3. Because we parted ways before the advent of Facebook, we have not saw one another since high school.

4. The soldiers have began their march on Tehran.

5. Scientific studies have showed that it's possible for a human to grow a red panda tail.

6. My mom told me that my brother had went to the park to play chess.

7. After the birds had flew south, the blizzard came and thrashed the trees in the forest.

8. The rooster's crow was a sign that the day had began.

9. If you had told me that the deadline was tomorrow, I would of begun the calculations.

10. By the time the parents got home, the baby broken the record player and was about to destroy the TV.

11. Had he won the lottery, he would of retired to a private beach in the south of France.

12. When Leonardo started the portrait, he did not know it would later became one of the most famous paintings in the world.

13. Tom knew that he should of kissed the girl, but he didn't have the courage.

14. Out of nowhere, China has became an economic superpower that other countries must depend on.

The most common verb-related error you'll see on the ACT is tense inconsistency. You need to ensure that the tenses in a sentence make sense. **Most of the time, that means changing everything to either past tense or present tense.**

Example 3

Wrong:	Whenever we stopped by the market, my mom always tries to negotiate the prices.
Correct:	Whenever we **stop** by the market, my mom always **tries** to negotiate the prices.
Correct:	Whenever we **stopped** by the market, my mom always **tried** to negotiate the prices.

Example 4

Wrong:	After winning Wimbledon in 2012, Federer regained the top ranking and declares himself the best in the world.
Correct:	After winning Wimbledon in 2012, Federer **regained** the top ranking and **declared** himself the best in the world.

Example 5

Wrong:	The end of World War II came when German forces surrender in Berlin and Italy.
Correct:	The end of World War II came when German forces **surrendered** in Berlin and Italy.
Rule:	Often times, dates or historical events in the question tell you the past tense is needed.

Example 6

Wrong:	Although the cheetah holds the record for fastest land animal, many other mammals outlasted it.
Correct:	Although the cheetah holds the record for fastest land animal, many other mammals **outlast** it.
Rule:	Statements of fact or of the way things are (things that are always true and will continue to be true) must be in present tense.

Example 7

Wrong:	In *Lord of the Flies*, Ralph and Jack fought over control of the island.
Correct:	In *Lord of the Flies*, Ralph and Jack **fight** over control of the island.
Rule:	When talking about what happens in a book, play, or movie, use the present tense for the main verbs.

There are some cases where verbs don't have to be consistent because of the meaning of the sentence. Sometimes we DO want to talk about two actions that happened in different time periods.

Example 8

Correct:	When I **was** young, I hated vegetables, but now I **love** them.
Correct:	Because he **was** late for the anniversary dinner, she **is** thinking about leaving him.

Both the above sentences are correct because the meaning **intends** for the verb tenses to be inconsistent. As you're checking for tenses on the ACT, make sure you take the meaning of the sentence into consideration. Don't be too robotic.

Tip

On the ACT, the answers to tense-related questions will almost always be the shortest ones. If you had the following answer choices, for instance:

A. NO CHANGE
B. jumped
C. had jumped
D. begun to jump

The answer would most likely be **B**. The reason this tip works is that most of the passages are in simple past or simple present, which means most of the verbs should be in simple past or simple present. In fact, you can usually guess the tense from the title of passage. Is it a history passage? Simple past. A narrative? Simple present. If the choices include both the simple past and the simple present, you'll have to look for the correct tense in the surrounding context.

Answer choices with *would* or *would have* are typically correct when dealing with hypotheticals:

- If I were rich, I **would** buy a Ferrari.

- If she had done her homework, she **would have** gotten an "A" this semester.

Exercise 2: Make the tenses consistent in the following sentences. Answers for this chapter start on page 202.

1. When Columbus and his crew discovered America in 1492, many Indian tribes welcome them graciously.

2. The United States is considered the melting pot because its inhabitants included immigrants from all over the world.

3. Although the giant panda's diet consists primarily of bamboo, most other bears hunted for their food.

4. Tolkien's *Lord of the Rings* trilogy tells the tale of Frodo, a hobbit who was charged with the task of destroying the one ring of power.

5. She bought her dress at Wal-Mart yet it impresses everyone at the party.

6. Every year he wishes for an end to world hunger and prayed for a cure for cancer.

7. Whereas astronomers focus on the stars to advance the frontier of science, astrologists studied the constellations to predict whether bad things will happen today.

Exercise 3: Answers for this chapter start on page 202.

1. The electric violinist put the speakers on full blast and <u>shaken</u> up the house.

   A. NO CHANGE
   B. shook
   C. had shook
   D. begun to shake

2. The incredible salary <u>had been</u> one of the reasons I am staying at my boring job.

   A. NO CHANGE
   B. will have been
   C. was
   D. is

3. I like to shop at the used bookstore because the people there are so friendly. It <u>was</u> a popular place to discover great books that can't be found elsewhere.

   A. NO CHANGE
   B. is
   C. had been
   D. was considered

4. The host presented the awards on the show and the winners <u>are</u> honored to receive them.

   A. NO CHANGE
   B. had been
   C. would have been
   D. were

5. When my uncle <u>has went</u> to buy a new computer, the salesman <u>told</u> him that he couldn't get a discount.

   A. NO CHANGE
   B. had went
   C. went
   D. goes

6. Showing us that his car has a GPS, the driver <u>claims</u> that he always knows the fastest route.

   A. NO CHANGE
   B. claiming
   C. having claimed
   D. has claimed

7. In 1869, Watson and Crick discovered something that <u>surprised</u> many scientists at that time – DNA.

   A. NO CHANGE
   B. had been surprised
   C. will have surprised
   D. surprises

8. Richard Branson has invested in many successful startups, built a global empire worth billions, and <u>flying</u> all across the world.

   A. NO CHANGE
   B. fly
   C. flew
   D. flown

9. While online tutorials make learning convenient and accessible, teachers <u>hold</u> students accountable in a way that promotes action and retention.

   A. NO CHANGE
   B. held
   C. had held
   D. holding

10. At the zoo, monkeys play on the handlebars and exotic birds <u>had chirped</u> in their elaborate cages.

    A. NO CHANGE
    B. chirp
    C. chirped
    D. could have chirped

11. Acupuncture starts with needles being inserted at the right locations. After that initial stage, the needles <u>had been</u> heated to strategically stimulate certain areas of the body.

    A. NO CHANGE
    B. have been
    C. were
    D. are

12. Last year, the teacher had chose the most difficult textbook, and the class average dropped steadily throughout the semester.

    A. NO CHANGE
    B. chose
    C. choose
    D. chosen

13. While we were on vacation, my brother and I will quietly creep out of our hotel room to go swimming with the sharks in the ocean.

    A. NO CHANGE
    B. quietly creep
    C. are quietly creeping
    D. quietly crept

14. Performing on the streets, I sing popular pop songs at the same time my partner play the guitar in the back.

    A. NO CHANGE
    B. played
    C. had played
    D. plays

15. When I went to Texas for my cousin's wedding, I drived over 200 miles to see the sites and avoid flying on a plane.

    A. NO CHANGE
    B. have driven
    C. drove
    D. driven

16. The residents of Colorado celebrated when their state would became the first to legalize marijuana.

    A. NO CHANGE
    B. had became
    C. becoming
    D. became

17. By 1999, the internet would of already drastically changed the way people around the world communicate.

    A. NO CHANGE
    B. had already drastically changed
    C. already drastically change
    D. has already drastically changed

18. Martin Luther King Jr. fought for racial equality and led the Civil Rights Movement. He called the American people to stand up for freedom, equality, and justice.

    A. NO CHANGE
    B. called on
    C. calls on
    D. calls

19. The makers of the *Angry Birds* game are now millionaires. John wishes he'd think of the idea before they did.

    A. NO CHANGE
    B. wished he had thought
    C. wishes he had thought
    D. wishes to have thought

20. During the Renaissance, the painters have experimented with different styles that combined the classics with new scientific knowledge.

    A. NO CHANGE
    B. have been experimenting
    C. had experiment
    D. experimented

Point of View

Keep the point of view the same within sentences and within paragraphs.

Example 1

Wrong:	If one does not believe, you will not succeed.
Correct:	If **one** does not believe, **one** will not succeed.
Correct:	If **you** do not believe, **you** will not succeed.

Example 2

Wrong:	If someone wants to play tennis, you should know how to serve.
Correct:	If **someone** wants to play tennis, **he or she** should know how to serve.
Correct:	If **you** want to play tennis, **you** should know how to serve.

Exercise: Keep the point of view the same in the following sentences. Answers are flexible. Answers for this chapter start on page 203.

1. The flight attendants demanded that we leave the plane even though you wanted to finish the movie.

2. Despite how hard salesmen try, sometimes you just can't get anyone you want to buy a house.

3. When you're married with your own kids, one's life becomes infinitely more complicated.

4. Even when we arrive ahead of time at the doctor's office, he makes you wait at least 15 minutes.

5. Although I chose to become a math teacher, you sometimes wonder what it would've been like to have been born a panda.

6. One must not disregard your moral compass when confronted with temptation.

7. In France, a tourist can spend a romantic night overlooking the Eiffel tower and you can also enjoy delicious coffee at all the cafes.

8. One is more likely to come back to this shop when they are treated with respect.

9. When I glanced into her eyes, one could see the tears she was holding back.

10. Registered voters will be notified of election time by a message to your email addresses.

11. To truly learn how computers work, we must take the time to study algorithms and how computers process them, regardless of whether one finds it interesting.

15

Commas

This chapter on commas is by far the important one in this book not only because it's the most tested topic on the ACT English section but also because it builds on previously covered topics such as subject-verb agreement, run-ons, and modifiers. We'll go over all the comma rules you need to know and give you examples and exercises that cover the full range of ways they can be tested.

1. Use a comma before a FANBOYS conjunction when joining two independent clauses.

Example 1

Wrong:	The neighbors upstairs are quite loud so I bought high-tech headphones to cancel out the noise.
Correct:	The neighbors upstairs are quite loud **,** so I bought high-tech headphones to cancel out the noise.

Exception

If the two independent clauses are short and clear, a comma is not necessary. For example,

The dogs barked and the wolves howled.

The ACT will not test this exception directly because it can be a matter of style, but it's a good thing to know.

Note that this rule only applies when joining two independent clauses. Conjunctions can be used in other ways that don't require commas, as in the following example.

Example 2

Wrong:	The thief stole my television, and jumped the fence.
Correct:	The thief stole my television/ and jumped the fence.

In Example 2, we have one subject performing two actions. Since we're not joining two independent clauses, we don't need a comma.

2. Use a comma after an introductory clause, phrase, or modifier.

Example 3

Wrong:	Although he is lactose intolerant he likes to eat pizza for lunch.
Correct:	Although he is lactose intolerant, he likes to eat pizza for lunch.

Example 4

Wrong:	Trapped in a mine the victims found it hard to see and breathe.
Wrong:	Trapped in a mine, the victims found it hard to see and breathe.

Example 5

Wrong:	At the end of the rainbow we saw a bowl of Lucky Charms cereal.
Correct:	At the end of the rainbow, we saw a bowl of Lucky Charms cereal.

Example 6

Wrong:	When I turn 16 I'm going to buy a car.
Correct:	When I turn 16, I'm going to buy a car.

Example 7

Wrong:	Because she's been so busy I haven't seen her in a month.
Correct:	Because she's been so busy, I haven't seen her in a month.

Most of the time, a comma is no longer required when an introductory dependent clause is moved to the end of the sentence. Note that the following sentences are punctuated correctly:

- I'm going to buy a car when I turn 16.
- I haven't seen her in a month because she's been so busy.

Clauses beginning with *after, as soon as, because, before, if, since, unless, until,* and *when* typically don't need a comma when they are at the end. Clauses beginning with *although, even though, though,* and *whereas* typically will. You don't need to memorize this list. As long as you're aware of it, it'll be pretty clear when you see this type of unnecessary comma on the ACT.

3. Use commas to separate three or more items in a series.

Example 8

Wrong:	His hobbies included jumping off planes, crashing helicopters and eating jellyfish.
Correct:	His hobbies included jumping off planes, crashing helicopters, and eating jellyfish.

Example 9

Wrong:	After college, James had three options: get a job, apply to graduate school or become a criminal.
Correct:	After college, James had three options: get a job, apply to graduate school, or become a criminal.

The comma between the last two items is sometimes called the serial or Oxford comma. Although some style guides make it optional, most require it. On the ACT, the Oxford comma is required.

4. Use commas to separate coordinate adjectives that describe the same noun.

Example 10

Wrong:	This school will train you to be a well-read, curious analytical individual.
Correct:	This school will train you to be a well-read, curious, analytical individual.

Two adjectives in a row are coordinate if you can answer yes to the following two questions:

- If the adjectives are written in reverse order, does the sentence still make sense?
- If the adjectives are written with *and* between them, does the sentence still make sense?

In Example 10, reversing the order (*analytical, curious, well-read individual*) makes sense, as does putting *and* in between them (*well-read and curious and analytical individual*). Therefore, the adjectives are coordinate and require commas in between.

Example 11

Wrong:	She went to a long, student orientation.
Correct:	She went to a long student orientation.

In Example 11, the adjectives *long* and *student* are not coordinate (we cannot reverse the order for instance), so the commas must be removed.

Example 12

Wrong:	Making sushi is a time-consuming complicated task.
Correct:	Making sushi is a time-consuming, complicated task.

Example 13

Wrong:	I like eating cold, strawberry shortcake.
Correct:	I like eating cold strawberry shortcake.

Example 14

Wrong:	My friend's dad is a lazy, complacent, parent.
Correct:	My friend's dad is a lazy, complacent parent.

Never put a comma between the final adjective and the noun.

Example 15

Wrong:	My friend's dad is a lazy, and complacent parent.
Correct:	My friend's dad is a lazy/ and complacent parent.

Never put commas between adjectives when they're already joined by *and*.

5. Use commas to set off nonrestrictive/nonessential elements.

Example 16

Wrong:	Great white sharks the most fearsome creatures of the sea are actually less dangerous than they appear.
Correct:	Great white sharks, the most fearsome creatures of the sea, are actually less dangerous than they appear.

The phrase *the most fearsome creatures of the sea* is **nonrestrictive** because it just adds additional description to the sentence; it's not essential. If we took it out, the sentence's core meaning would not change.

Example 17

Wrong:	The guy, cleaning the room, is the janitor.
Correct:	The guy/ cleaning the room/ is the janitor.

The phrase *cleaning the room* is a **restrictive** element because it specifies which guy. In other words, there are multiple guys in the room, and we need a restrictive phrase to limit the scope of who or what we're talking about.

Example 18

Wrong:	Runners around the world participate in the Boston Marathon which is 26 miles long.
Correct:	Runners around the world participate in the Boston Marathon, which is 26 miles long.

Example 19

Wrong:	The path, that we took yesterday, is 15 miles long.
Correct:	The path/ that we took yesterday/ is 15 miles long.

That is always used for restrictive/essential elements (commas are unnecessary) whereas *which* is usually used for nonrestrictive/nonessential elements (commas are necessary).

Example 20

Wrong:	Stephen King's first novel *Carrie* was a surprise success.
Correct:	Stephen King's first novel, *Carrie*, was a surprise success.

Example 21

Wrong:	The poem, *The Road Not Taken*, is one of Robert Frost's most famous works.
Correct:	The poem/ *The Road Not Taken*/ is one of Robert Frost's most famous works.

The title of the poem is an essential element because it specifies which poem is being referred to. If you took out the title, the sentence would lose its meaning. In Example 20, *Carrie* is nonessential because *first novel* already designates which book it is.

Example 22

Wrong:	Students, who work hard, will ace the ACTs.
Correct:	Students/ who work hard/ will ace the ACTs.

Example 23

Wrong:	Jonathan who works hard will ace the ACTs.
Correct:	Jonathan , who works hard , will ace the ACTs.

Make sure you understand the difference between Example 22 and Example 23.

Example 24

Wrong:	Next to the Japanese restaurant, I like, is the ice cream place.
Correct:	Next to the Japanese restaurant/ I like/ is the ice cream place.

The essential phrase *I like* is just the shortened version of *that I like*. The word *that* is sometimes omitted.

Example 25

Wrong:	Lions are carnivorous or meat-eating mammals.
Correct:	Lions are carnivorous , or meat-eating , mammals.

6. Use commas to set off transitions and intervening phrases.

This rule piggybacks off the previous one since most transitions and intervening phrases are nonessential to the sentences they're in.

Example 26

Wrong:	Some animals are nocturnal; for example the coyote hunts during the night.
Correct:	Some animals are nocturnal; for example , the coyote hunts during the night.

Example 27

Wrong:	When I told my parents I was pregnant, they were to my relief supportive and understanding.
Correct:	When I told my parents I was pregnant, they were, to my relief, supportive and understanding.

Example 28

Wrong:	Penguins unlike most other birds cannot fly.
Correct:	Penguins, unlike most other birds, cannot fly.

Example 29

Wrong:	Most bats are blind. Their sense of hearing however is amazing.
Correct:	Most bats are blind. Their sense of hearing, however, is amazing.

7. Use commas to set off direct quotations in dialogue.

Example 30

Wrong:	Confucius once said "Life is really simple, but we insist on making it complicated."
Correct:	Confucius once said, "Life is really simple, but we insist on making it complicated."

Example 31

Wrong:	"I will never cook for you again" the chef said.
Correct:	"I will never cook for you again," the chef said.

Example 32

Wrong:	My dad said, that he would buy me a car for Christmas.
Correct:	My dad said that he would buy me a car for Christmas.

Indirect quotations (rephrasings without quotation marks) do not require commas.

Exercise 1: In the following sentences, use the rules in this chapter to add or delete commas. Some sentences may be correct. Answers for this chapter start on page 204.

1. Gunpowder, which was invented in China during the Tang dynasty eventually spread to Europe through the Silk Road.

2. Jake had to answer quite a few boring, interview questions before he got the job offer.

3. Don and Marie, the architect who designed the building I live in went to the ball together.

4. I did what I did to improve the system not destroy it.

5. Drinking coffee scientists have discovered may help prevent heart disease.

6. I've decked out my laptop with a keyboard cover, pokemon stickers and a transparent case.

7. Our school's computer science club which was founded in 2000 has prompted other schools to start their own.

8. The company partnering with us is Amazon.

9. When dawn came we woke up to prepare for Kanyadaan, the initial step in a traditional Indian wedding ceremony.

10. He typed up the essay that was due the next day and threw it in his backpack.

11. Janice doodled on scrap paper while the teacher gave his lecture on trigonometry.

12. Unfortunately Syed ran out of time before he could get to the last question.

13. Maine is known for its juicy lobster rolls and its friendly laid-back residents.

14. I sold my car to a dealer who stripped it for parts and shipped them to China where scrap metal fetches a high price.

15. Mario dodged blazing fireballs, turtles with hammers and venus fly traps to rescue Princess Peach.

16. Nevertheless the world's resources cannot sustain the current rate of population growth.

17. Homer's poem, *The Iliad*, recounts the rise and fall of the great Greek hero, Achilles.

18. The tigers slowly, and quietly crept up on the antelopes, but they still couldn't catch them.

19. Ron had mentioned, that the place on the corner had really good strawberry ice cream.

20. *Interpreter of Maladies*, the 2000 Pulitzer Prize winner, is the book Tom chose for his book report.

21. After the fumes were gone the cleaners rearranged the furniture.

22. The research suggests that the craters on Mars may contain ice, but evidence of life is far from conclusive.

23. Jimmy's closest friend Chris Hernandez drove a 1998 Toyota Camry.

24. Standing in front of the customers, Debbie announced, discounts on all the clothing in the store.

25. Miyazaki's first film, *Lupin III*, was released in 1979.

26. On clear nights, we could see the silver shining stars in the sky.

27. Circling the parking lot like a predator on the hunt the driver anxiously waited for the next parking spot.

28. The rapid pace of technological development however has enabled more people to survive on less.

29. The panda is a, warm, gentle, animal that dines on bamboo shoots.

30. To make the workplace more environmentally conscious, we put solar panels, recycling bins and energy efficient dryers into place.

31. When Jacob stopped at the gas station, he realized that his wallet was back at home.

32. Roger knew the ball wasn't going in as soon as he hit it yet the fans shouted as if he had won the point.

33. If you put the eggs in the pan, and stir them for a minute, the cake will be perfect.

34. Mutual respect and communication are the foundations of a good relationship for better or worse.

35. The chef picked up the carrots from the grocery store, chopped them up with his knife and pushed them into the boiling pot of water.

36. The fan sitting in the fifth row on the right side of the stadium was dancing and screaming during every play.

37. Pete had to stay at the dull, drawn-out, play because his girlfriend was in it.

38. Polio was once a contagious devastating disease that wiped out small towns.

39. The mailman dropped off the package and I told my brother that his computer had arrived.

40. As the plane took off the flight attendants gave us emergency directions.

41. The boys finished their desserts and dashed out of the restaurant as soon as the waiter went back into the kitchen.

Exercise 2: Because the questions are restricted to the scope of this chapter, not all of them will have all four answer choices. Answers for this chapter start on page 204.

Origami

Origami originated in Japan, but today it is
$\underline{}_{1}$
practiced all over the world. Literally, the word
$\underline{}_{2}$
means "folding paper" and refers to the creation
of decorative creative, shapes and figures from pa-
$\underline{}_{3}$
per. Example creations include animals, lanterns
$\underline{}_{4}$
and boats. The easiest way to start with origami is
$\underline{}_{4}$
with a kit. Kits generally have lines and arrows to
show you where to make the fold, and how to ma-
$\underline{}_{5}$
nipulate the paper into the desired shape.

Another great way to get started is with an
origami book. These books have all sorts of great
designs with easy to follow instructions. Each de-
$\underline{}_{6}$
sign comes with pictures so that you know exactly
$\underline{}_{7}$
how and where to make each fold.

The most basic design, the one most people are
taught first, is the Japanese crane. Like most designs
$\underline{}_{8}$ $\underline{}_{9}$
it starts with a square piece of paper and eventually
$\underline{}_{9}$
turns into an intricate design that is tough to reverse
engineer.

1. **A.** NO CHANGE
   B. Japan but
   C. Japan, but,

2. **A.** NO CHANGE
   B. Literally the word
   C. Literally, the word,

3. **A.** NO CHANGE
   B. decorative, creative shapes
   C. decorative, creative, shapes
   D. decorative, creative, shapes,

4. **A.** NO CHANGE
   B. lanterns, and boats.
   C. lanterns, and, boats.

5. **A.** NO CHANGE
   B. fold, and,
   C. fold and

6. **A.** NO CHANGE
   B. designs, with

7. **A.** NO CHANGE
   B. so, that
   C. so, that,

8. **A.** NO CHANGE
   B. first is
   C. first is,

9. **A.** NO CHANGE
   B. designs, it

Although special origami paper can be bought at craft stores, any paper that can hold a fold can be used. You can even glue colored, tissue paper
<u>colored, tissue paper</u>
10
or aluminum foil to regular paper for an interesting look. Normal copy paper is okay for simple folds, but it's a bit too heavy for more delicate designs. Very heavy paper is ideal for <u>wet-folding which is</u>
11
a technique developed by Akira Yoshizawa in the early 1900s. Wet-folding allows you to manipulate the paper into <u>curves, and</u> other interesting designs
12
that can't be done with dry paper. The design holds its <u>shape, after</u> the paper dries.
13

The paper traditionally used in Japan is called *washi*, which refers to hand made paper but translates literally to "Japanese paper." It is much tougher than paper made from wood pulp. Washi is most commonly made from the bark of the gampi <u>tree, but</u> bamboo, wheat, <u>rice and hemp</u> are often
14   15
used as well.

10. A. NO CHANGE
     B. colored tissue paper
     C. colored tissue, paper
     D. colored, tissue, paper

11. A. NO CHANGE
     B. wet-folding, which,
     C. wet-folding, which

12. A. NO CHANGE
     B. curves and,
     C. curves and

13. A. NO CHANGE
     B. shape, after,
     C. shape after,
     D. shape after

14. A. NO CHANGE
     B. tree but
     C. tree, but,
     D. tree but,

15. A. NO CHANGE
     B. rice, and hemp
     C. rice, and hemp,
     D. rice and hemp,

16
Comma Abuse

A lot of the comma related questions on the ACT test you on what NOT to do with them. The previous chapter on commas already presented several comma misuses. This chapter lays out additional comma misuses you will have to be on the lookout for.

1. Don't separate the subject from the verb with a comma.

Example 1

| Wrong: | The meeting's purpose, is to bring all parties together. |
| Correct: | The meeting's purpose/ is to bring all parties together. |

Example 2

| Wrong: | The ships that are trapped at sea, set sail a week ago. |
| Correct: | The ships that are trapped at sea/ set sail a week ago. |

2. Don't use commas to separate compound elements that aren't independent clauses.

Compounds elements are things connected by *and*.

Example 2

| Wrong: | The director, and his crew set up all the equipment in the middle of the night. |
| Correct: | The director/ and his crew set up all the equipment in the middle of the night. |

Example 3

| Wrong: | The tsunami in Thailand resulted in thousands of deaths, and millions of dollars in damages. |
| Correct: | The tsunami in Thailand resulted in thousands of deaths/ and millions of dollars in damages. |

Example 4

Wrong:	Sean picked up the newspaper on the porch, and drove off in his Lamborghini.
Correct:	Sean picked up the newspaper on the porch/ and drove off in his Lamborghini.

3. Don't use a comma after the introductory phrase of an inverted sentence.

Example 5

Wrong:	At the bottom of hell, rest the devil and his minions.
Correct:	At the bottom of hell/ rest the devil and his minions.

4. Don't use a comma before a preposition (typically *at, for, in, of, on, to, with*).

This one is not a hard and fast rule, but on the ACT, **a comma before a preposition is almost always wrong**. This rule especially holds when the preposition is one that usually goes with its preceding words (e.g. the *of* in *consists of*). Some examples will clarify:

Example 6

Wrong:	She was waiting, at the train station.
Correct:	She was waiting/ at the train station.

Example 7

Wrong:	The police investigation, of the crime scene, didn't turn up any clues.
Correct:	The police investigation/ of the crime scene/ didn't turn up any clues.

Example 8

Wrong:	Robert wants to make changes, to the essay, before we submit it.
Correct:	Robert wants to make changes/ to the essay/ before we submit it.

Example 9

Wrong:	Rolex watches are designed, with elegance, style, and luxury in mind.
Correct:	Rolex watches are designed/ with elegance, style, and luxury in mind.

Example 10

Wrong:	Andy Murray, of Great Britain, competed intensely, for the gold medal in tennis.
Correct:	Andy Murray/ of Great Britain/ competed intensely/ for the gold medal in tennis.

5. Don't use a comma before an infinitive.

Like rule 4, this one is also not a hard and fast rule, but on the ACT, it comes pretty close.

Example 11

Wrong:	My cousins went to the rooftop, to get a better view of the city.
Correct:	My cousins went to the rooftop, to get a better view of the city.

Example 12

Wrong:	We must be conscious of our spending, to ensure we have enough for our vacation.
Correct:	We must be conscious of our spending, to ensure we have enough for our vacation.

Exercise 1: Remove unnecessary commas from the following sentences. Some sentences may be correct. Answers for this chapter start on page 207.

1. The train ran off the tracks that were twisted by the bandits, and tumbled down the cliff.

2. Having a large stock of water and canned foods, is quite important, especially during the apocalypse.

3. The public computers in the lab, have been moved due to vandalism.

4. Each of the students, and teachers, in the school will receive a handbook on proper conduct.

5. The bank told us that we would qualify for a credit card with a better interest rate, and greater rewards if we opened a savings account.

6. A vast majority of the questionnaire, covers issues that are not relevant to what we're studying.

7. Job placements were determined by test scores, calculated by the employer organization.

8. Martin Luther King Jr. believed that all people have a right to freedom, and that everyone should be treated equally.

9. The band members, at Newton High School, forgot to rehearse for their big concert.

10. William broke through the glass window, and hopped over the fence, to get away from the police.

11. All across China, where new housing projects accommodate the wealthy instead of the poor, protests are being staged at city government buildings.

12. The professor will deduct points off your total score, unless you're able to turn in the essay today.

13. In the game of life, the people who work hard and hustle, will always succeed in spite of their circumstances.

14. The roasted chicken was seasoned with a special mix of spices and cooked, to perfection.

15. A senior at the big accounting firm PWC pleaded not guilty to forging the books, claiming that it was his coworkers who did it.

16. Marjorie introduced the new students, to their dorm rooms for the year.

17. The restaurant that two hours ago had a line out the door, was now quiet and deserted.

18. The movie theater, which was permeated by the smell of popcorn, and illuminated by the motion picture, was 20 years old.

19. Each year, only schools with good classroom sizes, and a top test score average will receive funding.

20. The books that were sitting on the shelf, fell onto the floor below.

21. The photographer rushed, to the scene, to get the best shot of the actors on the red carpet.

22. Because he embraced failure instead of avoiding it, Chris quickly learned how to play the piano, speak Spanish, and solve the Rubik's Cube.

23. Beneath the electric chair that Eric sat in, was a knife that he used to cut himself free.

24. The kids were swimming out to the outlying island, when the great white shark approached.

25. Growing up in poverty, I often dreamed, of the luxury, that I was working towards.

26. The mayor has not been able to repair his reputation, since his dismissal from office.

27. Behind the dumpster, were squirrels, mice, and Tom, foraging for food.

28. Known for its noodle dishes, the restaurant down the street always has customers, most of whom are Asian.

29. Donations poured in to help the victims of the crash, and their families.

30. Having had his arm in a cast for a month, Jacob found it difficult, to type on his computer.

31. Joshua Grossman, a professor at NYU, and his associate claim that their research is definitive and trustworthy.

32. The greatest tennis players are the ones who have the courage, to play the big points with no restraint.

33. On the left wall of the living room, hung five paintings and a poster.

34. Joey sat in the waiting room, until his wife got out of the doctor's office.

35. I can't buy those new shoes, if the price is too high.

36. David wasn't able to play to the best of his ability, because of the foot injury.

37. Novak Djokovic, one of the best tennis players, of the modern era, is worshipped as a god in Serbia.

38. It was my father who inspired me, to pursue medicine as my course, of study.

Exercise 2: Answers for this chapter start on page 207.

The Five Lined Skink

When the weather starts to warm up, all thoughts turn to camping. I love camping in the wilderness. We built a little cabin nestled deep in the woods to get away from the hustle and bustle, of modern life. It is only accessible by foot, or all terrain vehicle. No road access at all. This is great for privacy but makes it difficult to drag in all of our gear. There is no running water, so everything we need has to be brought in. Everything we bring in, of course, has to be taken out.

The remoteness makes it the ideal location for nature watching: the deer crossing the beaver dam, the otters jumping and playing in the water, the little chipmunks scurrying here and there to gather nuts. Duck species ranging from the mallard, to the brown wood duck, can be seen at dusk. They like to sleep on small, quiet ponds, safe from predators that come out at night, such as the fisher, and the wolf.

1. **A.** NO CHANGE
   B. camping, in
   C. camping, in,
   D. camping in,

2. **A.** NO CHANGE
   B. woods, to
   C. woods, to,
   D. woods to,

3. **A.** NO CHANGE
   B. bustle of
   C. bustle of,
   D. bustle, of,

4. **A.** NO CHANGE
   B. foot or,
   C. foot or
   D. foot, or,

5. **A.** NO CHANGE
   B. in of course
   C. in of course,
   D. in, of course

6. **A.** NO CHANGE
   B. dam the otters
   C. dam the otters,
   D. dam, the otters,

7. **A.** NO CHANGE
   B. mallard to
   C. mallard to,
   D. mallard, to,

8. **A.** NO CHANGE
   B. duck, can,
   C. duck can,
   D. duck can

9. **A.** NO CHANGE
   B. ponds, safe,
   C. ponds safe,
   D. ponds safe

10. **A.** NO CHANGE
    B. fisher and,
    C. fisher and
    D. fisher, and,

Animal populations go in cycles. We have seen the number of small animals decline <u>steadily, over the course, of a few years</u> and then slowly replen-
11
ish again. The fisher eats <u>anything, including</u> por-
12
cupines. It is one of the few animals that can tackle the sharp <u>quills, and dig</u> into the flesh.
13

I like watching all of the animals, but I think the five lined skink is my <u>favorite, because</u> it is so
14
rare. The tiny lizard can usually only be seen in the spring. This is when the young start leaving the nest to explore. The young all have bright blue <u>lines,</u>
15
<u>along</u> their bodies and tails, which is how the lizard
15
got its name. As they get older, the females lose the blue color and the lines turn a light brown. Males keep the blue <u>tails, but</u> the lines on the body also
16
turn a light brownish color.

The skink is completely harmless. The little ones come <u>out, to</u> sun on the rocks. They dart out of
17
<u>sight in</u> a split <u>second, when</u> they detect the slight-
18   19
est movement. I have to be very <u>still, and quiet</u> to
20
get a glimpse of these cute little critters.

11. **A.** NO CHANGE
     B. steadily over the course, of a few years
     C. steadily, over the course of a few years
     D. steadily over the course of a few years

12. **A.** NO CHANGE
     B. anything including
     C. anything, including,
     D. anything including,

13. **A.** NO CHANGE
     B. quills and dig,
     C. quills and dig
     D. quills, and dig,

14. **A.** NO CHANGE
     B. favorite because
     C. favorite, because,
     D. favorite because,

15. **A.** NO CHANGE
     B. lines along
     C. lines along,
     D. lines, along,

16. **A.** NO CHANGE
     B. tails but
     C. tails, but,
     D. tails but,

17. **A.** NO CHANGE
     B. out, to,
     C. out to,
     D. out to

18. **A.** NO CHANGE
     B. sight, in
     C. sight in,
     D. sight, in,

19. **A.** NO CHANGE
     B. second when
     C. second when,
     D. second, when,

20. **A.** NO CHANGE
     B. still, and quiet,
     C. still and quiet
     D. still and quiet,

17

Apostrophes

Apostrophes serve two purposes—possession and contraction.

Possession

To show possession, always add an **'s** unless the noun is plural and ends in *s*, in which case add only the apostrophe.

Example 1

Wrong:	Tonys hat is on the floor.
Correct:	**Tony's** hat is on the floor.

Example 2

Wrong:	Louis' scarf is 3 feet long.
Correct:	**Louis's** scarf is 3 feet long.

Example 3

Wrong:	Both players's jerseys were soaked with sweat.
Correct:	Both **players'** jerseys were soaked with sweat.

Contraction

Apostrophes can also be used to take the place of missing words or letters. For example, *it's* is short for *it is* and *can't* is short for *cannot*. The following is a table of common contractions:

Contraction	stands for...
it's	it is
they're	they are
who's	who is
could've	could have
he's	he is
I've	I have
you're	you are
that's	that is

As you probably know, there are quite a few words that get commonly confused with possessives and contractions that sound the same. Here are the ones you need to know for the ACT:

it's vs. its

it's (contraction) – He told me that **it's** an alien from outer space.
its (possessive) – The poster fell from **its** spot on the wall.

they're vs. their vs. there

they're (contraction) – **They're** going to meet us at the restaurant.
their (possessive) – The students passed in **their** homework late.
there (location) – Jacob put the water bottle over **there**.

who's vs. whose

who's (contraction) – **Who's** that person sitting by himself?
whose (possessive) – I have a friend **whose** mother is an accountant.

Whenever you're on a question that deals with contractions, ALWAYS read the sentence with the uncontracted version to see if it makes sense.

Example 4

Wrong:	The book has a cool picture on it's cover.
Correct:	The book has a cool picture on **its** cover.

Would the uncontracted phrase *it is cover* make sense in Example 4? Nope. We need the possessive *its*.

Example 5

Wrong:	He is the actor whose most known for his role in *Batman*.
Correct:	He is the actor **who's** most known for his role in *Batman*.

In Example 5, we mean to say *who is* and can do so using the contracted version, *who's*.

Exercise: Answers for this chapter start on page 210.

1. Praised by critics for <u>it's having</u> innovative plot and cinematography, the director's first movie was a huge hit at the box office.

   A. NO CHANGE
   B. its
   C. it's
   D. its'

2. After the funeral was held for the brave soldiers, the general scattered their <u>bodies</u> ashes into the sea.

   A. NO CHANGE
   B. body's
   C. bodys
   D. bodies'

3. Writing code for applications and websites requires a lot of complexity to be stored in the <u>programmers mind</u> at any one time.

   A. NO CHANGE
   B. programmer's mind
   C. programmers' mind
   D. programmers mind

4. Because their families are wealthy, each of my <u>friends' houses</u> has a swimming pool.

   A. NO CHANGE
   B. friend's houses
   C. friends houses
   D. friends houses

5. I go to a school <u>who's</u> parking lot can accommodate only 10 cars.

   A. NO CHANGE
   B. whose
   C. that the
   D. where

6. The teacher told us that the <u>semester's grades</u> will be released a week from now.

   A. NO CHANGE
   B. semesters grades
   C. semesters' grades
   D. grade's for the semester

7. Every day, I look at the <u>weeks</u> deadlines and make sure I'm on track to meet them.

   A. NO CHANGE
   B. weeks'
   C. week's
   D. weeks's

8. After their meeting with the principal, <u>the teachers'</u> gossiped amongst themselves about who would be fired.

   A. NO CHANGE
   B. the teachers
   C. the teacher's
   D. the teachers's

9. Examining the mountain in front of them, the hikers were confident in <u>they're ability to climb its</u> rocky terrain.

   A. NO CHANGE
   B. they're ability to climb it's
   C. their ability to climb its
   D. their ability to climb it's

10. Known for his powerful hooks, Mike Tyson was once <u>one of boxings</u> most fearsome competitors.

    A. NO CHANGE
    B. boxings
    C. boxing's
    D. one of boxing's

11. Before the dancers could finish, a loud noise in the audience disrupted <u>their</u> rhythm and ruined the entire performance.

    A. NO CHANGE
    B. they're
    C. it's
    D. its'

12. Taylor took the frame down, added a fresh coat of paint on each of <u>it's</u> sides, and inserted a new picture.

    A. NO CHANGE
    B. its'
    C. its
    D. their

13. My friends love to eat. Inside <u>they're refriger-ator, there's</u> always a full stock of snacks and drinks.

    A. NO CHANGE
    B. they're refrigerator, theirs
    C. their refrigerator, theirs
    D. their refrigerator, there's

14. One end of the cable goes through the top opening of the wooden pole and the other end wraps around <u>it's</u> foundation.

    A. NO CHANGE
    B. its'
    C. its
    D. their

15. The deck of <u>Emily's parents's</u> yacht had been completely destroyed by the hurricane.

    A. NO CHANGE
    B. Emily's parents'
    C. Emily's parents
    D. Emilys parents'

16. The novel's protagonist, <u>who's</u> telekinetic powers are capable of mass destruction, is a seemingly quiet and shy girl.

    A. NO CHANGE
    B. whose
    C. who has
    D. with her

17. The water dripped down from the ceiling, hit the cabinet, and dripped onto the <u>rooms</u> floor.

    A. NO CHANGE
    B. room's
    C. rooms'
    D. rooms's

18. We will host a casino night where the players donate <u>their</u> winnings to charity.

    A. NO CHANGE
    B. there
    C. they're
    D. its

19. Because she was late to work, Joanne had to report to her <u>factorys'</u> director.

    A. NO CHANGE
    B. factory's
    C. factories'
    D. factories

20. After doctors found her lying unconscious on the floor, they rushed her to the <u>infirmary's</u> emergency room.

    A. NO CHANGE
    B. infirmaries
    C. infirmaries'
    D. infirmarys

18

Word Choice

One of the most commonly tested concepts is word choice, choosing the most appropriate word in context. Unfortunately, it's impossible to cover the infinite number of ways this concept can show up. After all, there are hundreds of thousands of words and no formulaic rules for why one word should be chosen over the other. Although you'll have to rely on your fluency in English for most of them, the ACT does not make these questions difficult. In fact, the answer must be clear enough so that it's not up to opinion. Here are a few general guidelines:

1. Choose lively and expressive words

What do I mean by expressive words? On the ACT, you might see a word choice question like:

With a thousand people staring at me, I suddenly felt the need for fresh air and <u>went</u> *outside.*

Which of the following choices best expresses the idea that the narrator left in a hurry?

A. NO CHANGE
B. went
C. moved
D. dashed

The answer here is **D** not only because it implies that the person was in a rush but also because *went* and *moved* are boring, everyday words. If the ACT wants an expressive word, don't choose a boring word.

2. Choose specific words

Here's an example:

Fish with bright colors have to be especially careful of dangerous <u>things</u> *that lurk in the sea.*

Which choice fits best in the context of this sentence?

A. NO CHANGE
B. animals
C. mammals
D. predators

The answer is **D**. The most specific words convey the most meaning, and on the ACT, the most meaningful words will usually be the answer.

3. Choose the word that's unlike the others

This guideline applies to "acceptable alternative" questions.

The tennis player smashed his racquet in disgust, <u>aggravated</u> by his poor performance.

Which of the following alternatives would NOT be acceptable?

A. angered
B. enraged
C. repelled
D. infuriated

The answer is **C**. The word *repelled* just doesn't quite fit here, especially when all the other choices share the same meaning.

4. Don't choose casual or informal language

Tired from the 20 mile hike, Yasmine retired to her tent and <u>snoozed.</u>

A. NO CHANGE
B. hit the sack.
C. slept.
D. dozed off.

The answer is **C**. The other answers are too informal.

5. Don't forget your grammar rules

Some questions look like they're testing you on word choice when they're actually testing you on grammar.

The zombies <u>raised</u> from their graves and hunted the survivors.

A. NO CHANGE
B. rise
C. rose
D. rised

A lot of students think this is a word choice question when it's not. Notice that choice **D**—*rised*—is not a word. Choice **B** is in the present tense when the sentence is in the past tense. Choice **A** uses the wrong verb; the meaning of *raise* is not quite the same as that of *rise*. The answer is **C**. Here's one more example:

I do my laundry <u>while</u> she does the dishes.

Which of the following alternatives would NOT be acceptable?

A. while
B. at the same time
C. as
D. then

The answer is **D**. Yes, all the other choices share the same meaning but more importantly, choice **D** would make the sentence a run-on. No matter what type of question you're on, always keep your grammar rules in mind.

Keep in mind that the guidelines above are just guidelines. Every question is different and not all of them will apply to every one. Your own judgment will be your best weapon once you've done enough practice.

Exercise 1: Answers for this chapter start on page 210.

Campbell's Thousand-Faced Hero

Joseph Campbell's 1949 comparative study of mythology, *The Hero with a Thousand Faces*, presents a fascinating concept that can be applied to many
<u>1</u>
of the great stories of modern times. He found that many hero stories <u>among</u> time and cultures <u>clone</u> a
<u>2</u>   <u>3</u>
similar pattern, a 17-stage journey, in fact. The three major <u>divisions</u> of this journey are the hero's depar-
<u>4</u>
ture, his initiation, and his return.

<u>In agreement with</u> Campbell's schema, every
<u>5</u>
hero receives a <u>plea</u> to adventure into the unknown,
<u>6</u>
usually inspired by a <u>vision</u> that changes the hero's
<u>7</u>
understanding of himself and his purpose in life. In *Star Wars*, Luke <u>learns</u> that his father was a Jedi
<u>8</u>
knight and receives his father's lightsaber from Obi-Wan Kenobi.

1. Which of the following alternatives would be LEAST acceptable?
   - A. theory
   - B. idea
   - C. thesis
   - D. opinion

2.
   - A. NO CHANGE
   - B. across
   - C. on
   - D. over

3.
   - A. NO CHANGE
   - B. recap
   - C. follow
   - D. redo

4. Which of the following alternatives would be LEAST acceptable?
   - A. parts
   - B. stages
   - C. phases
   - D. areas

5.
   - A. NO CHANGE
   - B. Pertaining to
   - C. According to
   - D. In relation to

6.
   - A. NO CHANGE
   - B. a ring
   - C. a call
   - D. an invitation

7. At this point, the author wants to indicate that the hero has gone through a dramatic transformation. Which choice most effectively accomplishes this goal?
   - A. NO CHANGE
   - B. revelation
   - C. goal
   - D. dream

8. Which of the following alternatives would NOT be acceptable?
   - A. NO CHANGE
   - B. discovers
   - C. finds out
   - D. detects

After his foster parents are killed, Luke chooses to embark with Obi-Wan on an adventure through distant galaxies. Similarly, in *The Matrix*, Neo is pre-sented with the truth that he has not been living in the real world, which is actually a barren wasteland.

He chooses to take "the red pill," unplugs from the civilized world he has known for his entire life, and enters a desolate reality.

    The initiation stage involves many trials, temptations, and failures. Luke Skywalker endures dangerous battles, undergoes difficult training with Yoda, and eventually faces the evil Darth Vader, as well as the truth that Vader is his father. In the process, he loses his hand and is nearly killed. Neo submits to intense training and self-questioning, which culminates in a fight with Agent Smith.

    After hammering away through great suffering and adversity, the hero returns as a new person with greater power and self-understanding, in possession of some knowledge, ability, or token that indicates his newfound mastery. Luke successfully faces Darth Vader and wins him back to the good side. Batman returns, and Neo rises from the dead with greater powers than before.

9. Which choice fits most specifically in the context of this sentence?
   - **A.** NO CHANGE
   - **B.** is shown
   - **C.** confronts
   - **D.** sees

10. Which of the following alternatives would NOT be acceptable?
   - **A.** elects
   - **B.** is forced
   - **C.** decides
   - **D.** opts

11. Which choice fits most specifically in the context of this sentence?
   - **A.** NO CHANGE
   - **B.** unpleasant
   - **C.** sad
   - **D.** painful

12. At this point, the author would like to suggest that Luke was successful in battle. Which choice most effectively accomplishes this goal?
   - **A.** NO CHANGE
   - **B.** triumphs through
   - **C.** suffers through
   - **D.** goes through

13.
   - **A.** NO CHANGE
   - **B.** furthermore
   - **C.** also plus
   - **D.** with

14.
   - **A.** NO CHANGE
   - **B.** hanging tough
   - **C.** sticking it out
   - **D.** persevering

15. Which of the following alternatives would NOT be acceptable?
   - **A.** conveys
   - **B.** points to
   - **C.** reflects
   - **D.** describes

Exercise 2: Answers for this chapter start on page 210.

Chivalry

In modern times, the word "chivalry" is generally assumed to refer to men treating women with respect and courtesy, opening doors for them, pulling out chairs for them, and giving up their seats on buses and in crowded rooms. In medieval times, however, the term transported a much richer
<u>1</u>
meaning that underlay the expectations placed on aristocratic men. The word derives from the French
<u>2</u>
word *chevalier*, which means "horseman." In general, it referred to any man who could allow to arm
<u>3</u>
himself and ride his own horse into battle–in other
<u>4</u>
words, a knight. In those days very few men were
<u>4</u>
able to do it, hence the association between chivalry
<u>5</u>   <u>6</u>
and the aristocracy.

1. **A.** NO CHANGE
    B. moved
    C. carried
    D. displayed

2. Which of the following alternatives would NOT be acceptable?
    A. extends from
    B. derives from
    C. comes from
    D. originates from

3. **A.** NO CHANGE
    B. afford
    C. provide
    D. bear the expense

4. **A.** NO CHANGE
    B. in which case,
    C. therefore,
    D. in summary,

5. **A.** NO CHANGE
    B. that
    C. those
    D. such

6. Which of the following alternatives would NOT be acceptable?
    A. NO CHANGE
    B. attachment
    C. connection
    D. link

Over time, what began as an idealization of knightly conduct during the Crusades of the 11th and 12th centuries <u>transformed</u> into a complex sys-
₇
tem of ethics governing a knight's behavior toward God, his lord, both his allies and his enemies, and women and children. The literature of the late middle ages, particularly the Arthurian legends, <u>shaped</u>
₈
the imaginations of <u>many</u> peasants to love and be-
₉
lieve in the ideal of the courtly knight. In *Sir Gawain and the Green Knight*, written in the late 1300s, Sir Gawain displays an almost obsessive desire to <u>ful-</u>
₁₀
<u>fill the chivalric code.</u> Other characters constantly
₁₀
reference his reputation as a knight known for both his <u>fantastic mind</u> in battle and his excellent man-
₁₁
ners.

7. All of the following are acceptable alternatives EXCEPT:
   - **A.** persisted
   - **B.** developed
   - **C.** turned
   - **D.** evolved

8. Which of the following alternatives would NOT be acceptable?
   - **A.** sparked
   - **B.** shaped
   - **C.** inspired
   - **D.** amped up

9. Which choice provides the most specific information?
   - **A.** NO CHANGE
   - **B.** a lot of
   - **C.** thousands of
   - **D.** tons of

10. Which of the following choices is LEAST acceptable?
    - **A.** NO CHANGE
    - **B.** achieve
    - **C.** honor
    - **D.** respect

11. **A.** NO CHANGE
    - **B.** know-how
    - **C.** smarts
    - **D.** prowess

Raymond Lull's 13th-century book on chivalry
<u>12</u>

details the ethical expectations, rules, and instruc-
<u>13</u>

tions a knight should follow. He was to be a man of

able body, good lineage, and wealth. He was to be <u>in</u>
<u>14</u>

<u>control of his abilities and his wealth,</u> giving aid to
<u>14</u>

those in need and protecting women and children.

He was to be loyal to his lord, courageous in his de-

fense, and a wise advisor. <u>Basically,</u> he was to be a
<u>15</u>

man of honor, who would stay true to his Christian

faith and keep his word at all costs.

This old notion of chivalry should not be a

relic of the past. After all, honor, loyalty, humility,

courage, and generosity are <u>relevant</u> in all aspects
<u>16</u>

of our increasingly global society. Perhaps the mod-

ern definition of chivalry should be <u>revisited.</u>
<u>17</u>

12. Which choice fits most specifically in the context of this sentence?

    A. NO CHANGE
    B. publication
    C. manual
    D. tome

13. Which of the following alternatives would NOT be acceptable?

    A. confirms
    B. lays out
    C. specifies
    D. describes

14. Which choice fits most specifically in the context of this sentence?

    A. NO CHANGE
    B. generous with
    C. courteous with
    D. responsible with

15. At this point, the author wants to emphasize that honor was the highest priority for a knight. Which choice most effectively accomplishes this goal?

    A. NO CHANGE
    B. First,
    C. Above all,
    D. Initially,

16. Which of the following alternatives would NOT be acceptable?

    A. NO CHANGE
    B. a big deal
    C. important
    D. essential

17. Which of the following alternatives would be LEAST acceptable?

    A. NO CHANGE
    B. revised.
    C. changed.
    D. varied.

19
Transitions

To demonstrate what transitions are and how they're used, let's consider the following sentence:

May's cookies are sweet and sugary. Sam eats them all the time.

In this sentence, it's understood that Sam eats May's cookies *because* they are sweet and sugary. Despite the implied cause and effect relationship here, the reader can't be completely sure. It could be that the two sentences represent two totally independent ideas: May's cookies are sweet and sugary, and it just so happens that Sam eats them all the time. To make the cause-and-effect relationship absolutely clear, we could insert a transition:

*May's cookies are sweet and sugary. **Therefore,** Sam eats them all the time.*

This is a bit of an extreme example, but it illustrates an important point—transitions have meaning. They express how two sentences or paragraphs relate to one another, and they make that connection explicit, even if it's a bit unnecessary to do so. In this case, the *therefore* is probably not needed, but suppose we wanted to imply that sweet and sugary were bad qualities:

*May's cookies are sweet and sugary. **Nevertheless,** Sam eats them all the time.*

With one word, we're able to shift the meaning entirely. Now, sweet and sugary cookies are unhealthy snacks to be avoided.

How sentences connect to one another comes naturally to most students. The hard part is staying aware of the full context. In this one made-up example, we can't be completely sure what the author's intended meaning is, but on the ACT, the author's intention will always be clear. Your job on ACT transition questions is to read the context, figure out the author's meaning, and choose the transition word that conveys that meaning. Always read the sentence before and the sentence after the one in question.

You'll typically see transitions at the start of sentences. And while there are many transitions out there, as long as you are familiar with the ones in the table below, you shouldn't need to memorize anything. In fact, this table includes almost all the transitions that have shown up on released past exams. The best way to get better is to practice and review, practice and review.

Common Transition Words		
Example	**Transition...**	**Similar Transitions**
I love eating vanilla ice cream. **However**, too much of it makes me sick.	presents an opposing point or balances a previous statement	fortunately, on the other hand, conversely, whereas, while, in contrast, on the contrary, yet
Math trains you to approach problems more analytically. **Furthermore**, it helps you calculate the minimum tip when you eat out.	adds new and supporting information	in addition, also, moreover, and, too, as well, additionally, not to mention
Pandas are rapidly becoming extinct. **In fact**, some experts predict that pandas will die out in 50 years.	gives emphasis to a point by adding a specific detail/case	as a matter of fact, indeed, to illustrate, for instance, for example
The state is facing a flu epidemic. **Consequently**, all hospital rooms are filled at the moment.	shows cause & effect	as a result, because, hence, therefore, thus, accordingly, so, for this reason
Granted, the ACT is a long and tedious exam, but it's necessary for college admissions.	concedes a point to make way for your own point	nevertheless, although, regardless, despite, even if, nonetheless, still, even so
Place the bread on an ungreased baking sheet. **Finally**, bake in a preheated oven for 10 minutes.	shows order or sequence	subsequently, previously, afterwards, next, then, eventually, before
Social security numbers uniquely identify citizens. **In the same way**, IP addresses identify computers.	shows similarity	similarly, likewise, by the same token
In conclusion, the world would be a happier place without nuclear weapons.	gives a summary or restatement	in summary, to sum up, in short, in other words

Some other transitions that didn't quite fit in the table are *meanwhile, instead,* and *otherwise.* If you understand all these transitions and how they're used, you should have no problem answering these questions on the ACT.

Exercise 1: Choose the best transition. Answers for this chapter start on page 211.

1. Although women in cities from New York to Boston demanded equality in academic opportunities, most East Coast universities did not yield to such demands. <u>In fact,</u> coeducational balance did not become a prominent issue for East Coast admissions officers until the 1960s.

    A. NO CHANGE
    B. In addition,
    C. For example,
    D. Be that as it may,

2. As it turned out, Senator Aldrich did not plan his Jekyll Island trip for relaxation purposes. <u>Therefore,</u> he confidentially planned the weeklong affair to confer with Wall Street executives for a specific purpose–to draft a banking reform bill that would create a centralized American banking system.

    A. NO CHANGE
    B. Nevertheless,
    C. Instead,
    D. Afterwards,

3. Some conservatives claim that America was founded as a Christian nation by devout men who sought to establish a system of law and governance based on the Bible. More secular voices, <u>in summary,</u> have argued that the "Christian nation" concept is a misnomer.

    A. NO CHANGE
    B. likewise,
    C. for instance,
    D. on the other hand,

4. The general knew that the price of victory was enormous. <u>Moreover,</u> there would be over a hundred battles and thousands of deaths by the time the war was over.

    A. NO CHANGE
    B. Yet,
    C. Eventually,
    D. Indeed,

5. Emily Dickinson is known for her reclusiveness, her isolation from the world outside her home. <u>Thus,</u> she did have numerous family members to interact with and keep her company when she needed it.

    A. NO CHANGE
    B. Meanwhile,
    C. Fortunately,
    D. As a result,

6. <u>Even as</u> Emily Dickinson was never recognized as the poet she was during her own lifetime, she is now known as one of the greatest poets ever.

    A. NO CHANGE
    B. Before
    C. Unless
    D. Although

7. Dogs use their excellent sense of smell to detect friends and foe around them. <u>Nevertheless,</u> bats rely on their incredible ears to navigate the world using echolocation.

    A. NO CHANGE
    B. In the same way,
    C. On the one hand,
    D. Otherwise,

8. Jonas became fascinated by the variety of seafood in Japan. <u>Nonetheless, the people</u> there ate everything from raw fish over rice, known as sushi, to dried squid and octopus.

    A. NO CHANGE
    B. Conversely, the people
    C. Additionally, the people
    D. The people

9. The cooks first beat the mixture until the batter comes together in the pan. The pan is then put into the oven and the cake is baked for 30 minutes. <u>Meanwhile,</u> the cake is taken out and put into a decorative box as it cools.

    A. NO CHANGE
    B. Secondly,
    C. Finally,
    D. In conclusion,

10. My cousin in Vietnam told me in advance that a gift would be arriving at my doorstep. <u>Nevertheless,</u> it surprised me to see a package from such a faraway place reach a small suburban town in Minnesota.

    A. NO CHANGE
    B. In fact,
    C. Furthermore,
    D. Therefore,

11. Many students at the university copy their homework assignments, store test answers in their calculators, and collude in groups. <u>Additionally,</u> professors now use multiple versions of their tests, along with questions that are open response and cannot be copied.

    A. NO CHANGE
    B. To illustrate,
    C. As a result,
    D. Just in case,

12. If nothing is done, many sea creatures will soon die off in the face of illegal hunting and the destruction of their natural habitats. <u>Similarly,</u> the leatherback turtle is predicted to be extinct within 20 years.

    A. NO CHANGE
    B. In other words,
    C. In contrast,
    D. In particular,

13. When I visited New York City for the first time, seeing all those densely packed streets didn't intimidate me. Regardless, they just reminded me of my childhood in Hong Kong, where I would walk from shop to shop selling newspapers.

    A. NO CHANGE
    B. They
    C. Similarly, they
    D. Finally, they

14. Even though they all serve sushi, there are many types of sushi restaurants in Japan. Accordingly, kaiten sushi restaurants use a conveyor belt from which customers can pick out what they want to eat.

    A. NO CHANGE
    B. Thus,
    C. Otherwise,
    D. For example,

15. The United States upholds free speech and the right to bear arms. In addition, the Singapore government bans the chewing of gum and fines its citizens if they forget to flush a public toilet.

    A. NO CHANGE
    B. In contrast,
    C. Otherwise,
    D. Similarly,

Exercise 2: Answers for this chapter start on page 211.

1. As most people associate fortune cookies with Chinese cuisine, they were developed entirely in America and are not at all a Chinese invention.

    A. NO CHANGE
    B. Otherwise
    C. However
    D. Even though

2. Global warming has lead to the melting of the polar ice caps, harming ecosystems and disrupting natural habitats that have existed for centuries. Even so, there has been a scramble to reduce carbon dioxide emissions and slow the rate of environmental change.

    A. NO CHANGE
    B. For this reason,
    C. Meanwhile,
    D. Be that as it may,

3. A vital part of any school curriculum, physical education gives students a much needed break in the middle of the day. Consequently, the classes promote healthy eating and exercise, something most Americans don't get enough of.

    A. NO CHANGE
    B. However,
    C. Likewise,
    D. Moreover,

4. One of the most densely populated areas in the world, Hong Kong is a city bustling with tourists and foreign businessmen, <u>not to mention</u> the 7 million people who live there.

    A. NO CHANGE
    B. furthermore
    C. don't forget about
    D. also plus

5. The President must maintain his position on this issue <u>provided that</u> the public does not think he is indecisive and easily swayed.

    A. NO CHANGE
    B. so that
    C. in spite of the fact that
    D. because

6. <u>Where</u> the government breaks up the monopoly of the cable companies to allow for more competition, service outages and high monthly charges will continue to be the norm.

    A. NO CHANGE
    B. If
    C. Unless
    D. As soon as

7. Sam likes to keep his finances in check with spreadsheets that track where he spends his money, <u>alternatively,</u> Juno impulsively spends money on things she doesn't need.

    A. NO CHANGE
    B. rather than
    C. so
    D. whereas

8. The Mongols are better equipped, have more men, and know exactly how to dismantle our defenses. <u>Anyway,</u> fighting them is a hopeless endeavor.

    A. NO CHANGE
    B. In short,
    C. Nevertheless,
    D. Specifically,

9. Guavas originated from Mexico or Central America and were distributed throughout tropical America and the Caribbean region. <u>They</u> are now cultivated in many different places around the world, including Africa and the Mediterranean coast.

    A. NO CHANGE
    B. Later, they
    C. For instance, they
    D. In summary, they

10. All over the world remain fantastic objects, vestiges of people or forces which the theories of archaeology, history, and religion cannot explain. <u>They</u> have found electric batteries many thousands of years old and strange entities in space-suits with platinum fasteners.

    A. NO CHANGE
    B. In addition, researchers
    C. In particular, they
    D. For instance, researchers

11. The idea that life can flourish only under terrestrial conditions has been made obsolete by space research. There are forms of life at the bottom of oceans that don't need oxygen.

    Which is the best phrase to add to the beginning of the second sentence?

    A. Even on Earth,
    B. As a specific example,
    C. Despite the findings,
    D. As a result of the research,

12. Both rock and pop can be considered movements in society; the motivations behind these movements, <u>in fact,</u> were not the same.

    A. NO CHANGE
    B. therefore,
    C. however,
    D. furthermore,

13. Four guys were brought together by a few corporate bigwigs to create an American version of The Beetles—The Monkeys. Little did the public know they were not even singing their own songs; they were lip-syncing the whole time. The Monkeys managed to top the charts and make young girls faint.

    Which of the following should be added to the beginning of the last sentence?

    A. Subsequently,
    B. All in all,
    C. Nevertheless,
    D. As a matter of fact,

14. Developed biomedical methods such as cloning are very controversial. <u>Due to this,</u> 93% of all Americans oppose cloning.

    A. NO CHANGE
    B. In fact,
    C. As you can see,
    D. In conclusion,

15. In any organ donation, blood types and other characteristics must match before organs can be transferred. <u>According to some people,</u> unexpected incompatibilities may exist, resulting in further medical problems.

    A. NO CHANGE
    B. In summary,
    C. Similarly,
    D. Even then,

20 Transitions II

In the previous chapter, we reviewed transition words such as *furthermore* and *however* and how they're used to explicitly connect ideas. Transitions, however, can be more than just one or two words—they can be entire sentences that guide the reader from one thought to another. The more complex ideas get and the more subtle the relationships between them become, the longer the transitions will tend to be. Take a look at the following paragraphs:

> By the time *Heart of Darkness* was published in 1902, a movement was already underway to expose the large-scale theft and murder occurring in the Congo. Dozens of missionaries had begun sending reports, including photographs, to bear witness to the violence. William Sheppard, an African-American Presbyterian, was one of these missionaries. He sent out shocking testimony of lands seized by force, of people living under a reign of terror, and of soldiers cutting off the hands of women and children.

> **An Englishman named E.D. Morel gathered the many reports and photographs and published them.** He gathered crowds to listen to eyewitness accounts of colonial atrocities. He lobbied the British Parliament to denounce the Belgian king's horrifying practices. This became the first modern humanitarian movement, and it successfully exposed the horrendous violence in the Congo. Historians estimate, however, that, by that time, between 10 million and 20 million Congolese people had lost their lives.

Take note of the bolded sentence. This sentence serves as a transition between the two paragraphs, but how do we know? **A good transition sentence references both preceding key terms or ideas and the ones following it.** In this case, the transition brings up not only *E.D. Morel*, who is the primary focus of the second paragraph but also the *many reports and photographs* that were the focus of the first paragraph.

When you're asked to choose the best transition between two paragraphs or even between two sentences within the same paragraph, always read above and below where the transition will be. The best transition will be the one that brings together the main elements on either side, leading from the previous topic to the next.

A few more examples:

1.

> Lambert confirmed that we as humans have a finite amount of mental energy and attention. Tough decision making, such as that used when following a diet, saps us of our ability to exercise the same discipline later on. **Based on this research, Lambert designed a diet that minimizes the need for discipline and protects against regression.** Her program has been used by everyone from celebrities to world-class athletes who vouch for its effectiveness.

The bolded sentence is an amazing transition between two topics in the same paragraph. The opening phrase *Based on this research* refers back to the statements on mental energy. In particular, the word *this* makes that link explicit. The *diet* that Lambert designed leads into the focus of the next sentence: the *program*. In short, this transition guides us from the research she did to the diet program she developed.

2.

> A professor at Harvard and an advocate of human rights, Dr. Joseph remains skeptical of charities that donate haphazardly to impoverished African communities, and **his position has gained traction among other scholars**. Many economists believe that these donations disrupt the local economy and potentially jeopardize businesses that would have to compete against the items being donated.

The bolded phrase is a transition that guides us from Dr. Joseph to other economists, explicitly laying out what the relationship is between them.

3.

> Zero population growth was an idea espoused by Dr. Ehrlich at Stanford in the 60's. His argument was that the Earth's resources would soon be exhausted and that everyone would suffer unless measures were taken to slow the rate of population growth. By the 70's, the idea had become mainstream. Everyone knew what zero population growth meant and its implications. People even took to the streets to raise awareness of the impending doom. **Despite the movement's popularity, the predicted apocalypse never happened.**
>
> The world today manages to support over 7 billion people and counting. Through ingenuity and innovation, the human race has developed such improved agricultural practices that increasingly more can be maintained with increasingly less. Technological developments such as the internet have allowed humans to be more efficient in both production and distribution.

The first paragraph talks about the rise of the zero population growth idea whereas the second paragraph talks about the world today. Notice how the bolded sentence serves as a transition between the two paragraphs, bridging them together. If you took out this sentence, the shift in topic between the paragraphs would be jarring and confusing for the reader.

4.

> Computer science is more than just working with computers. It involves computational thinking and algorithms, step-by-step solutions to complex problems. For example, calculating the shortest way from one location to another like a GPS would requires an algorithm. The subject requires patience and extreme attention to detail, especially when it comes to tracking down bugs and cleaning up code.
>
> **From an early age, I knew I wanted to study computer science and so all of my college planning revolved around it.** I asked my math and science teachers to write me recommendations for all the top universities that offered this major. My college essays focused on the applications that I had built and the fun I had on the robotics team. I talked extensively about my passion for problem solving in my interviews. Now I just have to wait for decisions to roll in.

The bolded sentence serves as a transition between what computer science is and the author's personal experience with college planning. Note that this sentence is also a great topic sentence. Hopefully by now, you're really seeing how these transitions work. Bad transitions will either miss the connection altogether or fail to relate both sides in a logical way.

Tip

When you're asked to insert the best transition between two sentences, look for words such as *this*, *that*, and *these*. These reference words must point to other nouns that exist in the surrounding context, which means the transition sentence itself may need to include them. In the last example, the second sentence of the second paragraph contains the words *this major*. But what is *this major*? Notice that the bolded transition defines what *this major* is—computer science. Because it supplies that definition, this is the transition you would pick as the answer if this were a question on the ACT.

Now on the ACT, you'll know you're being tested on these types of transitions when you see questions like this:

- Which choice most effectively guides the reader from the previous paragraph to this new paragraph?

- Which choice most effectively signals the shift from the preceding paragraph to this paragraph?

- Which choice would most effectively introduce this paragraph?

- Which choice would provide the most effective link between Sentences X and X?

- At this point, the writer wants to add a statement that would lead into the sentence that follows it. Which choice would best accomplish that purpose?

Exercise 1: Choose the best transition. Answers for this chapter start on page 211.

1. It's well known that cell phone usage correlates with a higher chance of vehicle accidents. <u>No matter how safely people drive, there will always be accidents.</u> Teenagers have the highest level of risk because they're the newest to driving. They're also the ones who tend to text the most. Older drivers, however, are generally more responsible and have the patience to wait.

    A. NO CHANGE
    B. Not all age groups, however, have the same level of risk.
    C. For that reason, many states require seat belt use by law.
    D. Road signs that encourage drivers to put their phones away are marginally effective at best.

2. Since I was a child, I've wanted to see the treasures that were supposedly hidden behind the stone wall. <u>My friends would always say that they'd one day start the journey over the wall, but they never found the courage.</u> Despite these failed attempts, I was determined to find a way in.

    A. NO CHANGE
    B. It's rumored that dragons lay in wait, guarding all the riches beyond imagination.
    C. Local tribesmen gossiped daily of the different ways they would try to get through.
    D. Many men had lost their lives trying to scale it and a half-finished underground tunnel had been given up on years ago.

3. Jacobsen LLC. is a cupcake company that does about a million dollars every year, but <u>the bulk of the revenue doesn't come from the cupcakes that are sold in the stores.</u> Much of the money actually comes from corporate accounts that make sizeable orders for their premier events.

    A. NO CHANGE
    B. customers aren't aware of its finances.
    C. management intends to triple that number in the coming few years.
    D. most orders aren't for the signature cupcake that it promotes.

4. Of all the Indian tribes, the Wampagees designed the most elaborate masks, but their purpose is still unknown. <u>Perhaps the Wampagees created the masks for their ritual dances, which were performed every month for good luck.</u> As one of the smaller tribes, they had to repeatedly stave off invaders that wanted to claim their land. In order to survive, the Wampagees must have sought ways to deal with enemies other than direct combat.

    A. NO CHANGE
    B. Members of the tribe were extremely superstitious.
    C. Some speculate that the masks were worn in times of war to intimidate competing tribes.
    D. They could've been used solely as decorative items, a form of art to line the walls of their huts.

5. The busiest season for our travel agency is spring, cherry blossom season in Japan. During this time, <u>visitors line up outside our doors for the discounts that we offer.</u> Some are headed solely for the temples while others are interested in the local sushi joints and the fascinating shopping malls.

    A. NO CHANGE
    B. the trees in the public parks are in full bloom.
    C. many of the hotels are fully booked.
    D. we arrange plans for hundreds of tourists eager to explore the sites.

6. There were some days when I loved taking public transportation, and other days when I didn't. On a good day, I would sit back and enjoy the coffee sold at the corner store. Today being a good day, I watched an old Vietnamese woman with a cluster of plastic shopping bags gripped tightly in her hand like a cloud of tiny white bubbles. Next to her was the lonely businessman staring longingly across the aisle at the beautiful Mexican girl in the tight jeans standing with her back to him.

    A. NO CHANGE
    B. study the other passengers.
    C. listen to the music stored on my phone.
    D. read the paper for most of the commute.

7. The decline in Pennetta's form, however, is not without its causes. Two years ago, the Italian was involved in a bike accident that left her arm with a serious concussion. Doctors said that a full recovery was possible. During the long break, the tennis star kept up a light practice routine and proclaimed that she would come back to the sport stronger than ever.

    A. NO CHANGE
    B. She didn't play any tournaments for the rest of the year.
    C. She used the most advanced treatments of physiotherapy to nurse it back to health.
    D. It crossed her mind a few times after the injury that she may never play professionally again.

8. Serena Williams has come a long way since her childhood days in California. Tournament after tournament, year after year, she continues to prove her dominance over the sport of tennis. Although she cannot equal Maria Sharapova's endorsements, she maintains a crushing 17-2 head-to-head record over the number two Russian. In fact, no other female athlete in any other sport can rival Serena's winnings.

    A. NO CHANGE
    B. she finds the time for projects outside of tennis, such as designing fashionable athletic clothing.
    C. her career prize money exceeds 56 million dollars, almost double that of Sharapova.
    D. her matches command the highest TV ratings, her popularity among American tennis fans being at an all time high.

9. Many students pursuing their doctorate degrees are disheartened by the amount of research professors have to do to maintain their positions, but research is much more than poring over books and writing articles. As a biology professor, I conduct interviews with experts, collect samples from the ocean, and perform experiments in the lab.

    A. NO CHANGE
    B. the compensation and career stability make it worthwhile.
    C. the universities are unwilling to change their requirements.
    D. it shouldn't be thought of as a burden.

10. My doctor has told me that I need to go on a strict diet, no unnecessary snacks and definitely no junk food. I know that controlling calorie intake is important when trying to lose weight. Just last night, even after I had finished my dinner, I drove to the grocery store and wolfed down an entire cheesecake in the parking lot.

    A. NO CHANGE
    B. I also exercise daily to improve my health.
    C. I forced myself to throw away all the chips and candy from the kitchen cabinet.
    D. I try to heed his advice, but it's difficult.

11.   Boston has become the central hub for food, tourism, and entertainment in New England. New businesses and restaurants are popping up all over the place and its sports teams pack the stadiums every week.

      The reasons for Boston's growth can be traced back to excellent state policy decisions a decade ago. Old brownstones, once affordable to even those on government welfare, are being listed for thousands of dollars. Many people who prefer single studios now have no choice but to find roommates to soften the cost of living.

   A. NO CHANGE
   B. Despite the city's modern appeal, Boston's cultural and historical significance cannot be ignored.
   C. Rents for apartments have been on the rise due to the booming economy.
   D. Boston also has a large variety of housing options.

12. A major component of a pilot's flight training is preparing for emergency situations. However, it is not practical to rehearse all the scenarios that might occur. Often, a candidate demonstrates excellent flying skills, but loses composure when under pressure.

   A. NO CHANGE
   B. It is vital that all cabin crew know basic first aid in the event that a passenger becomes ill.
   C. All important flight instruments, such as the course deviation indicator, must be regularly monitored by the co-pilot.
   D. Therefore, assessors will look for candidates who can adjust calmly to unexpected events.

13. The Great Pyramid of Giza is best enjoyed by taking the desert approach on camelback or on foot. Not only does it offer a better view of the monuments, but it also costs much less. On busy days, there are so many visitors that it's impossible to reach the main entrance by the city route.

   A. NO CHANGE
   B. avoids most of the tourist traffic.
   C. provides a local experience.
   D. passes by the Giza plateau, which is home to many fascinating desert animals.

14. The last few years have seen an abundance of new microbial species being discovered. While many discoveries occur in the comfortable surroundings of university research laboratories, still many more are made out in the field. Scientists have developed special vessels to withstand the extreme pressures found at these depths.

   A. NO CHANGE
   B. in jungles and lakes.
   C. on the planet's surface.
   D. on the deep ocean floor.

15. Sherlock Holmes would sometimes use a loose network of casual spies called the "Baker Street Irregulars." These were young boys who provided intelligence to Holmes on an ad hoc basis. After all, even a detective as great as Sherlock Holmes needs help sometimes. But in the event that the amateur sleuths provided a clue of some special importance, they might just find themselves in receipt of a full dollar!

   A. NO CHANGE
   B. His assistant Watson, however, was the primary companion on most of his cases.
   C. Their reward for such services was 25 cents a day.
   D. It wouldn't be until the final novel that they would play a crucial role in the mystery.

Exercise 2: Choose the best transition. Answers for this chapter start on page 211.

1. Crystals will form, but only under certain conditions. <u>The correct temperature and pressure need to be maintained throughout the procedure.</u> Please ensure that at least one member of your team is responsible for monitoring these key metrics.

   A. NO CHANGE
   B. Vapor formation is entirely natural, so there is no need to worry about any condensation.
   C. The experiment could be ruined by a lack of preparation.
   D. As in any lab experiment, it's hard to keep a completely controlled environment.

2. One way of beating the casinos is to learn the art of card counting. <u>It's actually not illegal, but most casinos won't allow it at their tables.</u> Memorizing all the possible card combinations and how to play them can take up to a year.

   A. NO CHANGE
   B. The challenge with this tactic is that it looks much easier to do than it really is.
   C. By betting only small stakes, you have a greater chance of winning in the long-term.
   D. Roulette wheels are a game of pure chance, and no amount of practice will help you get an edge on the house.

3. The reality is that the oil boom of the past 10 years caused a spike in the population levels of socially advanced western nations. <u>Clean water is considered to be a major factor in the population growth as well.</u> Due to the boom, the majority of central banks in Europe have now upgraded their economic forecasts for the coming years.

   A. NO CHANGE
   B. However, this growth may be unsustainable.
   C. Population levels in South Asia will soon outstrip those in the United States.
   D. It also caused unprecedented growth in industries such as steel making, retail, and agriculture.

4. To vote for your favorite comedy show at this year's TV Awards, you will need to visit our website and click on the appropriate link. <u>Only one vote per IP address can be entered.</u> Any more than one vote, and the extra votes will not be counted. Please see our full terms and conditions at the bottom of the page.

   A. NO CHANGE
   B. The best shows don't always win their category.
   C. Voting fraud was a major problem at last year's ceremony.
   D. The list of categories will be published one week before the voting opens.

5. My approach to in-game tactical decisions has always been to leave them to the captain on the field. <u>Because the stakes are high, we train hard all throughout the week.</u> If I were to start giving orders from the stand, I'd be better off putting on a shirt and getting out there myself.

   A. NO CHANGE
   B. Every good football manager should have a number of tactical variations at their disposal.
   C. The role of the manager should be to prepare the team beforehand.
   D. Our team has been on the road for much of the month.

6. This husband-and-wife team turned a dingy off-road café into one of London's most chic eateries in less than two years. <u>The location has a lot of foot traffic and is frequented by tourists and locals alike.</u> The danger, of course, is that a move somewhere else might kill its unique vibe.

    A. NO CHANGE

    B. Finding the best ingredients is so much easier being close to some of the best fish markets in Smithfield.

    C. Prices in London are now so high that renting premises in the capital can be off-putting to new businesses.

    D. Due to their success, they're now thinking of moving locations to accommodate their rapidly increasing number of customers.

7. Our company is independent–our first priority is you, the customer, and your concerns. <u>Most of our competitors will not ship directly to your door.</u> If you find a lower price on the same product, tell us and we'll match it.

    A. NO CHANGE

    B. We know that what's most important to you is getting the best quality for the best price.

    C. Other manufacturers will try and cut costs by using cheap and substandard parts, but not us.

    D. Our products can be purchased in most retail stores.

8. There is an unusual type of racquet game known as "royal ball." <u>The game is played with small, wooden racquets and a ball consisting of hand-rolled cloth.</u> Because the equipment is so different, even professional tennis players have a hard time adjusting to this quirky sport.

    A. NO CHANGE

    B. Different styles of service are given different names, depending on their type.

    C. The courts are not symmetric, like they are in lawn tennis.

    D. Spectators will often sit in an enclosed gallery immediately adjacent to the court.

9. The BAC Concorde made her maiden flight on March 2nd, 1969. <u>When it finally took off, the passengers were relieved because they were already running late due to the weather conditions.</u> Indeed, only one other supersonic transport aircraft had ever been used safely and successfully in commercial transport.

    A. NO CHANGE

    B. The pilot and co-pilot were to give interviews afterwards.

    C. Expectations were high, but with two previously failed attempts to take her to the skies, nothing was guaranteed.

    D. The control tower was situated at the southern end of the runway.

10. Rumors began to circulate and the excitement began to build; the discovery could very well be an unknown composition by the late playwright Anton Chekov. The manuscript was immediately handed over to experts at the Russian State Library, who <u>examined every inch of it in the lab.</u> The samples were frauds conceived by a counterfeiter.

    A. NO CHANGE

    B. came back with disappointing results.

    C. were world-renowned for their work in forensics.

    D. told the public that a thorough investigation could take months.

11. Caves come into existence through an erosion process that takes place at, or below, the ground-level. There are several different types of caves, depending on the excavation mechanics involved in their creation. These formations are downward growing straws, created by the slow dripping of water from cavern roofs.

    A. NO CHANGE
    B. Caves discovered in France contain evidence of prehistoric habitation.
    C. Some caves contain limestone structures within them, called stalactites.
    D. It is the junction between different rock layers where caves are most likely to form.

12. Parkour involves moving quickly and unhindered over objects and obstacles found within the urban landscape. The sport is extremely intense and can result in severe injuries. Since its beginnings in the military, it has quickly spread in popularity among civilians, and now parkour stages many internationally recognized competitions every year.

    A. NO CHANGE
    B. Originating in France in the 1980s, the pastime began as a form of training for soldiers in the French army.
    C. Most martial arts are rarely found outside of the military arena.
    D. It eventually gave rise to its more inclusive version now known as free-running.

13. The British Swimming Championships saw another record fall before the final day. Oddly enough, Adam Peaty almost didn't qualify for the second round the night before. The previous record stood at 58.46, set by Cameron van der Burgh three years earlier. Peaty now adds the British title to his haul of silverware and is setting his sights on Olympic gold in Rio in 2016.

    A. NO CHANGE
    B. Speaking after the event, Peaty's coach praised the support he had received from Sport England and the Amateur Athletics Association.
    C. The practice pool was closed to the finalists, which some claim hampered their preparation for the race that night.
    D. Adam Peaty broke the 100m breaststroke world record with a time of 57.92 seconds.

14. Philosophers have long speculated that the machines we build today could tomorrow evolve an intelligence that threatens our dominance in the world. Their musings have been the basis for many science fiction novels and movies. Everywhere we look, we already see evidence of our dependence on technology. Digital maps direct us from one place to another, social networks keep us connected to our friends, and 3-D printers allow anyone to make almost anything.

    A. NO CHANGE
    B. Robotic control systems still rely on human input to function correctly.
    C. They might not be as crazy as we think.
    D. Computers thus far have failed to demonstrate physical self-replication.

15. *The Adventures of Huckleberry Finn* is one of Mark Twain's most famous literary creations. The story of a young boy and his adventures along the Mississippi with a runaway slave has long been a part of the great pantheon of American literature. In his defense, Twain is simply satirizing the views that would be found objectionable today, and he does so by using language that sometimes seems unsavory to our modern ears.

    A. NO CHANGE
    B. However, it is preferable to have first read *The Adventures of Tom Sawyer* before tackling this weighty tome.
    C. Still, readers often criticize its allegedly racist use of the local dialect.
    D. The book brings up issues of race, family, and friendship that should be confronted in every high school curriculum.

21

Sentence Improvement

About 3-6 questions on the ACT English section will require you to improve a particular sentence by reordering the words for clarity and proper grammar.

These questions usually go like this:

- *The best placement for the underlined portion would be:*
- *All of the following would be acceptable placements for the underlined portion EXCEPT:*

Sometimes, the whole sentence is underlined and you're picking out the entire sentence from the answer choices.

General Strategy

- Place the underlined portion after the thing it applies to.
- If you're picking out an entire sentence, ensure any misplaced or confusing phrases are placed after the things they apply to.
- IMPORTANT: Always read the sentence for its meaning and make sure it makes sense.

Example 1

During summer camp, I would talk to the other campers about friends back home <u>living in the cabin.</u>

The best placement for the underlined portion would be:

A. where it is now.
B. after the word *talk*.
C. after the word *campers*.
D. after the word *friends*.

Who's living in the cabin? The campers. Therefore, we should put the underlined phrase after *campers*, answer **C**.

Example 2

As young kids, we would hide from our parents <u>in the kitchen next to the river of the abandoned house.</u>

    A. NO CHANGE
    B. next to the river in the kitchen of the abandoned house.
    C. in the kitchen of the abandoned house next to the river.
    D. in the kitchen of the river next to the abandoned house.

The placements of the three prepositional phrases (*in the kitchen, next to the river, of the abandoned house*) are very important. The original sentence makes it seem like there's a river going through the house (*river of the abandoned house*). Answer **B** makes it seem like the river is in the kitchen. Answer **D** makes it seem like the river has its own kitchen. The answer is **C**.

Example 3

Many strains of microbes found in the deep ocean <u>deadly to life</u> have evolved to survive in conditions on the planet's surface.

The best placement for the underlined portion would be:
    A. where it is now.
    B. after the word *conditions.*
    C. after the word *survive.*
    D. after the word *surface.*

The author's intent is to say that these microbes survive in conditions that would normally be deadly to life on the surface (i.e. humans). Therefore, we place the phrase next to what it applies to—*deadly* next to *conditions* and *life* next to *on the planet's surface.* The answer is **B**.

Example 4

Roulette wheels are a game of pure chance <u>on the house,</u> and no amount of memorization will help you get an edge.

The best placement for the underlined portion would be:
    A. where it is now.
    B. after the word *memorization.*
    C. after the word *get.*
    D. after the word *edge.*

The phrase *on the house* applies to *edge,* meaning an advantage over the casino. Therefore, we place the phrase after *edge,* answer **D**.

Some phrases can be placed in multiple places. In these cases, the general strategy in this chapter won't be of help to you; you'll have to use your own judgment, as in the following example.

Example 5

In the current economy, downsizing our workforce would not be advisable.

Assuming capitalization is revised accordingly, all of the following would be acceptable placements for the underlined portion EXCEPT:

    A. where it is now.
    B. after the word *workforce*.
    C. after the word *advisable*.
    D. after the word *downsizing*.

Placing the underlined phrase between *downsizing* and *our workforce* would make for an awkward interruption. The answer is **D**.

Example 6

The managing director at the accounting firm declared a schedule to modernize its operations during the board meeting with all the staff.

    A. NO CHANGE
    B. The managing director at the accounting firm, during the board meeting with all the staff, declared a schedule modernizing its operations.
    C. During the board meeting with all the staff, the managing director at the accounting firm declared a schedule to modernize its operations.
    D. The managing director at the accounting firm declared that its operations were scheduled to be modernized during the board meeting with all the staff.

Take a look at the sentence. This is where reading for the meaning is really important. By placing the phrase *during the board meeting with all the staff* after *operations*, the author makes it seem like the operations will be modernized by the time the meeting is over, that it will happen DURING the meeting. This, of course, is nonsensical. Answer **D** is wrong because of the same reason. Answer **B** makes it seem like the schedule itself will be the thing that modernizes the operations. The answer is **C**.

Example 7

Timothy swung his racquet just as his tennis teacher instructed over and behind his left shoulder.

    A. NO CHANGE
    B. Over and behind his left shoulder, Timothy swung his racquet just as his tennis teacher instructed.
    C. Just as his tennis teacher instructed, swinging his racquet over and behind his left shoulder, as did Timothy.
    D. Timothy swung his racquet over and behind his left shoulder, just as his tennis teacher instructed.

In the original sentence, it's the phrase *over and behind his left shoulder* that's awkwardly placed. It makes it sound like the teacher was standing behind Timothy's left shoulder, giving him instruction, whereas the author's intent is to say that Timothy swung his racquet over and behind his left shoulder. Answer **B** makes it sound like Timothy himself was over and behind his left shoulder, which is nonsense. Answer **C** is extremely awkward and is missing a subject. The answer is **D**.

Exercise 1: Determine the best placement for the underlined portion. Answers for this chapter start on page 213.

1. Over the past several years, schools have strived to meet the new education guidelines of exams <u>for the development</u>.

    A. where it is now.
    B. after the *strived*.
    C. after the word *meet*.
    D. after the word *guidelines*.

2. That county is so impoverished that most students can pay <u>barely</u> for lunch in school.

    A. where it is now.
    B. after the word *students*.
    C. after the word *can*.
    D. after the words *school*.

3. Check with the landlord of the building to see if the apartment will be available for viewing at night <u>before your trip</u>.

    A. where it is now.
    B. before the word *check* (assuming proper capitalization and punctuation).
    C. after the word *available*.
    D. after the word *viewing*.

4. On the campus map was <u>for researchers</u> a lab in the main building next to the park.

    A. where it is now.
    B. after the word *map*.
    C. after the word *lab*.
    D. after the word *park*.

5. This bill set the quantitative goal of <u>raising</u> the minimum wage in the country from eight dollars to eleven dollars.

    A. where it is now.
    B. after the word *goal*.
    C. after the word *wage*.
    D. after the word *country*.

6. Mr. Smith spotted a bird sitting on a telephone wire near his house <u>that he could not recognize</u>.

    A. where it is now.
    B. after the word *bird*.
    C. after the word *sitting*.
    D. after the word *wire*.

7. He found a pie on the top shelf of the refrigerator <u>baked by his wife</u>.

    A. where it is now.
    B. at the beginning of the sentence (assuming proper capitalization and punctuation).
    C. after the word *pie*.
    D. after the word *shelf*.

8. A feudal lord <u>during the Medieval ages</u> would oversee the work of hundreds of peasants.

   The underlined portion could be placed in all of the following EXCEPT:

   A. where it is now.
   B. at the beginning of the sentence.
   C. after the word *work.*
   D. after the word *peasants.*

9. Research has suggested that eating fruit <u>in particular</u>—watermelon—might help to reduce the risk of skin cancer by providing essential vitamins to skin cells.

   A. where it is now.
   B. after the word *watermelon.*
   C. after the word *help.*
   D. after the word *cells.*

10. The typical four-door sedan is now prevalent because assembly lines and automation have made <u>profitable</u> production of large numbers of these cars.

    A. where it is now.
    B. after the word *production.*
    C. after the word *large.*
    D. after the word *cars.*

11. In 1903, Marie Curie became the first woman to win the Nobel Prize in physics. In 1911, <u>for a second time</u> she became the first person to win it.

    A. where it is now.
    B. after the word *became* in the second sentence.
    C. after the word *person.*
    D. at the end of the second sentence.

12. The gap <u>at the top</u> between the salaries of executives of the corporate ladder and those of the people at the bottom has only increased over recent decades.

    A. where it is now.
    B. after the word *executives.*
    C. after the word *ladder.*
    D. after the word *increased.*

13. Environmentalists who protect the southern lakes justify doing so on the grounds <u>from oil companies</u> that such lakes are cultural landmarks.

    A. where it is now.
    B. after the word *protect.*
    C. after the word *lakes.*
    D. after the words *doing so.*

14. In a desperate search for his phone, Adam looked in backpacks, drawers, old boxes—<u>hanging</u> even in the pockets of laundry.

    A. where it is now.
    B. after the word *even.*
    C. before the words *pockets of.*
    D. after the words *pockets of.*

15. To reduce pollution in Beijing, China instituted limits on the amount of carbon dioxide that could be released <u>into the sky</u>.

    A. where it is now.

    B. after the word *pollution*.

    C. after the word *limits*.

    D. after the words *carbon dioxide*.

Exercise 2: Answers for this chapter start on page 213.

1. Scientists are thinking about various methods for slowing the accumulation <u>of high levels of the atmosphere in methane.</u>

    A. NO CHANGE

    B. of high levels of methane in the atmosphere.

    C. of the atmosphere in high levels of methane.

    D. of methane in high levels of the atmosphere.

2. <u>The fire station was located by the river that was made of red brick.</u>

    Which of the following is LEAST acceptable?

    A. NO CHANGE

    B. Made of red brick, the fire station was located by the river.

    C. The fire station that was made of red brick was located by the river.

    D. Located by the river, the fire station was made of red brick.

3. I gave the scraps of meat <u>to the dog which had been left on the dinner plates.</u>

    A. NO CHANGE

    B. which had been left to the dog on the dinner plates.

    C. which had been left on the dinner plates to the dog.

    D. to the dog on the dinner plates which had been left.

4. <u>Our neighbor, who enjoys Halloween more than any other occasion, gave us lots of candy dressed in a vampire costume.</u>

    A. NO CHANGE

    B. Dressed in a vampire costume, our neighbor, who enjoys Halloween more than any other occasion, gave us lots of candy.

    C. Our neighbor, who enjoys Halloween more than any other occasion dressed in a vampire costume, gave us lots of candy.

    D. Our neighbor, who enjoys Halloween dressed in a vampire costume more than any other occasion, gave us lots of candy.

5. The author <u>discusses the happiness of dogs by explaining dog psychology in the first chapter and the best way to take care of them.</u>

    A. NO CHANGE

    B. discusses the happiness of dogs when he explains dog psychology in the first chapter and discusses the best way to take care of them.

    C. discusses the happiness of dogs and the best way to take care of them when he explains dog psychology in the first chapter.

    D. explains dog psychology in the first chapter, discusses the happiness of dogs, and discussing the best way to take care of them.

6. The marathon went extremely well this year, with each of the competitors <u>shaving off his own best time by several minutes.</u>

    A. NO CHANGE
    B. off several minutes by shaving his own best time.
    C. off his own best time by shaving several minutes.
    D. shaving several minutes off his own best time.

7. For all their discussions about the environment, oil companies <u>have so far spent very little to prevent toxic waste.</u>

    A. NO CHANGE
    B. have spent very little to so far prevent toxic waste.
    C. have so far spent to prevent very little toxic waste.
    D. have very little spent to prevent toxic waste so far.

8. When the earthquake hit our city, my friend and I were <u>so frightened that we fell out of our chairs almost.</u>

    A. NO CHANGE
    B. so almost frightened that we fell out of our chairs.
    C. so frightened almost that we fell out of our chairs.
    D. so frightened that we almost fell out of our chairs.

9. Because part of the fun of travel is getting lost and exploring the sites, <u>it is a bad idea to decide everything in advance.</u>

   Which of the following would be the MOST acceptable alternative to the underlined portion?

    A. it is a bad idea in advance to decide everything.
    B. it is a bad idea to decide in advance everything.
    C. deciding everything in advance is a bad idea.
    D. deciding everything is a bad idea in advance.

10. To limit the harm done to the ozone layer, some countries control <u>freon in the use of refrigerators as a liquid coolant.</u>

    A. NO CHANGE
    B. the use of freon as a liquid coolant in refrigerators.
    C. the use of freon in refrigerators as a liquid coolant.
    D. refrigerators as a liquid coolant in the use of freon.

11. <u>Shown by me how to cook the noodle dish with various sauces, I was taught by Julia how to bake brownies.</u>

    A. NO CHANGE
    B. Showing Julia how to cook the noodle dish with various sauces, she taught me how to bake brownies.
    C. Teaching me how to bake brownies, Julia was shown by me how to cook the noodle dish with various sauces.
    D. I showed Julia how to cook the noodle dish with various sauces, and she taught me how to bake brownies.

12. The contestant should be banned from our lives for his opinion that television drew criticism.

    A. NO CHANGE
    B. The contestant drew criticism from our lives that television should be banned for his opinion.
    C. The contestant drew criticism for his opinion that television should be banned from our lives.
    D. The contestant drew criticism that his opinion should be banned from television for our lives.

13. Engineers must have experience to build applications effectively if they are to learn in fixing software bugs.

    A. NO CHANGE
    B. if they are to learn to build applications effectively in fixing software bugs.
    C. in fixing software bugs to build applications effectively if they are to learn.
    D. in fixing software bugs if they are to learn to build applications effectively.

14. A gruesome scene of violence should be avoided by those who don't want to see a picture on the front page.

    A. NO CHANGE
    B. On the front page is a picture that should be avoided by those who don't want to see a gruesome scene of violence.
    C. By those who don't want to see a gruesome scene of violence, on the front page is a picture that should be avoided.
    D. On the front page is a gruesome scene of violence that should be avoided by those who don't want to see a picture.

15. You will find that the tires are flat and if you take a closer look at one of these cars, the tank is out of fuel.

    A. NO CHANGE
    B. The tank is out of fuel if you take a look at one of these cars, and you will find that the tires are flat.
    C. The tires are flat and you will find that the tank is out of fuel if you take a look at one of these cars.
    D. If you take a closer look at one of these cars, you will find that the tires are flat and the tank is out of fuel.

22
Placement

Every sentence and every paragraph has its place. Sure, sometimes the order in which you present your thoughts might not matter, but more often than not, it will impact the meaning and clarity of what you have to say.

Let's first talk about sentence placement. On the ACT, you'll encounter questions that read like this:

- *For the sake of the logic and coherence of this paragraph, Sentence 4 should be placed:*

- *The most logical and effective place to add this sentence would be after Sentence:*

- *This sentence would most logically be placed after:*

And then your answer choices will consist of the number labels of the sentences or paragraphs in the passage.

The most important thing is to read the sentences before and after the insertion point. So if you're considering inserting the given sentence after sentence 5, make sure to read sentences 5 and 6. Those sentences will often be the deciding factor. If they support the given sentence or clearly transition to or from it, you know you've arrived at the answer.

Handling these types of questions is a lot like selecting the best transition, except you're now working backwards. Instead of choosing which sentence to insert, you're figuring out the best place to insert a given sentence. All the same thinking you exercised back in those transition chapters carries over to these questions.

In particular, look for these cues:

1. *this, that, these, those*

Example 1

[1] During a visit to my son's school, I was able to eat lunch in the cafeteria. [2] When I went there at noon, students were lined up single file to pick out their meals. [3] There were four counters, each serving something different. [4] I picked up a side of salad at the first, some rice at the second, and a chicken sandwich at the third. [5] At that point, I was eager to find a seat and enjoy my meal. [6] What made me upset, however, was the fourth counter, which was serving cake, ice cream, and cookies. [7] I called up the school office to file a complaint, but nobody would listen to me. [8] The fourth counter was the most popular one in the cafeteria.

Upon reviewing this essay and realizing that some information has been left out, the writer composes the following sentence:

> Desserts like these are bound to make students unhealthy.

The most logical and effective place to insert this sentence would be:

- **A.** after Sentence 2.
- **B.** after Sentence 3.
- **C.** after Sentence 4.
- **D.** after Sentence 6.

When you read the sentence in question, your first thought should be *Desserts like what? What are these?* The sentence only makes sense if it's placed next to another sentence that defines what *these* are. The only sentence that does so logically is Sentence 6 (*cake, ice cream, and cookies*), answer **D**.

Example 2

[1] After a year of living on futons and eating ramen, the founders at Hourglass decided that antique watches weren't profitable enough to sustain a business. [2] Instead, they decided to invest in modern designs, create new watches, and market them at a discount online. [3] Hourglass soon skyrocketed to success. [4] Within a year, it broke ten million dollars in revenue and announced its intent to expand overseas. [5] A lot of existing watch companies are now looking to buy out this company that was once on the verge of bankruptcy. [6] With those plans in place, the company began to attract the young and fashionable crowd, as well as celebrities looking for the next trend.

For the sake of the logic and coherence of the paragraph, Sentence 6 should be:

- **A.** placed where it is now.
- **B.** placed after Sentence 1.
- **C.** placed after Sentence 2.
- **D.** placed after Sentence 4.

Note that Sentence 6 refers to *those plans*, so your natural thought should be *What plans?* Sentence 6 only makes sense if it's placed next to another sentence that defines what *those plans* are. The only sentence that does so logically is Sentence 2 (*invest in modern designs, create new watches, and market them at a discount online*), answer **C**.

2. Nouns or pronouns in need of clarification

Example 1

[1] The Large Hadron Collider, the most powerful particle collider in the world, was built to test theories of particle physics. [2] In particular, it was used to prove the existence of the Higgs Boson, a new type of particle that helps explain why things have mass. [3] The Collider is based at the CERN Laboratory and contains four types of detectors. [4] Having more than one detector carry out the same tests gives scientists the ability to cross-check results and identify any anomalies in the data they generate.

Upon reviewing this essay and realizing that some information has been left out, the writer composes the following sentence:

> Two of them, the ATLAS and CMS detectors, are very similar and can run the same class of experiments.

The most logical and effective place to insert this sentence would be:

- **A.** after Sentence 1.
- **B.** after Sentence 2.
- **C.** after Sentence 3.
- **D.** after Sentence 4.

The key word is *them*—what's *them*? Detectors, obviously. So we must put this sentence after one that brings up detectors, Sentence 3. The answer is **C**. The important take-away here is that *them* was a pronoun in need of a clarifying reference.

The first cue in this chapter—*this, that, these, those*—is just a more specific version of this second cue. After all, *this, that, these,* and *those* are all pronouns that are in need of a reference that clarifies them.

Example 2

[1] Hong Kong has long been criticized for its citizens' taste for rare ocean delicacies, especially shark fin soup. [2] People pay hundreds of dollars to enjoy one bowl of the soup, which symbolizes wealth and power. [3] But overfishing and a love for seafood have disrupted many underwater habitats in Asia, endangering much of the marine life, including local sharks. [4] Last October, the Hong Kong government decided to prohibit all imports of shark fin. [5] Biologists are closely monitoring the shark population to see if it recovers.

Upon reviewing this essay and realizing that some information has been left out, the writer composes the following sentence:

> Environmental activists praised the ban as a crucial step towards protecting the underwater ecosystem in Asia, but more should be done.

The most logical and effective place to insert this sentence would be:

- **A.** after Sentence 2.
- **B.** after Sentence 3.
- **C.** after Sentence 4.
- **D.** after Sentence 5.

The noun that needs clarification here is *the ban*. Reading the sentence by itself, we're not sure what *the ban* refers to. That's why we need to place this sentence next to one that provides that clarification, Sentence 4, which specifies that it's a shark fin ban. The answer is **C**.

3. Chronological order

Example 1

[1] The Mongols tried to conquer Vietnam at various points in the second millennium. [2] The first time, they were repelled by the unknown landscape and intemperate climate. [3] When they came back better prepared, the Vietnamese scared them off by setting fires to their encampments. [4] The Mongols finally succeeded twice in the late 13th century, but mysteriously left each time. [5] It wasn't until the 19th century that the Vietnamese were fully conquered—by the French. [6] On their third return, they were routed by the genius of the Vietnamese generals at the battle of Bach Dang.

For the sake of the logic and coherence of the paragraph, Sentence 6 should be:

  A. placed where it is now.
  B. placed after Sentence 1.
  C. placed after Sentence 2.
  D. placed after Sentence 3.

This is an example of putting things in chronological order, from first to last. Sentence 6 begins with *On their third return*, which means that it should be placed after the narrator has talked about the first and second times. The second time the Mongols tried to conquer Vietnam is discussed in Sentence 3, so the answer is **D**.

Example 2

[1] John dusted himself off and returned to the tractor for a flashlight and a length of rope. [2] We tied the end of the rope to the rear of the tractor. [3] I lead the line for John while he went down for a look around. [4] He had discovered one of the largest cave systems in all of New York State. [5] It would take years to map and would be an adventure even more profitable than the original goal that had lead us to discover it.

Upon reviewing this essay and realizing that some information has been left out, the writer composes the following sentence:

> When John returned to the surface, he was grinning ear to ear.

The most logical and effective place to insert this sentence would be:

  A. after Sentence 1.
  B. after Sentence 2.
  C. after Sentence 3.
  D. after Sentence 4.

Consider the logical sequence of events. The sentence in question states that "John returned to the surface," which means he had to have gone below the surface sometime before that point. Sentence 3 is the only place where that event is stated. The answer is **C**. Why not place it later, after Sentence 4, for example? Because placing the sentence after Sentence 3 then allows Sentence 4 to explain why John was "grinning ear to ear." Also note that the first half of the paragraph is action, whereas the latter half is more reflection. The given sentence belongs in the "action" half.

4. Lead/Topic Sentences

Example 1

[1] Clinical studies have shown that squatting is better than any other lower-body movement for muscle hypertrophy. [2] In fact, the rate of muscle growth can be up to three times as fast if squats are done correctly as part of a regular workout routine. [3] The back-squat is considered the king of all bodybuilding movements. [4] Most injuries in the gym, however, stem from accidents caused by poor form. [5] As a result, runners will rarely use squats as part of their training.

For the sake of the logic and coherence of the paragraph, Sentence 3 should be:

  A. placed where it is now.
  B. placed before Sentence 1.
  C. placed after Sentence 4.
  D. placed after Sentence 5.

Sentence 3 is a good example of a lead sentence—a more general sentence that leads into more specific details or supporting evidence, sort of like a topic sentence. It sets the stage for the more specific reasoning in sentences 1 and 2. The answer is **B**.

The only reason I like to call it a lead sentence rather than a topic sentence is that most students think a topic sentence must start a paragraph. Lead sentences, however, can be in the middle of the paragraph. Take a look at the following example:

Example 2

[1] My freshman year of college was quite intimidating. [2] Not only did I have to adjust to a new setting, but I also had to make sure I did well in my classes. [3] Professor Kwok always had a weird experiment to illustrate the concept of the day. [4] One time, he made a bomb out of liquid nitrogen so that we could put the Gurney equations to the test. [5] The entire building had to evacuate after the explosion set off the sprinkler system.

Upon reviewing this essay and realizing that some information has been left out, the writer composes the following sentence:

> I had many teachers, but my favorite was my math professor.

The most logical and effective place to insert this sentence would be:

  A. after Sentence 1.
  B. after Sentence 2.
  C. after Sentence 4.
  D. after Sentence 5.

The sentence in question is a lead sentence—it introduces what the author will talk about next, his math professor. Because everything after Sentence 2 talks about Professor Kwok, after Sentence 2 is exactly where the sentence should be inserted. The answer is **B**. This lead sentence is essentially a transition sentence.

5. Supporting Sentences

A supporting sentence is the opposite of a lead sentence. It offers additional details and specific facts or examples in support of a more general statement that comes before it. Let's take a previous example and change the question:

Example

[1] My freshman year of college was quite intimidating. [2] Not only did I have to adjust to a new setting, but I also had to make sure I did well in my classes. [3] I had many teachers, but my favorite was my math professor. [4] Professor Kwok always had a weird experiment to illustrate the concept of the day. [5] One time, he made a bomb out of liquid nitrogen so that we could put the Gurney equations to the test. [6] The entire building had to evacuate after the explosion set off the sprinkler system.

Upon reviewing this essay and realizing that some information has been left out, the writer composes the following sentence:

> To teach us about speed and rates of change, he swung a bowling ball from the ceiling until it collided with the door.

The most logical and effective place to insert this sentence would be:

A. after Sentence 1.
B. after Sentence 3.
C. after Sentence 4.
D. after Sentence 5.

The sentence in question is a supporting sentence—it provides an example that backs up some point made before it. Because it's an example of one of Professor Kwok's "weird experiments," it belongs after Sentence 4. The answer is **C**. The sentence should not be placed after Sentence 5 because it would interrupt Sentences 5 and 6, which belong together (Sentence 6 further describes the incident brought up in Sentence 5). Note that Sentence 4 is itself a supporting sentence to Sentence 3, but it's a lead sentence to the one we're inserting.

6. Transition words

Example

[1] Barbary falcons are a particular kind of hunting bird used in the desert kingdom of Saudi Arabia. [2] Their nimble flight mechanics make them the perfect predators for hunting smaller birds. [3] Although they live in dry open hills and deserts, they make their nests on cliffs and breed throughout the year. [4] The Barbary falcon is often mistaken for the peregrine falcon, even though the former has a smaller wingspan.

Upon reviewing this essay and realizing that some information has been left out, the writer composes the following sentence:

> However, they are less valuable for catching land based mammals like foxes or mice, as their larger size often warns potential prey of their approach.

The most logical and effective place to insert this sentence would be:

- **A.** after Sentence 1
- **B.** after Sentence 2
- **C.** after Sentence 3
- **D.** after Sentence 4

Note the word *However*. This indicates that wherever the sentence is placed, it must serve to offset or counter the sentence before it. The best insertion point is after Sentence 2, answer **B**. While barbary falcons are the "perfect predators for hunting smaller birds," they are "less valuable for catching land based mammals." Side by side, the two sentences offer a strength and then a weakness, which makes the *However* fit quite logically.

Paragraph placement questions—you'll encounter at most two in the entire section—deal with putting a paragraph in the right place within a passage. The approach is very much the same as in sentence placement questions, except you'll be looking for the cues on a paragraph-to-paragraph level, rather than a sentence-to-sentence level.

For example, each paragraph will have its own distinct focus, but you'll still be looking for transitions that guide the reader from one to another in a logical way. You'll still be looking for dates and time words like *before, now,* and *finally* to place paragraphs in chronological order. You'll still have to be conscious of the relationships between paragraphs, whether one leads into the next one or supports the one before it. If you get good with sentence placement questions, you'll be well prepared for paragraph placement questions.

Example

[1]

Fred went up first to make sure none of the caribiners had come loose or overly worn under the weather. Scott couldn't wait to harness up and start the climb. The others weren't so enthusiastic. I told them we could make the two day hike back the way we came or climb up and be at the clubhouse within a few hours. Before we knew it, we were celebrating at the clubhouse.

[2]

The answer came quite quickly during the first hike. It was clear these kids—Tony, Lisa, Scott, Sara, Tim—did not want to be there. They grudgingly made their way through the trails, throwing rocks and breaking branches. The pace could not have been slower. After many hours of whining and complaining about being tired and hungry, the first day finally came to an end.

[3]

As part of a new program, our state decided to give first time offenders the choice of a three day hike through the mountains or a month of detention. Because my partner Fred and I give guided hiking tours through the mountains, we were chosen to be the tour guides for this program. Three days in the wilderness with five juvenile delinquents was not exactly what we had in mind when we started our hiking business. Then again, how hard could it be?

[4]

A few months later I asked the kids to see if our little hiking trip in the mountains had changed anything. I was pleased to hear that no one has been in trouble since. I can't wait to take on the next batch.

[5]

Over the course of the next day, their attitudes started to change. With each step, the children began to realize that their lives were in our hands. After all, they would have to rely on us for help if they got lost or fell. They had to either listen or risk serious injury. Towards the end of the hike, we presented the final challenge—the wall. There were other paths we could have taken, but we like to challenge our guests with a little mountain climbing. The cliff is only twelve feet high, so even an inexperienced climber can easily reach the top.

The most effective and logical ordering of the paragraphs in the passage is:

  A. 3, 1, 2, 4, 5

  B. 3, 2, 5, 1, 4

  C. 3, 1, 2, 5, 4

  D. 1, 3, 2, 5, 4

On the ACT, you won't get a question exactly like this, but you'll get questions that ask you where to place a certain paragraph. By the time you get to those questions, you will have read most of the passage. You'll have some idea of what each paragraph is about, which will make it much easier. But for learning purposes, let's say we haven't read this passage at all. The first thing I would do is scan the first sentence of each paragraph, which typically provides some clue of where it should be placed. Looking at paragraph 2, we read *The answer...*, which indicates it should be placed after a paragraph that ends in a question or dilemma: paragraph 3.

Paragraph 5 starts with *Over the course of the next day...*, which implies the previous paragraph should discuss the previous day. The paragraph that does this turns out to be paragraph 2, which ends with the words *the first day finally came to an end*. So far, we have 3, 2, and 5.

If you look at paragraph 4, *A few months later* is a sign that whatever's in that paragraph happened last, so it should be placed at the end. Paragraph 1 starts with *Fred went up first* and goes on to discuss the details of climbing, which means it should be placed after a paragraph that mentions that activity, paragraph 5. Finally, we have 3, 2, 5, 1, 4: answer **B**.

Exercise 1: Answers for this chapter start on page 213.

1. [1] Machines that play chess have been around for a long time, but never have they been as powerful as they are today. [2] Given that level of computing power, they usually win. [3] But a new type has been designed that is intended to lose. [4] The idea is aimed at novice players, who would benefit from a boost in confidence by beating a computer. [5] Grandmaster Garry Kasparov thinks the new machine is a great invention and intends to use it with his beginner students in the near future. [6] They are now able to perform millions of calculations within seconds in order to determine what moves to play.

    For the sake of the logic and coherence of the paragraph, sentence 6 should be:

    A. placed where it is now.
    B. placed after sentence 1.
    C. placed after sentence 2.
    D. placed after sentence 4.

2. [1] Chloe smiled, but didn't reply to his joke. [2] Erik searched her face for a clue as to what she was thinking. [3] Silently, they strolled on, Erik walking a little behind her in the dying light of the day. [4] Chloe turned to ask him something, but he was gone. [5] She called his name, but no response. [6] She knew then that she'd lost him forever.

    For the sake of the logic and coherence of the paragraph, sentence 6 should be:

    A. Placed where it is now.
    B. Placed after sentence 1.
    C. Placed after sentence 2.
    D. Placed after sentence 4.

3.   [1] Four workmen stand on a road in front of a small steel-mill. [2] They have a tricky problem. [3] How do they lift a weighty piece of machinery onto the second floor of the factory without the aid of a mechanical vehicle? [4] Even if it could be held up, it would be impossible to carry it up the steep, narrow stairs to where it needs to be fitted. [5] It is extremely heavy, too heavy to lift.

For the sake of the logic and coherence of the paragraph, sentence 5 should be:

   A. placed where it is now.
   B. placed after sentence 1.
   C. placed after sentence 2.
   D. placed after sentence 3.

4.   [1] The Prince built a barracks adjacent to the castle and stationed a garrison of men there to carry on the assault in his absence. [2] After he left north to negotiate with Edwin of Lancaster, the soldiers surprised the opposing province in a daring, early morning ambush. [3] According to the rules of medieval chivalry, he could not be pursued by the Prince's soldiers once he was there. [4] But the soldiers ignored these conventions, stormed the monastery, and captured him. [5] The duke escaped and fled to a nearby monastery.

For the sake of the logic and coherence of the paragraph, sentence 5 should be:

   A. Placed where it is now.
   B. Placed after sentence 1.
   C. Placed after sentence 2.
   D. Placed after sentence 3.

5.   [1] The drier conditions of the Ice Age suited one of the larger mammal species that made it to the Central American archipelago—the tree sloth. [2] However, there were a number of evolutionary relatives of this creature that didn't survive. [3] Was it the animal's unusual metabolism that gave the tree sloth a competitive advantage? [4] We can't know for sure. [5] What we do know from fossil findings is that the morphological characteristics of this kind of sloth are the same today as they were fifteen thousand years ago.

For the sake of the logic and coherence of the paragraph, sentence 5 should be:

   A. placed where it is now.
   B. placed after sentence 1.
   C. placed after sentence 2.
   D. placed after sentence 3.

6.   [1] The city was established in 1781, when a group of Spanish colonialists came up from Mexico and built a small town of mud houses with red tile roofs. [2] Would you recognize the name El Pueblo de Nuestra Senora La Reina de Los Angeles de Porciuncula? [3] You've probably heard of it before. [4] In fact, it's the Spanish name for what is now known as the city of Los Angeles. [5] It wasn't until 1847, after the Mexican-American War, that the city came under U.S. control, with the signing of the Treaty of Cahuenga finally confirming American ownership and the name change to Los Angeles.

For the sake of the logic and coherence of the paragraph, sentence 1 should be:

   A. placed where it is now.
   B. placed after sentence 2.
   C. placed after sentence 4.
   D. placed after sentence 5.

7.   [1] Plantation owners typically divided their fields between coffee beans and the native rubber crop. [2] In the 1800s, however, a coffee crop disease which spread throughout the region wiped out much of the farmland devoted to it. [3] The renewed taste for coffee elsewhere meant that it didn't take long for Sri Lanka's farms to recover with a complete shift to coffee production. [4] New, blight-resistant strains were re-planted where old ones had been decimated. [5] During that time, coffee was becoming more and more popular overseas, with the middle-class in America selecting it as its drink of choice. [6] Those who remembered the earlier blight thought this reliance on one export was foolish, but their warnings would go unheeded.

For the sake of the logic and coherence of the paragraph, sentence 5 should be:

   A. placed where it is now.
   B. placed after sentence 2.
   C. placed after sentence 3.
   D. placed after sentence 6.

8.   [1] In Spanish soccer teams, to score without the right aesthetic and technique is almost frowned upon. [2] Juande Ramos, the Real Madrid coach who previously led Seville to the UEFA Cup final in 2006, disagrees. [3] His utilitarian approach to management–to win at all costs, even if it isn't pretty–has predictably lost him favor with the fans. [4] But silverware and trophies are what count in the long-run, and many journalists, and even some spectators, are beginning to warm to him. [5] The Spanish believe that a victory in soccer must be achieved in style, that winning with flair is the only way to win.

For the sake of the logic and coherence of the paragraph, sentence 5 should be:

   A. placed where it is now.
   B. placed after sentence 1.
   C. placed after sentence 2.
   D. placed after sentence 3.

9.   [1] The Earth's poles may appear permanent, but they have reversed many times in the planet's history. [2] The North becomes the South, and the South becomes the North. [3] It is not known why this happens, just that it does. [4] Without this vital physical clue, it would've been impossible to tell whether this phenomenon had really occurred. [5] Magnetized rock on the ocean floor serves as a record for the changing orientation of the Earth's magnetic field.

For the sake of the logic and coherence of the paragraph, sentence 5 should be:

   A. placed where it is now.
   B. placed after sentence 1.
   C. placed after sentence 2.
   D. placed after sentence 3.

10.   [1] Many people mistakenly believe a wave is just a mass of water careening across the surface of the sea. [2] There's a much deeper science behind it. [3] If one observes a bird bobbing on the waves, it appears as if it's going to be carried away to another place. [4] If one keeps on looking, however, it looks like it's actually staying in the same place, not heading towards shore or anywhere else. [5] If they could just find a way to replicate the motions of an ocean wave in laboratory conditions, they could begin to investigate this peculiar phenomenon in more detail.

Upon reviewing this paragraph and realizing that some information has been left out, the writer composes the following sentence:

It was this lack of movement that first gave scientists an insight into how waves behave.

The most logical and effective place to insert this sentence would be:

A. after sentence 1.
B. after sentence 2.
C. after sentence 3.
D. after sentence 4.

11.   [1] The ships developed out of a maritime "arms-race" of sorts, in what was a unique set of economic circumstances at the time. [2] Tea drinking was quickly replacing beer as the national drink of England, and the tea came mostly from China. [3] Buyers were desperate to be the first to try a new variety of tea arriving in port, and so the ships that could deliver their cargo the fastest could charge the highest prices. [4] One such merchant was the flamboyant Irving Ironhammer, who had made his name in the cotton trade and now sought his riches from tea plantations in remote areas of China, far up the Yangtze River.

Upon reviewing this paragraph and realizing that some information has been left out, the writer composes the following sentence:

Merchants were willing to invest in building the sleekest ships to compete with one another.

The most logical and effective place to insert this sentence would be:

A. after sentence 1.
B. after sentence 2.
C. after sentence 3.
D. after sentence 4.

12.   [1] Oil is utilized in many industrial processes. [2] It provides fuel for heavy machinery used in the agriculture and farming sectors. [3] Much of the oil we extract from nature provides energy for the nation's power stations, which in turn provide heat and light for our homes and places of work. [4] It might surprise some people to discover that crude oil is also a crucial part of the plastic manufacturing process. [5] Hydrocarbons found in oil are the raw ingredients used to synthesize common household necessities, such as kitchenware and furniture. [6] They are also increasingly being used to create sophisticated biomedical devices, such as pacemakers and artificial limbs.

For the sake of the logic and coherence of the paragraph, sentence 5 should be:

A. placed where it is now.
B. placed after sentence 2.
C. placed after sentence 3.
D. placed after sentence 6.

13.   [1] The active ingredient in this medicine is Chlorphenamine Maleate. [2] Symptoms of an allergic reaction include itching, streaming eyes, and a blocked nose. If you suffer from hayfever, allergies, or insect bites, this drug may be of help. [3] Remember, do not give this medicine to anyone else whom it has not been prescribed to by a health professional. [4] Do not take this medication if you are taking any other treatment that your pharmacist or doctor has not been informed of.

Upon reviewing this paragraph and realizing that some information has been left out, the writer composes the following sentence:

> An antihistamine, the drug blocks the effects of a compound that can cause allergic reactions in some people.

The most logical and effective place to insert this sentence would be:

A. after sentence 1.
B. after sentence 2.
C. after sentence 3.
D. after sentence 4.

14.   [1] They reached the door of the hunting lodge. [2] Daisy dropped her bucket and looked around. [3] No one had been here for a long time. [4] She really couldn't remember. [5] The door was still unlocked, just as it had been when they were there last year. [6] She peered through the dusty window. [7] The bed had been made. [8] Had she left it like that?

For the sake of the logic and coherence of the paragraph, sentence 4 should be:

A. placed where it is now.
B. placed after sentence 2.
C. placed after sentence 5.
D. placed after sentence 8.

15.   [1] Because of his reputation as a great artist, Michelangelo was eventually pardoned and resumed work for the Medicis again. [2] During this period, he spent time crafting the tomb of Lorenzo de Medici. [3] His sculpture of Lorenzo seeks to capture the inner personality of the dark, pensive, and brooding man. [4] Indeed, Lorenzo's nickname, "The Thoughtful One," wasn't given to him for no reason.

Upon reviewing this paragraph and realizing that some information has been left out, the writer composes the following sentence:

> He would never finish the project during his lifetime, but scholars still acknowledge it as one of his finest pieces ever.

The most logical and effective place to insert this sentence would be:

A. after sentence 1.
B. after sentence 2.
C. after sentence 3.
D. after sentence 4.

Exercise 2: Answers for this chapter start on page 213.

1.   [1] India is a land of riches. [2] Precious metals and priceless stones have been mined from the earth there for as long as anyone can remember. [3] Yet the natural bounty that gave rise to its wealth has also brought with it a dark side. [4] However, the people have not surrendered so easily; even Alexander the Great was driven out, never to return. [5] Invaders have sought to conquer her lands to possess the riches underground.

For the sake of the logic and coherence of the paragraph, sentence 5 should be:

   A. placed where it is now.
   B. placed after sentence 1.
   C. placed after sentence 2.
   D. placed after sentence 3.

2.   [1] One of the saddest stories in Greek mythology is that of Echo the nymph. [2] Echo liked to have the last word in every conversation, but upon upsetting the goddess Hera, her punishment was to never speak again, except to repeat the last words spoken by other people. [3] But Narcissus cared only for himself and sat admiring his reflection on the surface of a pond until he died. [4] Echo was heartbroken and died not long after, the only remaining trace of her being the anguished cry heard between the mountains of her home. [5] One day, she encountered the handsome Narcissus and was smitten with his youth and beauty.

For the sake of the logic and coherence of the paragraph, sentence 5 should be:

   A. placed where it is now.
   B. placed after sentence 1.
   C. placed after sentence 2.
   D. placed after sentence 3.

3.   [1] Along the beaches of the Pribilof Islands is a sea creature prized for its luxuriant fur. [2] The bulls, or males, arrive first. [3] Snorting and threatening other males, they battle for prime territory. [4] Then, packs of females return to the islands, completing their winter migration from the north. [5] The bulls pack them into harems and spend the rest of their time defending their territory and mating with the females.

Upon reviewing this paragraph and realizing that some information has been left out, the writer composes the following sentence:

> Northern fur seals, as they are known, gather here every year to play out their violent breeding ritual.

The most logical and effective place to insert this sentence would be:

   A. after sentence 1.
   B. after sentence 2.
   C. after sentence 3.
   D. after sentence 4.

4.   [1] Many of Charles Dicken's characters are as famous today as they were when he wrote them into his books over a century ago. [2] Despite the great fortunes he made from his writings, Dickens always felt a special concern for the plight of the poor. [3] Characters like Tiny Tim and Oliver Twist portray the harsh lives that children suffered in Victorian times. [4] Dickens himself had a childhood not unlike those depicted in *A Christmas Carol* or *The Old Curiosity Shop*. [5] He never forgot those times and used the experiences as a resource for his works of fiction.

Upon reviewing this paragraph and realizing that some information has been left out, the writer composes the following sentence:

> After his father went to debtors' prison, young Charles had to work long hours in dismal conditions to pay back what the family owed.

The most logical and effective place to insert this sentence would be:

   A. after sentence 1.
   B. after sentence 2.
   C. after sentence 4.
   D. after sentence 5.

5.   [1] It is impossible to differentiate between cane sugar and beet sugar. [2] Cane molasses are what we know as the treacle in our puddings and desserts. [3] Beet molasses are not typically consumed by humans but go towards producing cattle food when mixed with beet pulp. [4] Both cane and beet molasses can be used to produce alcohol as well. [5] However, the molasses obtained from each are somewhat different.

For the sake of the logic and coherence of the paragraph, sentence 5 should be:

   A. placed where it is now.
   B. placed after sentence 1.
   C. placed after sentence 2.
   D. placed after sentence 3.

6.   [1] In 1849, the British government repealed the British Navigation Acts and opened up previously inaccessible tracts of the global marketplace to foreign traders. [2] Suddenly, merchants in the United States and all over Europe were free to compete with British businessmen on level terms, and they wasted no time in building even faster ships to capitalize on the situation. [3] They were still admired, but their aura of invincibility had gone. [4] The golden age of the British vessel was over; the new age of the steam ship was just around the corner.

Upon reviewing this paragraph and realizing that some information has been left out, the writer composes the following sentence:

> Soon, the ships of Great Britain were no longer the envy of the world.

The most logical and effective place to insert this sentence would be:

   A. after sentence 1.
   B. after sentence 2.
   C. after sentence 3.
   D. after sentence 4.

7.   [1] You do not want to be overly relaxed when executing a maneuver. [2] But nor do you want to be too tense. [3] You should be able to "relax into tension," to enable proper breathing while exerting sufficient muscle strength. [4] The concept seems like an oxymoron, but once you begin kettlebell training, you will start to understand. [5] In kettlebell training, you must keep a special balance between tension and relaxation.

For the sake of the logic and coherence of the paragraph, sentence 5 should be:

A. placed at the beginning of the paragraph.
B. placed after sentence 1.
C. placed after sentence 2.
D. placed after sentence 3.

8.   [1] The Brazilian portion of the Amazon is enormous, but it contains only about 7 percent of the country's population. [2] Much of that 7 percent is concentrated around the town of Belen. [3] Belen is known mostly for its tree farming industry. [4] Somehow, the seeds of its magnificent trees were stolen and later taken abroad where they were grown in special tree-nurseries, ending the monopoly Belen had enjoyed. [5] The timbers from that region of the Americas were once the finest in the world.

For the sake of the logic and coherence of the paragraph, sentence 5 should be:

A. placed where it is now.
B. placed after sentence 1.
C. placed after sentence 2.
D. placed after sentence 3.

9.   [1] It was once believed that fermentation was caused by little creatures living within substances in which gases or acids are formed. [2] Louis Pasteur discovered that it was actually due to tiny organisms floating in the air. [3] He tested his hypothesis by heating a liquid, like wine or milk, very rapidly. [4] He found that the microorganisms that soured the liquid were killed and that further contamination depended on whether the bottle was open to the air. [5] This process of treating foods with heat, pasteurization, still bears his name to this day.

For the sake of the logic and coherence of the paragraph, sentence 5 should be:

A. placed where it is now.
B. placed after sentence 1.
C. placed after sentence 2.
D. placed after sentence 3.

10.   [1] Tanks have been used as fighting vehicles in every modern war. [2] Compared to the latest designs, which incorporate electric range-finding devices and laser gun-control technology, those older models may seem like relics of the past. [3] Nevertheless, human beings are still required to drive the machines, no matter how technologically advanced they currently are. [4] But with automation science and remote-controlled drone-like piloting now being developed, tanks may become independent weapons of destruction sooner than we think.

Upon reviewing this paragraph and realizing that some information has been left out, the writer composes the following sentence:

> Early versions were pedal-powered and demanded a great deal of physical effort to propel them.

The most logical and effective place to insert this sentence would be:

A. after sentence 1.
B. after sentence 2.
C. after sentence 3.
D. after sentence 4.

11.   [1] The cat is often portrayed as a creature of leisure, stretching itself before a cozy fire, or curled up beside its owner. [2] Yet this animal, though it appears tame, is still a semi-wild pet, not reliant on its "master" as much as we'd like to think. [3] The cat has hardly changed in 4000 years of domestication. [4] Many farm cats, for instance, are fed sporadically so that they keep on catching mice and other countryside rodents.

Upon reviewing this paragraph and realizing that some information has been left out, the writer composes the following sentence:

Its hunting instinct is still strong.

The most logical and effective place to insert this sentence would be:

A. after sentence 1.
B. after sentence 2.
C. after sentence 3.
D. after sentence 4.

12.   [1] The tabor is a small, drum-like instrument. [2] It can be held aloft with one hand, or rested in the crook of an arm. [3] Should the musician play both instruments at the same time, he or she would use crooked drumsticks to make it easier to blow the pipe. [4] Evidence from manuscript records shows that the tabar was used nearly 1000 years ago. [5] It is even mentioned in some of Shakespeare's plays!

Upon reviewing this paragraph and realizing that some information has been left out, the writer composes the following sentence:

Beaten with either a drumstick or the palm of an opposing hand, the tabor would sometimes be accompanied by a flute or three-holed pipe, often played by the same musician.

The most logical and effective place to insert this sentence would be:

A. after sentence 1.
B. after sentence 2.
C. after sentence 4.
D. after sentence 5.

13.   [1] Soil provides a medium in which plants and other living things can grow. [2] The basis of all soil is rock. [3] These particles, over time, mix with other rocks, plants, bacteria, and a variety of organic materials. [4] The resulting soil rarely comprises more than a layer 10 inches thick, but it is a complete, functioning, living environment in and of itself. [5] When water and wind break rock down, finer and finer pieces are formed.

For the sake of the logic and coherence of the paragraph, sentence 5 should be:

A. placed where it is now.
B. placed after sentence 1.
C. placed after sentence 2.
D. placed after sentence 3.

14.   [1] Numerology is the belief that numbers have an inherent mystical dimension over and above their significance to mainstream mathematics. [2] There was a strong belief around that time that the universe could be understood through numbers, though this stemmed from a religious concept of the divine, in which man could be united with God through numerical relationships. [3] The idea was that the human understanding of numbers was a God-given attribute, put there to better appreciate the world that God created. [4] Yet it would be the early Church councils of the 4th century AD that eventually condemned this notion as superstitious nonsense, a move that many people today might find hard to believe. [5] Despite its unscientific character, numerology has a history going back to the Pythagorean school of philosophers of the 6th century BC.

For the sake of the logic and coherence of the paragraph, sentence 5 should be:

A. placed where it is now.
B. placed after sentence 1.
C. placed after sentence 2.
D. placed after sentence 3.

15.   [1] There is still no definitive cause of aging. [2] One theory is that cells have a pre-determined lifetime. [3] Some cells, like those that make up skin and blood, can be replaced, while others, such as nerve cells, cannot. [4] If a cell is damaged, and it cannot be replaced, it is lost forever. [5] This division process allows subsequent generations of cells to carry errors caused during replication. [6] These errors may degrade the quality of the duplicated cells, leading to what we know of as aging.

Upon reviewing this paragraph and realizing that some information has been left out, the writer composes the following sentence:

But cells that can be replaced do so by splitting in two.

The most logical and effective place to insert this sentence would be:

A. after sentence 2.
B. after sentence 4.
C. after sentence 5.
D. after sentence 6.

Exercise 3: Some of the following questions will ask you to order all paragraphs. You won't see these on the ACT, but they serve as the best training for all other paragraph ordering questions. Answers for this chapter start on page 213.

1.

[1]

There are people of other religions in India too, notably Muslims, who remained after the partition of Pakistan from the territory after the Second World War in 1947. Christians, Sikhs, and a few Buddhists are also accounted for. Jains, devotees of Jainism, make up a small community of believers in India. Once a large religious presence in the region, Jains suffered sporadic persecution, and the combination of rivalry from other sects of Hinduism and loss of royal patronage meant their numbers dwindled over the years.

[2]

Despite the many conquests of India's lands, the Hindu religion has persisted and to this day exerts the greatest influence on the population of 1.2 billion people. The faith is practiced in different forms, but all share common concepts and central ritual techniques. Some sects of Hinduism are associated with specific geographical locations. For instance, Pashupata Shaivism is followed mainly in the northern state of Gujarat, whereas devotees of Shaiva Siddhanta are normally found in the southern regions, where they have maintained distance from foreign aggressors.

[3]

India is a land of riches. Precious metals and priceless stones have been mined from the earth there for as long as anyone can remember. Yet the natural bounty that gave rise to its wealth has also brought with it a dark side. Invaders have sought to conquer her lands to possess the riches underground. However, the people have not surrendered so easily; even Alexander the Great was driven out, never to return.

[4]

Many ritual practices of Hinduism take place both within the home and at the temple. The temple is a place to bring the gods and man together, and the design of the temple space seeks to illuminate the ideas and beliefs of Hinduism. In this way, motifs inscribed on walls can symbolically present concepts such as the dharma and karma, guiding the believer to contemplate various aspects of the faith. Temples also contain idols, often serving as the focal point of the whole construction.

[5]

Prior to Alexander's ill-fated attempt on the sub-continent, the Indian lands were successfully invaded by the Aryans. A fair-skinned folk, they came from the northern passes, between the Vindhya Range and the Himalayas. They brought with them the *Rig-Veda*, a poem credited with being the founding text of the Hindu religion. Invasions over land continued for thousands of years, right up until the British and Portuguese fleets arrived in the 1700s.

The most effective and logical ordering of the paragraphs in the passage is:

A. 2, 1, 5, 4, 3
B. 3, 1, 4, 5, 2
C. 3, 5, 2, 4, 1
D. 5, 3, 2, 4, 1

2.

[1]

Later, in 1534, when Michelangelo was nearly 60 years old, Paul III became Pope. He traveled to Rome and began working on arguably his most famous painting, *The Last Judgment*. During this time, he met Vittoria Colonna, whom he held feelings for even after her death.

[2]

Upon completing the Sistine Chapel, Michelangelo underwent a period of great despair. Florence during that time was enmeshed in political rivalries, and despite Michelangelo's desire to work on the burial chamber of Pope Julius II, he himself got caught up in the intrigue and machinations of state. When Julius died in 1513, Rome soon fell to Charles V, and Pope Clement VII, who succeeded Julius, was locked away, and Michelangelo's patrons, the Medicis, were expelled from Florence.

[3]

Because of his reputation as a great artist, Michelangelo was eventually pardoned and resumed work for the Medicis. During this period, he spent time crafting the tomb of Lorenzo de Medici. He would never finish the project during his lifetime, but scholars still acknowledge it as one of his finest pieces ever. His sculpture of Lorenzo seeks to capture the inner personality of the dark, pensive, and brooding man. Indeed, Lorenzo's nickname, "The Thoughtful One," wasn't given to him for no reason.

[4]

Vittoria had a great impact on Michelangelo. It was said that she inspired him to grow a deep and renewed interest in the divine. This was reflected in his choice of subject matter for two of his last pieces— the *Crucifixion of St. Peter* and the *Conversion of St. Paul*. Michelangelo depicts Paul as an old and suffering man, perhaps suggesting his own state of mind during that time.

[5]

Florence once again reverted to a republic, but instead of following the Medicis into exile, Michelangelo remained where he was. Impulsive as always, he soon changed his mind and went to Venice but returned to Florence again not long after. Sadly for Michelangelo, the political situation had changed in Florence; the republic had fallen, Pope Clement VII and the Medicis had returned to power, and Michelangelo was forced to go into hiding.

The most effective and logical ordering of the paragraphs is:

A. 2, 5, 3, 1, 4
B. 2, 5, 1, 3, 4
C. 5, 2, 3, 4, 1
D. 3, 2, 5, 1, 4

3.

[1]

Many bird varieties can be found on the ground too. The quail is known to hide in dense foliage but can be harried out of the meadow grass to be seen dancing over the low brush in little bursts of intense flying. This game bird can be identified by its sandy color and its "quik-ik-ik" call.

[2]

If the butterflies or the flying birds prove too elusive for you, then keep your eyes peeled for another meadow resident—the humble spider. Look for glistening webs in the morning dew or the frantic shimmering of its captured prey. If you wait long enough, you might glimpse the gruesome spectacle of the spider immobilizing an unfortunate fly, plunging its poisoned fangs into the insect's body. You'll realize nature is beautiful, but also cruel. It's that cycle of life again, continuing on its merry way.

[3]

Bird life flourishes in both the meadows and the towns, the creatures having adapted more successfully to the spread of man's advances into the countryside. Sparrows are abundant around the sprawling farmsteads, and if you're lucky you might just spot the Italian variety with its white cheeks and distinctive beak. Those with keen ears might also hear the skylark, its high-pitched song soaring over the tree-tops.

[4]

Summer is a time for long country walks, picnics, and ball games in the open meadow. But if you stop, listen, and look a little closer, you'll realize you are not alone. The fields are buzzing with the natural world—honeybees gathering nectar for winter reserves, butterflies mating and laying eggs, caterpillars crawling out for the first time. The cycle of life continues every day.

[5]

But life is fragile for insects everywhere, and many species face the continual threat of extinction. The swallowtail butterfly uses its cunning camouflage to hide from predators, but predators aren't the only danger; the onward expansion of farmland and urban developments are destroying breeding sites, and the loss of these native creatures is a very real possibility.

The most effective and logical ordering of the paragraphs is:

   A. 3, 4, 5, 2, 1
   B. 3, 5, 4, 1, 2
   C. 4, 3, 5, 2, 1
   D. 4, 5, 3, 1, 2

4.

[1]

Everywhere we go, oil is ubiquitous. It forms the basis of detergents, cleaning liquids, and anti-freeze products we use in our cars. It's also found in cosmetics and perfumes, and even paint, medicines, chewing gum, and explosives. Oil is literally the substance on which our modern lives depend. The importance of oil means that we need to guarantee our access to it. Exploration of new oil fields is a perpetual concern, and new ways of extracting oil and gas from the ground are continually being developed.

[2]

Imagine nine bath tubs, filled to the brim with thick, black liquid. This is the amount of crude oil the average person in the world uses in just one year. If you live in a developed nation like France, you use twice that much. A person living in the United States, the biggest consumer of oil worldwide, uses even more than that.

[3]

So what is crude oil used for? Well, only a very small portion of it is used by individuals as actual oil. If you own a car or other mechanical device, you'd need it for lubrication, but most of its uses are found elsewhere.

[4]

Oil is used in heavy industrial processes, for public transport, and in agriculture and farming businesses. For instance, it's a crucial part of the plastic manufacturing process, which is used to produce man-made fibers and household necessities such as kitchenware and furniture. It also fuels power stations, which provide heat and light for our homes and places of work.

[5]

Scientists are now thinking about completely novel ways of producing oil. Some are even suggesting that we make oil ourselves. Researchers in China claim that microorganisms, such as yeast, could generate oil-like byproducts through their internal metabolic processes, which could then be harvested and used by humans. Techniques such as this don't just promise us more oil; they also make for a more environmentally friendly method of production.

For the sake of logic and coherence, Paragraph 1 should be placed:

A. where it is now.
B. after Paragraph 2.
C. after Paragraph 3.
D. after Paragraph 4.

5.

[1]

For millennia, the secrets of the ocean waves have puzzled mankind. What exactly are waves, and how do they form? How are they propagated across vast swathes of the planet? What allows a wave to be of different magnitudes and sizes? These and many other mysteries have remained unsolved until recently.

[2]

Marine scientists have used the latest and most sensitive measuring devices to research the behavior of waves. There is still much to be learned, but the fundamental details of the life-cycle of an ocean wave are already known. We know how they form, how they move, and how they decay once they reach the shore. It is upon this basic knowledge base that oceanographers seek to improve.

[3]

To explain the to-and-fro phenomenon of floating objects, researchers began creating artificial waves in giant water tanks. They used pieces of cork placed at different locations in the tank to measure the motion of the waves. Through painstaking experiments, they were able to catalogue reams of data that gave the researchers a better idea of what was going on.

[4]

When the data were analyzed, the scientists found that as the wave moved towards a certain cork, the cork rose but remained in the same location after the wave had passed. It did not travel across the surface of the water! The top layer of the ocean was moving up and down by itself.

[5]

Many people mistakenly believe a wave is just a mass of water careening across the surface of the sea. There's a much deeper science behind it. If one observes a bird bobbing on the waves, it appears as if it's going to be carried away to another place. If one keeps on looking, however, it looks like it's actually staying in the same place, not heading towards shore or anywhere else. It was this lack of movement that first gave scientists an insight into how waves behave. If they could just find a way to replicate the motions of an ocean wave in laboratory conditions, they could begin to investigate this peculiar phenomenon in more detail.

For the sake of logic and coherence, Paragraph 5 should be placed:

   A. where it is now.
   B. after Paragraph 2.
   C. after Paragraph 3.
   D. after Paragraph 4.

6.

[1]

Not far down the river Thames, a few miles from the capital of London, in a specially built dry dock, rests one of the last ships from a bye-gone maritime era. Considered the most famous clipper of all time, she is named after the witch in the poem *Tam-o-Shanter*, Robert Burn's gothic tale of drunken Scots and haunted churches.

[2]

Like the other clipper ships of that era, she was exceedingly fast. Built to lightweight standards, clippers took their name from their ability to "clip" days off the journey time taken by lesser vessels. The ships stole the imagination of a thrilled nation that marvelled at their record-breaking speeds.

[3]

Clippers developed out of a maritime "arms-race" of sorts, in what was a unique set of economic circumstances at the time. Tea drinking was quickly replacing beer as the national drink of England, and the tea came mostly from China. Buyers were desperate to be the first to try a new variety of tea arriving in port, and so the ships that could deliver their cargo the fastest could charge the highest prices. Merchants were willing to invest in building the sleekest ships to compete with one another.

[4]

In 1849, the British government repealed the British Navigation Acts and opened up previously inaccessible tracts of the global marketplace to foreign traders. Suddenly, merchants in the United States and all over Europe were free to compete with British businessmen on level terms, and they wasted no time in building even faster ships to capitalize on the situation. Soon, the ships of Great Britain were no longer the envy of the world. They were still admired, but their aura of invincibility had gone. The golden age of the British vessel was over; the new age of the steam ship was just around the corner.

[5]

The ship is the *Cutty Sark*. One glance at her smooth, flowing lines, her towering masts, bedecked with bleached white canvas, and it is obvious why she is regarded as a thoroughbred of the seas.

For the sake of logic and coherence, Paragraph 5 should be placed:

  A. where it is now.
  B. after Paragraph 1.
  C. after Paragraph 2.
  D. after Paragraph 3.

23
Relevance & Purpose

Relevance

On the ACT, you'll encounter a lot of questions that boil down to one or more of the following about a given sentence:

- Is it relevant in context?
- What does it accomplish?
- Does it accomplish the goal in question?
- Should it be added or deleted?

For example, you'll see something like this:

> At this point, the writer is considering adding the following sentence:
>
> > Joe then confronted Jane about the money she owed him.
>
> Should the writer make this addition?
>
> **A.** Yes, because the information clarifies Joe's reasoning for his actions.
> **B.** Yes, because the information helps explain how Joe and Jane originally met.
> **C.** No, because the additional information distracts the reader from the main point of the essay.
> **D.** No, because it's unclear whether Joe wanted to argue with Jane.

When tackling these types of questions, always answer the yes or no part first. Is it relevant? Should it be added or deleted? Yes or no. Don't even read the rest of the words in the answer choices. In your mind, just answer yes or no. That way, you've halved the number of choices under consideration. Usually it's pretty obvious whether a sentence is relevant.

Only after you have answered yes or no should you think about the why (why or why shouldn't the sentence be added?). The reason for doing this is to prevent the answer choices from influencing your reasoning, because once you answer yes or no, you instinctively develop your own reason which you can then compare with the two remaining answer choices. Letting the reason you thought up yourself guide you to the correct answer choice is extremely effective—your instincts are often right. Reading the full answer choices before you've had time to think for yourself has a way of playing with your mind.

If your reason doesn't line up with the reasons in the two remaining answer choices, it's a sign you need to reconsider the yes or no part.

Most irrelevant sentences come in the form of random facts that come out of nowhere. Here are some examples (irrelevant parts are italicized):

- Last Monday, I went to my high school reunion. I was excited about meeting old acquaintances and friends. *Afterwards, I went back home with my wife.* I had lost touch with them after so many years.

- My dad runs a bakery in Boston's Chinatown, *but there's also a Chinatown in Toronto.* He sells freshly baked pork buns, egg tarts, and cakes to the locals everyday.

- Because *All the King's Men* was released as a movie before I could read the book, *which is often available in used book stores,* I decided to watch the movie first. I wish I hadn't though because the book turned out to be far more entertaining.

- Since its inception, Cathay Pacific airlines has served millions of customers worldwide. *Obviously, flying is faster than driving.* The company continues to offer world class service, comfortable seating, and delicious meals on all flights.

The best way to spot irrelevance is to evaluate the key words in the sentence in question. If those key words aren't referred to in some way in the previous sentence or the following sentence, chances are that it's irrelevant. Notice in the respective examples above that:

- There is no reference to *home* or *wife* in the surrounding sentences.

- There is no reference to *Toronto* in the surrounding sentences.

- There is no reference to *used book stores* in the surrounding sentences.

- There is no reference to *driving* in the surrounding sentences.

Also notice how the italicized portions interrupt the flow of the passage; they are abrupt shifts in topic. Relevant content will stay on topic; irrelevant content will not.

Another sign that something is irrelevant is a sudden shift in scope—how general or specific something is. The last example above starts out by talking about one specific airline, Cathay Pacific, but all of a sudden, it jumps into something extremely general, that flying is faster than driving. Be wary of these sudden shifts in scope.

At the end of the day, there is no magic formula for determining whether something is relevant. After lots of practice, your intuition will be your best guide.

Purpose

Ok, so now you've determined whether something is relevant or not. Sometimes, you'll have to answer why. In addition to the relevance questions mentioned above, these questions can take the form of:

- If this sentence were deleted, the essay would primarily lose:

- Suppose the writer had decided to write an essay discussing.... Would this essay successfully fulfill the writer's goal?

- In this paragraph, the writer intends to.... Given that all the choices are true, which one would best accomplish the writer's intention?

- At this point, the writer wants to add a sentence that would.... Which of the following sentences would best accomplish this?

Here are some typical reasons for including/not deleting something:

- because the additional detail explains why. . .
- because if readers understand. . . , they will also understand why. . .
- because it can help the reader have a better understanding of. . .
- because the information shows. . .
- because the information explains the reference to. . .
- because it informs the reader. . .
- because it provides important background information

Here are some typical reasons for not including/deleting something:

- because it would distract readers from the main focus of the essay
- because it provides information that is included elsewhere in the essay
- because it fails to explain the connection between. . . and. . .
- because it is inconsistent with the tone/style of this essay
- because it does not provide specific enough information about. . .

Tip

The most common reason by far for not including/deleting something is irrelevance. If the question asks whether to add a given sentence and your answer is no, the reason will likely be that it distracts the reader or that it's irrelevant to the focus of the essay, so gravitate towards that answer choice first.

When you encounter purpose questions, always read the surrounding sentences and determine what function the given sentence plays. It will usually fall under one of the following categories:

- conclusion of a paragraph or essay
- further description
- effective transition
- specific evidence or supporting detail
- an explanation of a certain term or phenomenon
- introduction of a topic
- emphasis of a previous point

Again, there is no magic formula for consistently determining what the purpose of a sentence or essay is. A lot of it comes down to logic and judgment, which is best improved through practice.

Exercise 1: Answers for this chapter start on page 216.

Fishing on Grandmother's River

My favorite place to visit during my childhood was my grandparents' house, which overlooked a coastal river in North Carolina. [1] I spent many summers there fishing from the dock in the peaceful mornings and evenings when the river had calmed to a still surface broken only by the jumping mullets.

[2]

Flowing over a mucky, silty bed, the river usually appeared a dark bluish-brown. We couldn't see the bottom, so we fished with bobbers floating above the wormed hook. Who can express the excitement of a small child when he sees the bobber jerk down suddenly, its whiteness turning golden in the brown murk? [3] I experienced this excitement more times than I can recall, though I eventually learned to temper my joy when I more often than not pulled up an empty hook, <u>which became</u>
<u>4</u>
<u>rustier with every use.</u>
<u>4</u>

1. The writer is considering deleting the following phrase "which overlooked a coastal river in North Carolina" from the preceding sentence and ending it with a period. If it were deleted, the essay would primarily lose:

   A. important descriptive details.
   B. a comparison with a later idea.
   C. an explanation of a key term.
   D. an indication of the narrator's future travel plans.

2. At this point, the writer is considering adding the following sentence:

   A mullet is a chiefly marine fish that is widely caught for food.

   Should the writer make this addition?

   A. Yes, because it describes what the narrator was fishing for.
   B. Yes, because it clarifies a term that the reader may not be familiar with.
   C. No, because it distracts the reader from the focus of the essay.
   D. No, because there is no indication that the narrator eats mullets for food.

3. At this point, the writer is considering adding the following sentence:

   Not many can.

   Should the writer make this addition?

   A. Yes, because it addresses an important question that readers would like the answer to.
   B. Yes, because it gives a sense of how many people can express a certain level of excitement.
   C. No, because it is unnecessary to address a rhetorical question that is used to convey an experience.
   D. No, because it provides information that is already mentioned elsewhere in the essay.

4. Given that all of the choices are true, which one provides the most relevant information at this point in the essay?

   A. NO CHANGE
   B. one of the many I had bought at the store.
   C. which I had planned on replacing.
   D. a clear sign that the fish had escaped with the bait.

Sometimes, my sisters and I would sit together and wait <u>for hours on end.</u> With every fresh catch,
                                    5
we ran over to each other to celebrate, happy that our patience had paid off. Our hooks would bring in bream, bass, and even flounders that had washed in with the brackish water of high tide. 6 We let the smaller ones go but collected the bigger ones.

7 My parents enjoyed crabbing from the dock, using old chicken bones with scraps left on them as the bait. If we ever got drowsy waiting for the next bite, they would sneak up behind us with a crab in hand and scare us awake. 8

5. At this point, the writer wants to show the extent of his patience while he caught fish. Given that all of the choices are true, which one best accomplishes that goal?

   A. NO CHANGE
   B. while we chatted about books we had read.
   C. until one of us felt a tug.
   D. for a while.

6. The writer is considering deleting the preceding sentence. If the writer were to make this deletion, the essay would primarily lose:

   A. a cautionary detail to warn of the dangers of fishing during high tide.
   B. an indication of the fish the narrator tried to avoid.
   C. information regarding what types of fish the narrator caught.
   D. a transition to the narrator's later discussion of eels.

7. At this point, the writer is considering adding the following phrase to the end of the preceding sentence:

   for what would become a delicious meal back at the house

   Should the writer make this addition?

   A. Yes, because it expresses how hungry the narrator was after a long day of fishing.
   B. Yes, because it explains why the bigger fish were kept instead of let go.
   C. No, because it contradicts the narrator's earlier point that he would rather keep the fish as pets than eat them.
   D. No, because it goes beyond the scope of the essay, which focuses on fishing and not eating.

8. At this point, the writer is considering adding the following sentence:

   They also did a lot of other things for their own amusement.

   Should the writer make this addition?

   A. Yes, because it reinforces the parents' personalities as they are portrayed.
   B. Yes, because it reveals just how boring crabbing and fishing can be.
   C. No, because it digresses from the main focus of the paragraph.
   D. No, because it suggests that the narrator didn't have any fun, which is not true.

One afternoon, I felt a great tug on the line and excitedly began reeling it in. I thought for sure I had caught a good-sized fish, but instead it was a long, muscular, snake-like creature that flailed and twisted, flapping its tail of a body against the wood. [9] An oily substance covered every place it touched, leaving a powdery, slate-blue residue upon drying. [10] Too disgusted to touch it, I trapped the eel under my foot. Meanwhile, my sis-

ter was reeling in a large catch of her own. Once
                    11
it looked dead, we brought it to my grandmother, who had us leave it in a bucket for her gardener, who liked receiving food as gifts.
                    12

9. If the writer were to delete the phrase "long, muscular, snake-like" from the preceding sentence, the sentence would primarily lose:

   A. description that foreshadows what will eventually happen.
   B. emphasis on how odd the narrator's taste in fish are.
   C. details that reinforce the contrast between what the narrator expected and his actual catch.
   D. an indication of the type of fish the narrator typically caught.

10. The writer is considering deleting the preceding sentence. Should the writer make this deletion?

    A. Yes, because it distracts the reader from the main focus of the essay.
    B. Yes, because it's unclear whether the narrator is describing a fish or an eel.
    C. No, because it provides additional description that helps explain the narrator's reaction to the eel.
    D. No, because it provides details that support the idea that fishing is not always enjoyable.

11. A. NO CHANGE
    B. During that time, my sister was reeling in a large catch all by herself.
    C. Meanwhile, my sister caught something large on her own.
    D. OMIT the underlined portion.

12. Given that all of the choices are true, which one provides the most relevant information with regard to the gardener?

    A. NO CHANGE
    B. who was referred to us by a friend.
    C. who often bought clams at the seafood market.
    D. who thought of eels as a delicacy.

That evening, when we came up to the house for dinner, the gardener called us over. "I thought you said you killed that eel," he said. "We did," I answered. He pointed to the bucket: the eel was thrashing like it was possessed. Apparently, eels are hard to kill, <u>a fact I could've looked up in a book.</u>
₁₃
We all had a good laugh about it. Then he sliced it in half and threw a piece onto the frying pan.

| 14 |

13. **A.** NO CHANGE
   B. and it's a typical problem that other fishermen have.
   C. something I couldn't have predicted.
   D. OMIT the underlined portion and end the sentence with a period.

14. Suppose the writer had decided to write an essay discussing the best locations for fishing in North Carolina. Would this essay successfully fulfill the writer's goal?

   A. Yes, because the essay provides details of a location in which the narrator has caught a lot of fish.
   B. Yes, because the essay limits itself to describing a river in North Carolina.
   C. No, because the essay narrates a childhood experience in one particular location, with no indication it is one of the best fishing spots.
   D. No, because the essay focuses on the best way to fish, and not the best locations for fishing.

Exercise 2: Answers for this chapter start on page 216.

The Economics of the Black Death

Life for an English peasant during the feudal era was brief and taxing. Treated as slaves, peasants performed many tasks for their rich lords. [1] In return, peasants had places to live, a little bit of land to scrape a living from, and the lord's protection. There was very little chance that peasants would rise above their social class—imagine how they must have felt. [3]

they must have felt.
___
2

1. At this point, the writer is considering adding the following phrase to the end of the preceding sentence (adding a comma after *lords* and ending the sentence with a period):

   providing them with food, clothing, weaponry, and any other materials the nobles wanted

   Should the writer make this addition?

   A. Yes, because it offers specific details that help readers understand a broad statement.
   B. Yes, because it helps clarify the basic needs of the feudal lords.
   C. No, because it distracts the reader from the focus of the essay.
   D. No, because it gives examples that are a minor portion of the peasants' work.

2. Given that all of the following statements are true, which one provides the most relevant information at this point in the essay?

   A. NO CHANGE
   B. they played games together to pass the time.
   C. bread and porridge was the typical meal.
   D. a middle class was nearly non-existent.

3. Which choice, if inserted here, would most effectively and appropriately lead the reader from the topic of this paragraph to that of the next?

   A. When peasants got sick, there was very little that could be done to help them.
   B. With social structures seemingly set in stone, no one could have predicted the violent changes that soon came.
   C. Because of their short lifespans, peasants usually got married at an early age.
   D. Peasants would save as much as they could, so that their children would have better lives than they did.

From 1346 to 1353, the Black Death, carried by rats and fleas, decimated Europe, killing as many as one-third of its inhabitants. [4] But this disease, a massive pandemic of bubonic plague, also reshaped the social landscape and brought new opportunities to impoverished workers. [5] It was a matter of simple economics.
$$\underline{\qquad}$$
6

4. At this point, the writer wants to add a sentence that would further emphasize the catastrophic impact of the Black Death. Which of the following sentences would best accomplish this?

   A. It likely originated in the dry plains of Central Asia.
   B. Symptoms included acute fever and the vomiting of blood, with death approaching two to seven days later.
   C. Everyone lived in fear as family members lost their loved ones and even whole villages were wiped out.
   D. Because doctors at the time could not explain the cause, people turned to religion and fanaticism.

5. At this point, the writer wants to add a question that would mirror the reader's likely skepticism of the Black Death's positive impact. Which of the following would best accomplish this?

   A. Could death be a solution to most problems?
   B. So how exactly did such a terrible disaster end up helping the very group of people it killed?
   C. How did peasants react to these sudden changes in society?
   D. How come the feudal lords, with all their power, weren't able to prevent the rise of the peasants?

6. **A.** NO CHANGE
   B. economics, the study of money.
   C. economics, which most peasants were unaware of.
   D. economics, and that's it.

The feudal lords relied on their peasants to supply all their wants and needs. [7] As the plague raged on, they had fewer and fewer people to work their lands and manufacture the goods their lifestyle required. Though the plague struck both rich and poor, the disparity in their population sizes meant that the plague had disproportionate effects on the demand for labor and on the supply of labor. There were fewer nobles to begin with, and they were better equipped to shield themselves from the dying masses, so they were insulated from the sadness 8 and chaos around them. The much larger population of workers, on the other hand, decreased significantly, reducing the labor supply by the millions. [9]

7. At this point, the writer is considering adding the following sentence:

   They were addicted to snacking on caviar and wearing fancy robes.

   Should the writer make this addition?

   A. Yes, because it further illustrates the extravagance of the feudal lords.
   B. Yes, because it offers examples of a typical feudal lord's daily activities.
   C. No, because it is inconsistent with the tone and focus of the paragraph.
   D. No, because the basic needs of the feudal lords were more important than the luxuries they enjoyed.

8. Given that all of the following statements are true, which one provides the most relevant information at this point in the essay?

   A. NO CHANGE
   B. the peasants had even more reason to harbor resentment towards them.
   C. their daily routines were, for the most part, uninterrupted.
   D. their demand for labor did not change radically.

9. The writer is considering deleting the phrase "by the millions" from the preceding sentence (ending it with a period). If the writer were to make this deletion, the paragraph would primarily lose:

   A. a detail that conveys the immense wealth of the feudal lords.
   B. the magnitude of an important consequence.
   C. a figure that specifies the size of a population.
   D. information that is repetitious and unnecessary.

As a result, the peasants now had the ability to leave the lords they worked for. 10 There were many other lords eager to find new workers to replace the dead ones. While life remained rather grim for them, peasants had suddenly gained mobility and the ability, however small, to seek better employment and better lands. For those who survived, it's as happy an ending as anyone could have hoped for. 12

---

10. At this point, the writer is considering adding the following phrase to the end of the preceding sentence (ending the sentence with a period):

without putting their livelihoods at risk

Should the writer make this addition?

    A. Yes, because it offers an example of the daily struggles faced by peasants.
    B. Yes, because it makes explicit why peasants were previously tied to their lords.
    C. No, because it shifts the focus of the paragraph from the lords to the peasants.
    D. No, because it contradicts a point made in a previous paragraph.

11. Which of the following sentences would best conclude this essay?

    A. NO CHANGE
    B. It's too bad they had to contend with the trauma left by the plague.
    C. This change in the social landscape laid the ground work for the middle class and the fall of the feudal system.
    D. Many were able to start their own businesses as independent blacksmiths, merchants, and cooks.

12. Suppose the writer had decided to write an essay discussing the effects the Black Death had on the feudal system. Would this essay successfully fulfill the writer's goal?

    A. Yes, because it explains how the Black Death empowered the peasant class to improve their lives.
    B. Yes, because it describes the devastation from the perspective of a feudal lord.
    C. No, because it focuses only on the daily lives of the working class and not the entire feudal system as a whole.
    D. No, because it fails to mention any specific people who managed to climb the social hierarchy.

Exercise 3: Answers for this chapter start on page 216.

Harvesting Asparagus

Asparagus is not like other vegetables. ☐1 Because it's more difficult to grow asparagus from seeds, farmers typically buy crowns, dormant roots ready to be planted. ☐2 They place them in deep trenches, wait several years for them to mature, and then finally cut the plants in the spring, <u>when artichokes are also in season.</u> I learned about the entire
                            3
process one year when I applied for a job on a busy asparagus farm during harvest time. There was asparagus on this farm that was ready to be harvested.

☐4

1. At this point, the writer is considering adding the sentence:

   It isn't planted in the spring to be harvested in the fall.

   Should the writer make this addition?

   A. Yes, because it emphasizes the importance of the seasons in growing vegetables.
   B. Yes, because it provides specific justification for a previous statement.
   C. No, because it does not specify which vegetables follow the usual harvest schedule.
   D. No, because it does not clarify when asparagus is planted and harvested.

2. The writer is considering deleting the phrase "dormant roots ready to be planted" from the preceding sentence (ending it with a period). If the writer were to make this deletion, the essay would primarily lose:

   A. details that are irrelevant to the topic of the essay.
   B. information to support the point that farmers do not like asparagus.
   C. an explanation of a term that the reader may be unfamiliar with.
   D. a transition that leads the reader to the next sentence.

3. Given that all of the following statements are true, which one provides the most relevant information at this point in the essay?

   A. NO CHANGE
   B. my favorite season of the year.
   C. when they've grown strong enough to be harvested.
   D. just in time for the opening of the farmer's market in many cities.

4. The writer is considering deleting the preceding sentence. Should the writer make this deletion?

   A. Yes, because it offers information that is repetitive and obvious to the reader.
   B. Yes, because it is inconsistent with the style and tone of the essay.
   C. No, because it reinforces the difference between asparagus and other vegetables.
   D. No, because it helps establish the setting of the essay.

The pay wasn't much but I saw the job as an
<u>opportunity to learn about farming and agriculture.</u>
5
The manager explained to me that the crowns had been planted five years ago. During the first year, asparagus can look like a field of weeds. Those weeds have to be cut down so that they don't sap the nutrients from any developing asparagus roots. The next spring, small sprouts, also known as spears, start appearing but none of them should be picked as the plants are still establishing themselves in the soil. They grow a little bit each year but are cut down because they still aren't tall enough for harvest. During this phase, <u>it's difficult to predict how many plants will survive long enough to fully mature.</u>
6

5. At this point, the writer would like to convey the fact that he was fortunate to get the job. Given that all of the choices are true, which one best accomplishes that goal?

   A. NO CHANGE
   B. Before I got hired, I introduced myself to all the crew members, who all thought I'd work well with them in a team.
   C. On my first day of work, I felt intimidated by the long stretches of farmland that we needed to clear.
   D. Despite my inexperience, I landed the job because there was a larger yield than the farm anticipated.

6. At this point, the writer wants to reinforce the idea that growing asparagus is a delicate process that requires a lot of attention. Which of the following most effectively accomplishes that goal?

   A. NO CHANGE
   B. fertilizer can be especially helpful in stimulating their growth.
   C. farmers must check everything from the moisture in the soil to the diameter of the spears to ensure they are growing properly.
   D. a lack of sunlight can lead to a variety known as white asparagus.

In the next phase, when the spears are a few inches apart, the asparagus is ready to be harvested. [7] As with all vegetables, some of the plants are ready to be cut before others. This is why one harvest can last up to six weeks. Farmers get up by five in the morning everyday to avoid the midday heat.

8

Spears are cut or snapped just above soil level, leaving benign stubs. The spears are then collected in crates for cleaning and packaging. [9] Five years to wait for one crop to mature seems like a very long time, but once it is established, it can keep on reproducing for up to twenty years. Working on this farm was a great learning experience, but I haven't been able to eat asparagus since. [10]

7. The writer is considering deleting the following phrase from the preceding sentence:

    when the spears are a few inches apart,

    Should the writer make this deletion?

    A. Yes, because it unnecessarily repeats information from earlier in the passage.
    B. Yes, because it does not describe any other aspects of the asparagus.
    C. No, because it specifies an important condition that is relevant to the sentence.
    D. No, because it establishes that spears are the outgrowth of an asparagus plant.

8. Given that all of the choices are true, which one most clearly provides a reason for the prior statement in this sentence?

    A. NO CHANGE
    B. to brush their teeth.
    C. to the sound of rooster's crow.
    D. to find breakfast waiting for them.

9. At this point, the writer is considering adding the following sentence:

    Asparagus grows the best when the nights are cool and the days are hot.

    Should the writer make this addition?

    A. Yes, because it elaborates on the conditions needed for the successful growing of asparagus.
    B. Yes, because it explains why asparagus is grown only in certain regions of the world.
    C. No, because it diverts the reader's attention from the harvesting process back to the growing process.
    D. No, because it contradicts the writer's previous point that asparagus needs stable conditions to grow in.

10. Suppose the writer had decided to write an essay focusing on his personal experience working on a farm. Would this essay successfully fulfill the writer's goal?

    A. Yes, because it explains why the author wanted to work on a farm.
    B. Yes, because it describes some of things he learned by working with his team members.
    C. No, because the writer was unqualified to work on a farm.
    D. No, because it focuses much more on the general process of growing one vegetable than the writer's own experiences.

24

Dashes & Colons

You will almost always see dashes or colons on the ACT, though they'll be tested on only one or two questions at most.

The Dash

The dash (—) serves two purposes:

1. To set off and emphasize interrupting phrases or in-between thoughts, sometimes for dramatic effect

Examples:

- All our kitchen equipment—from the steel pans used for sauces to the premium-grade oven—had to be sold to cover our losses.

- The Loch Ness Monster—a sea creature that is rumored to exist but has never been found—supposedly comes out only during the winter.

- When my teacher found the cookies I was hiding—all 154 of them—she ate them all herself.

- Frank took the goldfish from the bowl, carried it to the bathroom, put it in the toilet—and dropped it.

- My cousin was a world-class wrester—he still is—but now he focuses on coaching others.

If you just keep this first purpose of dashes in mind, you'll be fine on the ACT, because the second purpose is just a more specific version of the first one.

2. To signal a list, restatement, or additional detail

Examples:

- I like to walk everyday—not for exercise, but for alone time.

- The city is full of people you would never meet in my hometown—bums, actors, models, the crazy, the oddly dressed.

- Consider the amount of paper that's wasted by unnecessary printing—a hundred thousand pages, three times as much as what our competitors use.

- Everywhere we traveled in Kyoto there were vending machines—some served green tea while others carried only juice.

The Colon

Colons are used after an independent clause to direct attention to a list, a noun phrase, or another independent clause that summarizes or clarifies the first. Obviously those uses overlap with the dash's, but a dash is more dramatic than a colon. You'll never be tested on whether a dash should be used instead of a colon, since the two are somewhat interchangeable. **What you should know is that a colon can only come after an independent clause.**

Examples:

- A classic eggs benedict breakfast should include the following ingredients: poached eggs, english muffins, bacon, and hollandaise sauce.

- Tokyo is one of the cleanest cities in Asia: the street cleaners sometimes have no work to do.

- Cambridge is home to two of the best universities in the world: MIT and Harvard.

- I had no choice but to utter the truth in front of the judge: my brother was guilty.

Note 1

Again, it's important you know that colons can only follow an independent clause. Therefore, all of the following are incorrect, even though they may seem like correct uses of the colon:

- The dangerous animals you have to watch out for are: lions, tigers, and pythons.
- The evidence consists of: emails, text messages, and phone calls.
- The local bakery sells many delicious desserts such as: cheesecake, lemon tarts, and brownies.

None of the examples above need the colon.

Note 2

Semicolons, which are mainly used to join two independent clauses, can also be used to separate a list that contains a lot of potentially confusing punctuation:

- My favorite snacks are Pringles, which are chips in a can; ice cream, especially during the summer; and bread, usually with hummus on the side.

Exercise: Answers for this chapter start on page 217.

1. The Rolex Daytona, the most luxurious watch ever <u>released,</u> sells for a staggering half a million dollars.

   A. NO CHANGE
   B. released
   C. released:
   D. released—

2. My brother is a decent tennis <u>player, he serves well:</u> but his forehand could be hit with a bit more accuracy.

   A. NO CHANGE
   B. player—he serves well—
   C. player, he serves well—
   D. player and he serves well

3. I practice scales on the piano <u>everyday—not because I want to,</u> but because I have to.

   A. NO CHANGE
   B. everyday; not because I want to
   C. everyday not because I want to;
   D. everyday, not because I want to;

4. As the country becomes increasingly health conscious, fast food chains are removing a number of artificial ingredients from their <u>offerings:</u> sodium nitrite, aluminum silicate, canthaxanthin, and monosodium glutamate.

   A. NO CHANGE
   B. offerings;
   C. offerings
   D. offerings,

5. Google's search engine is not only effective but also <u>easy to use,</u> the home page is nothing more than a search field.

   A. NO CHANGE
   B. easy to use:
   C. easy to use,
   D. used easily:

6. Strange rainbow lights seem to emanate from the ground in photographs taken of the town, but no one knows where they come from. <u>This phenomenon remains one</u> of science's unsolved mysteries.

   A. NO CHANGE
   B. This phenomenon, remains one
   C. This phenomenon: remains one
   D. This phenomenon remains one,

7. The handbook lays out the most common mistakes when it comes to <u>writing;</u> lack of structure, having nothing to say, and repetitiveness.

   A. NO CHANGE
   B. writing,
   C. writing
   D. writing:

8. While I was on my trip to Thailand, Claire went on a shopping spree to <u>buy</u> a new car and a new wardrobe without my permission.

    A. NO CHANGE
    B. buy:
    C. buy;
    D. buy,

9. The size of the universe is hard to fully <u>comprehend:</u> there are more stars in space than there are grains of sand on all of Earth's beaches.

    Which of the following alternatives would be LEAST acceptable?

    A. NO CHANGE
    B. comprehend;
    C. comprehend—
    D. comprehend. Since

10. Environmentalists have marched into the streets to protest the country's lax attitude towards deforestation, which has proven to be devastating to the local deer <u>population: only</u> twenty sightings in the past year.

    A. NO CHANGE
    B. population, and only
    C. population; only
    D. population. Only

11. What you should remember from this whole ordeal <u>is: that there</u> can be no progress without sacrifice.

    A. NO CHANGE
    B. is that there
    C. is, that there
    D. is that there,

12. The greatest accomplishment in professional tennis is winning all four grand slam tournaments in a single <u>year, the Australian Open, Roland Garros</u> (held in France), Wimbledon (held in Britain), and the U.S. Open.

    A. NO CHANGE
    B. year, the Australian Open, Roland Garros,
    C. year: the Australian Open, Roland Garros
    D. year: the Australian Open, Roland Garros,

13. Raised in a family that had toiled day after day on a <u>farm.</u> Andrew Blomfeld liked to hire people that were hard workers, even if they lacked talent.

    A. NO CHANGE
    B. farm,
    C. farm:
    D. farm;

14. Benjamin Franklin was introduced to democratic ideals when he read one of the most influential works of his <u>time;</u> John Locke's *Two Treatises of Government*.

    A. NO CHANGE
    B. time, about
    C. time:
    D. time

15. The kitchen was <u>renovated: with</u> new marble tiles, extra cabinets and cupboards, and a stainless steel sink.

    A. NO CHANGE
    B. renovated, with
    C. renovated with
    D. renovated with:

16. Of all the things the President could have done to improve the economy, he chose to shift his attention to the one thing that was considered <u>irrelevant to undertake</u> health care.

    A. NO CHANGE
    B. irrelevant:
    C. irrelevant to
    D. irrelevant against

17. Even though he killed hundreds of innocent people, the fighter pilot was portrayed <u>as</u> a hero back at home.

    A. NO CHANGE
    B. as,
    C. as:
    D. as;

18. Designed with the user in <u>mind. The</u> new phone features a slick interface for accessing all your important notes, emails, and contacts.

    A. NO CHANGE
    B. mind, the
    C. mind: the
    D. mind the

19. While most students at MIT use their intellect to better the <u>world for example, creating vaccines for deadly viruses,</u> some are using their exceptional math skills to beat the card games in Vegas.

    A. NO CHANGE
    B. world: for example, creating vaccines for deadly viruses,
    C. world, for example, creating vaccines for deadly viruses
    D. world—for example, creating vaccines for deadly viruses—

25

You and Me Errors

Example 1

Question:	You and me should go out on a date.
Cross Out:	~~You and~~ me should go out on a date.
Use Ear:	Which is more natural? *Me should go out on a date?* OR *I should go out on a date?*
Answer:	**You and I** should go out on a date.

Example 2

Question:	This hose will protect you and I from the blazing fire.
Cross Out:	This hose will protect ~~you and~~ I from the blazing fire.
Use Ear:	Which is more natural? *This hose will protect me?* OR *This hose will protect I?*
Answer:	This hose will protect **you and me**.

Note 1

After *between* or *among*, it's always the *you and me* form, NOT *you and I*. For example,

Hey! Between **you and me**, Jack has a huge crush on Marissa.

Note 2

When dealing with these errors, never use the reflexive pronoun forms (e.g. *myself, himself, herself*). For example, the following sentences are incorrect:

- Jackie loved to borrow things from her brother and myself. *(correct: her brother and me)*
- Her brother and myself loved to loan things to Jackie. *(correct: Her brother and I)*

Exercise: Correct the following sentences. Answers for this chapter start on page 217.

1. It's a good thing that the coach knows that you and him work well as a team.

2. Ron knows that himself and his son must work together if the family business is to succeed.

3. Why is it that they always complain about you and I?

4. To meet the deadline, the President and them need to come to some sort of an agreement.

5. My sister says her and her friends rarely text message each other.

6. It's hard to get through the school day when the class bully considers my friends and myself his source of lunch money.

7. The neighbors next door and us could not be any more different.

8. Her dogs and herself got lost when they took a wrong turn in the forest.

9. To think that there's a special relationship between you and I is stupid indeed.

10. He can't stand how fast you and me talk.

11. After grabbing a drink, she plopped herself between the rest of the girls and I.

12. The girl scouts and me went out to sell cookies in the neighborhood.

13. You are safe with the prison guards and I.

14. The coach's extreme resentment towards the opposing team and I disturbed even his own players.

15. The secrets between myself and her are starting to come to light as the investigation continues.

26 Idioms

Idioms are phrases that are correct just because that's the way we say them. There's no rhyme or reason behind them and the right preposition can depend on the meaning of the sentence. Some are downright obvious because they sound so unnatural but some can be tough to spot, especially if you haven't encountered the idiom before.

Example 1

Wrong:	He is regarded **to be** an awesome speaker.
Correct:	He is regarded **as** an awesome speaker.

Example 2

Wrong:	That painting is similar **with** the red one.
Correct:	That painting is similar **to** the red one.

Example 3

Wrong:	She is suspicious **towards** me.
Correct:	She is suspicious **of** me.

Example 4

Wrong:	I have an interest **towards** fishing.
Correct:	I have an interest **in** fishing.

Example 5

Wrong:	He deserves **receiving** a gold medal.
Correct:	He deserves **to receive** a gold medal.

Exercise 1: Correct the idiom errors below. Answers for this chapter start on page 218.

1. I don't care about your opinion towards me.

2. Your ability in getting the perfect cards has caught the attention of casino surveillance.

3. The Olympic athlete was capable in climbing Mt. Everest.

4. The public was opposed against the war.

5. The children were prohibited against playing outside at dark.

6. Unless you comply to those food safety standards, we will shut you down.

7. Those who don't abide with the rules are often the ones who successfully innovate.

8. China is becoming an economic hegemony against foreign rivals who dare to compete.

9. By taking good care of pandas, zoos have succeeded to save pandas from extinction.

10. I hope you are aware about the raccoons that are living in your basement.

11. She has lived in Broome street for over fifty years.

12. After the pause, they resumed to play football until nightfall.

13. Paralyzed, Robert couldn't help but watching the thief steal the car.

14. He was inclined in accepting the new job offer, but wanted to wait.

15. The young graduate yearned towards the days when he didn't have to worry about the bills.

Exercise 2: Answers for this chapter start on page 218.

1. When I first started running as a child, I never thought that I'd ever get the chance <u>to be representative of</u> my local club at the Sydney regional finals.

   A. NO CHANGE
   B. in representing
   C. in representation of
   D. to represent

2. Unfortunately, injury has kept me bed-ridden <u>for</u> the rest of the season.

   A. NO CHANGE
   B. in
   C. at
   D. with

3. So I kept <u>towards</u> working at it, and ran the best times I had in years.

   A. NO CHANGE
   B. with
   C. on
   D. about

4. The weather took a turn for the worse, but as we made the first part of the ascent, hope <u>in success</u> was still strong.

   A. NO CHANGE
   B. of success
   C. to succeed
   D. to succeeding

5. Wearable technologies will make a huge impact <u>towards</u> the global smartphone marketplace in the coming years.

   A. NO CHANGE
   B. at
   C. on
   D. against

6. Dubai is home to one of the world's tallest buildings, which attracts its fair share <u>for</u> adrenaline junkie base-jumpers.

   A. NO CHANGE
   B. in
   C. with
   D. of

7. Spot welding relies <u>on</u> the heat caused by electrical resistance to fuse metal pieces together.

   A. NO CHANGE
   B. against
   C. by
   D. in

8. Spot welding is preferred <u>against</u> friction welding when fixing broken pipes.

   A. NO CHANGE
   B. over
   C. to
   D. more than

9. We more often observe loose allegiances between smaller gangs, <u>consisting in</u> various nationalities and ethnicities.

   A. NO CHANGE
   B. made up of
   C. made up in
   D. making up of

10. The President praised the initiative <u>in raising</u> funds from sources other than government grants.

    A. NO CHANGE
    B. for raising
    C. to raise
    D. on the raise of

11. To the avant-garde, innovation is a necessary component <u>about</u> greatness.

    A. NO CHANGE
    B. with
    C. of
    D. to

12. After speaking with our lawyers, we successfully petitioned <u>with</u> the patent office.

    A. NO CHANGE
    B. to
    C. towards
    D. OMIT the underlined portion.

13. Magnetic inductors are more efficient than wind power <u>by</u> a watt-by-watt basis.

    A. NO CHANGE
    B. on
    C. regarding
    D. as

14. The Mongols and the Chinese both tried to conquer Vietnam at various points <u>on</u> the second millennium.

    A. NO CHANGE
    B. upon
    C. in
    D. from

15. Irish dancing can trace its origins back to the time of the Druids, when it was believed that ritual processions should take place <u>in honoring</u> the sun spirit.

    A. NO CHANGE
    B. to honor
    C. of honoring
    D. for the honoring of

27
Who vs. Whom

Now's a good time to introduce an error you'll probably encounter just once on the ACT, but probably hundreds of times in your life: *who* vs. *whom*.

Rule

Use *whom* after a preposition (*to, for, of,...*). Use *who* for all other cases. Note that this rule is not always correct, but it's easier to memorize and it will get you through all ACT questions related to this error.

Example 1

Wrong:	Jane is the girl for **who** I brought these gifts.
Correct:	Jane is the girl for **whom** I brought these gifts.
Correct:	Jane is the girl **whom** I brought these gifts for.

Note the exception to the rule in the second correct version. Sometimes, the preposition (*for*, in this case) is moved to someplace later in the sentence, so just watch out. Here's another example of this:

Example 2

Wrong:	The chaperones **who** the students were assigned to made sure they walked in a single file.
Correct:	The chaperones **whom** the students were assigned to made sure they walked in a single file.
Correct:	The chaperones **to whom** the students were assigned made sure they walked in a single file.

In the example above, the preposition to look out for is *to*. Notice that the preposition can be moved back in front of the *whom*.

Example 3

Wrong:	The boys **whom** robbed the store should be thrown in jail.
Correct:	The boys **who** robbed the store should be thrown in jail.

Example 4

Wrong:	To **who** should I send these flowers?
Correct:	To **whom** should I send these flowers?

Example 5

Wrong:	The librarian yelled at the boy **whom** never returned his books.
Correct:	The librarian yelled at the boy **who** never returned his books.

Example 6

Wrong:	He is the man **who** I love.
Correct:	He is the man **whom** I love.

This is an example of an exception to the rule. Because *the man* is the object of your love, we have to use *whom*. These cases pretty much never come up on the ACT, so just trust in the rule above. However, knowing this exception will give you added confidence on the small chance it actually comes up.

Exercise: Answers for this chapter start on page 219.

1. The agency recruited overseas teachers (*who/whom*) would be able to demonstrate a native fluency in English.

2. At Kim's birthday party were millionaires and celebrities, some of (*who/whom*) had flown in from New York to attend.

3. Julie's math teacher was a graduate student (*who/whom*), after completing his finance degree, decided to get into teaching instead.

4. The police officers, (*who/whom*) were eating donuts at the time, didn't hear the cries for help.

5. The girl (*who/whom*) Dave was matched with was unimpressed by his sense of humor.

6. Anyone (*who/whom*) has read the book will say that it's much better than the movie.

7. Reflecting on all her past accomplishments, the winner thanked everyone with (*who/whom*) she had been associated.

8. Can you tell the boys (*who/whom*) are at the door to go away?

9. The girls with (*who/whom*) I'm going shopping need to borrow money.

10. I want to hire those chefs (*who/whom*) cooked the perfect pasta at the restaurant we ate at last week.

28

Adverbs vs. Adjectives

An adjective is a word that describes a noun (person, place, or thing):

> The **mighty** panda trampled through the jungle. (*mighty* describes the noun *panda*)

An adverb describes a verb, adjective, or even another adverb:

- The panda **mightily** trampled through the jungle. (*mightily* describes the verb *trampled*)
- The panda, an **incredibly** fierce beast, trampled through the jungle. (*incredibly* describes the adjective *fierce*)
- The panda tears through leaves **incredibly** quickly. (*incredibly* describes the adverb *quickly*, which describes *tears*)

Unlike adjectives, adverbs usually describe the *how* of an action and end in *ly* 99% of the time. On the ACT, you will see incorrectly used adjectives that should be turned into adverbs and vice versa. All you have to do is add *ly* to turn adjectives into adverbs and remove the *ly* to turn adverbs back into adjectives. This error seems obvious when it's pointed out, but if you're not looking for it, it's very easy to miss because we sometimes omit the *ly* in conversations and we don't read sentences as carefully as we should. It's not a common topic on the ACT, but they will throw it in from time to time.

Example 1

Wrong:	She did poor on the exam.
Correct:	She did **poorly** on the exam. (*poorly* describes the verb *did*)

Example 2

Wrong:	The elegant dressed vampire befriended her on Facebook.
Correct:	The **elegantly** dressed vampire befriended her on Facebook. (*elegantly* describes the adj. *dressed*)

Example 3

Wrong:	She speaks so loud that I can't hear anything you're saying.
Correct:	She speaks so **loudly** that I can't hear anything you're saying. (*loudly* describes the verb *speaks*)

Rule

A special rule applies when dealing with the four "sense" verbs - *taste, smell, look, feel*. Ask yourself if the verb is actively being performed. Is the subject actively smelling or looking at something? If so, use the *-ly* ending. If the verb's job is to describe something (*The pizza tastes awful*), then don't use the *-ly* ending.

Example 4

Wrong:	The salad tastes badly.
	Is the salad bad at tasting things with its "tongue"? No.
Correct:	The salad tastes **bad**.

Example 5

Wrong:	The roses smell pleasantly.
	Are the roses actively smelling with their "noses"? Nope.
Correct:	The roses smell **pleasant**.

Example 6

Wrong:	Because he didn't like his job, the postman always looked angrily.
	Did the postman look with his eyes or are we describing his appearance? Describing his appearance.
Correct:	Because he didn't like his job, the postman always looked **angry**.

Example 7

Wrong:	The postman looked angry at the little kids who got in his way.
	Did the postman look with his eyes or are we describing his appearance? In this case, he looked with his eyes.
Correct:	The postman looked **angrily** at the little kids who got in his way.

Example 8

Wrong:	She felt badly about cheating on the test.
	Did she feel badly with her fingers? Nope.
Correct:	She felt **bad** about cheating on the test.

Exercise: Correct the following sentences. Some may be correct. Answers for this chapter start on page 219.

1. The rapid changing movements of the tides often catch some sea animals by surprise.

2. He's been sent to therapy three times because he acts so impulsive.

3. He attributed the dramatic score improvement to his incessant studying.

4. I am impressed by how cleanly your dog smells.

5. The Camry runs a lot more efficient than the Hummer.

6. Please listen close to the words I'm about to say to you.

7. Because he drove so careful, cars behind him would get impatient.

8. He threw the baseball so quick that his teammate couldn't react in time to catch it.

9. You need to get some rest because you look awfully today.

10. The iPod is the most clever designed music player to date.

11. The waiter acted so gracious in serving our table that we left him a huge tip.

12. The plane flew direct from New York to Seoul.

13. The astonishing high height from which he fell only made his survival story more miraculous.

14. After I finished my final exams, I felt less uneasily about my grades.

15. Grammar usually comes so natural to us that we don't think about it in conversation.

16. My dog walks so incredibly awkward that I no longer have the patience to take him out everyday.

29

Comparatives vs. Superlatives

Example 1

Wrong:	Between the lion and the tiger, the tiger is the most fierce and the most strong. Between the lion and the tiger, the tiger is the fiercest and the strongest.
Correct:	Between the lion and the tiger, the tiger is the **fiercer** and the **stronger**. Between the lion and the tiger, the tiger is **more fierce** and **more strong**.

Example 2

Wrong:	Among all the bears in the world, the panda bear is stronger. Among all the bears in the world, the panda bear is more strong.
Correct:	Among all the bears in the world, the panda bear is **most strong**. Among all the bears in the world, the panda bear is **strongest**.

Rule 1

Comparing two things requires the *-er* ending or *more*.
Comparing three things or more requires the *-est* ending or *most*.

Rule 2

Between is used only for comparing two things. Use *among* to compare more than two things.

Exercise: Correct the following sentences. Answers for this chapter start on page 220.

1. Harry Potter and Frodo Baggins both rise to the challenges in their magical worlds, but I think Frodo has the most courage.

2. Of all the essays I've read, this one has the better chance of impressing admissions.

3. The raspberry pie is my favorite between the four of them.

4. China is not only the biggest of all the Asian countries but also the one with more historical culture.

5. Of the two main types of books out there, Jose finds non-fiction to be the most enlightening.

6. Because they're so smart and diligent, it's hard to tell which of the two frontrunners is most likely to be valedictorian.

7. There are no secrets among the the president and vice president.

30
Review Cheat Sheet

This chapter consists of a lot of incorrect example sentences from previous chapters. They cover most of the concepts you'll encounter on test day, so it's a great review for the day before the test. See if you can fix these sentences without looking back at the corresponding chapter. Answers are at the end of this chapter.

Subject-Verb Agreement

- The diner near the dorms which (*houses/house*) the students (*serves/serve*) breakfast all day.

- The widely recognized red coloring of stop signs everywhere (*alerts/alert*) people who can't even read them to stop.

- Each team made up of one girl and one boy (*has/have*) to reenact a scene from Romeo and Juliet.

- Her jewelry, in addition to her pokemon cards, (*was/were*) stolen by the robber.

- Beside the bins, where one could smell the stench of rotten eggs, (*was/were*) a pack of philosophy majors gathering cans for recycling.

Run-ons

- He was hungry, he bought a Chipotle burrito.

- In New York, the train system is difficult to learn, however the food is fantastic and diverse.

- He believed that a career in nursing would guarantee a stable job, Joseph applied to medical school.

Modifiers

- The magician dazzled and surprised the audience members wearing a cloak and top hat.

- Decorated with colorful ornaments and stars, we took pictures by the Christmas tree.

- After missing an easy goal, the crowd booed the soccer player.

Fragments

- In the middle of the night, when most people are sleeping while I sneak to the kitchen to eat.

- Although pandas are one of the most likable mammals but are one of the most rare.

Redundancy

- The reason why red pandas have ringed tails is because they are relatives of both the giant panda and the raccoon.

- After hearing the spy's information, the general knew that an attack was imminent in the future.

- In her biography about her life, she writes about overcoming poverty and fear.

- It's only on the night before the test that I wish my notes had been more clearer.

Parallelism

- That she looks beautiful and her charm help her get out of speeding tickets.

- In chess, remember these three goals: get your pieces to the center, capture the opposing pieces, and attacking the opposing king.

- The 300 men trained diligently, screamed fiercely into battle, and valiantly fights.

Pronoun Reference

- Whenever Jason and Alexander sit down at a buffet, he eats way more food.

- Even if a student gets in early, they still have to maintain good grades during senior year.

- At the police station, they found a pile of cash stashed in her bra.

- Although it is small and furry, koalas are able to protect themselves from predators by quickly climbing trees.

Tense Errors

- Although the cheetah holds the record for fastest land animal, many other mammals outlasted it.

- Whenever we stopped by the market, my mom always tries to negotiate the prices.

- She bought her dress at Wal-Mart yet it impresses everyone at the party.

- The rooster's crow was a sign that the day had began.

- Jay, with no care whatsoever, has repeatedly swam in the polluted East River.

Shift in Point of View

- Even when we arrive ahead of time at the doctor's office, he makes you wait at least 15 minutes.

- If someone wants to play tennis, you should know how to serve.

- If one does not believe, you will not succeed.

Commas

- I did what I did to improve the system not destroy it.

- Drinking coffee scientists have discovered may help prevent heart disease.

- I've decked out my laptop with a keyboard cover, pokemon stickers and a transparent case.

- Our school's computer science club which was founded in 2000 has prompted other schools to start their own.

- The panda is a, warm, gentle, animal that dines on bamboo shoots.

- The mailman dropped off the package and I told my brother that his computer had arrived.

- As the plane took off the flight attendants gave us emergency directions.

- Each year, only schools with good classroom sizes, and a top test score average will receive funding.

- The public computers in the lab, have been moved due to vandalism.

- Each of the students, and teachers, in the school will receive a handbook on proper conduct.

- I can't buy those new shoes, if the price is too high.

Apostrophes

- Tonys hat is on the floor.

- Louis' scarf is 3 feet long.

- Both players's jerseys were soaked with sweat.

- The book has a cool picture on it's cover.

- He is the actor whose most known for his role in *Batman*.

Dashes & Colons

- Consider the amount of paper that's wasted by unnecessary printing, a hundred thousand pages, three times as much as what our competitors use.

- The handbook lays out the most common mistakes when it comes to writing, lack of structure, having nothing to say, and repetitiveness.

- What you should remember from this whole ordeal is: that there can be no progress without sacrifice.

- Cambridge is home to two of the best universities in the world MIT and Harvard.

You and Me Errors

- The girl scouts and me went out to sell cookies in the neighborhood.

- You are safe with the prison guards and I.

- After grabbing a drink, she plopped herself between the rest of the girls and I.

Idioms

- The Olympic athlete was capable in climbing Mt. Everest.

- The public was opposed against the war.

- The children were prohibited against playing outside at dark.

- Unless you comply to those food safety standards, we will shut you down.

Who vs. Whom

- The agency recruited overseas teachers (*who/whom*) would be able to demonstrate a native fluency in English.

- Jane is the girl for (*who/whom*) I brought these gifts.

- The chaperones (*who/whom*) the students were assigned to made sure they walked in a single file.

Adverbs vs. Adjectives

- The astonishing high height from which he fell only made his survival story more miraculous.

- The rapid changing movements of the tides often catch some sea animals by surprise.

- You speak so loud that I can't hear what you're saying.

Comparatives vs. Superlatives

- Between the lion and the tiger, the tiger is the fiercest and the strongest.

- China is not only the biggest of all the Asian countries but also the one with more historical culture.

- Harry Potter and Frodo Baggins both rise to the challenges in their magical worlds, but I think Frodo has the most courage.

Model Answers to the Review Cheat Sheet:

Subject-Verb Agreement

- The diner near the dorms which **house** the students **serves** breakfast all day.

- The widely recognized red coloring of stop signs everywhere **alerts** people who can't even read them to stop.

- Each team made up of one girl and one boy **has** to reenact a scene from Romeo and Juliet.

- Her jewelry, in addition to her pokemon cards, **was** stolen by the robber.

- Beside the bins, where one could smell the stench of rotten eggs, **was** a pack of philosophy majors gathering cans for recycling.

Run-ons

- He was hungry, **so** he bought a Chipotle burrito.

- In New York, the train system is difficult to learn; however the food is fantastic and diverse.

- **Because** he believed that a career in nursing would guarantee a stable job, Joseph applied to medical school.

Modifiers

- **Wearing a cloak and top hat,** the magician dazzled and surprised the audience members.

- We took pictures by the Christmas tree, **which was decorated with colorful ornaments and stars.**

- After **he missed** an easy goal, the crowd booed the soccer player.

Fragments

- In the middle of the night, when most people are sleeping, ~~while~~ I sneak to the kitchen to eat.

- Although pandas are one of the most likable mammals, **they** are one of the most rare.

Redundancy

- ~~The reason why~~ Red pandas have ringed tails ~~is~~ because they are relatives of both the giant panda and the raccoon.

- After hearing the spy's information, the general knew that an attack was imminent ~~in the future~~.

- In her biography ~~about her life~~, she writes about overcoming poverty and fear.

- It's only on the night before the test that I wish my notes had been ~~more~~ clearer.

Parallelism

- **Her beauty** and her charm help her get out of speeding tickets.

- In chess, remember these three goals: get your pieces to the center, capture the opposing pieces, and **attack** the opposing king.

- The 300 men trained diligently, screamed fiercely into battle, and **fought valiantly**.

Pronoun Reference

- Whenever Jason and Alexander sit down at a buffet, **Jason** eats way more food.

- Even if a student gets in early, **he or she** still **has** to maintain good grades during senior year.

- At the police station, **the officers** found a pile of cash stashed in her bra.

- Although **they are** small and furry, koalas are able to protect themselves from predators by quickly climbing trees.

Tense Errors

- Although the cheetah holds the record for fastest land animal, many other mammals **outlast** it.

- Whenever we **stop** by the market, my mom always tries to negotiate the prices.

- She bought her dress at Wal-Mart yet it **impressed** everyone at the party.

- The rooster's crow was a sign that the day had **begun**.

- Jay, with no care whatsoever, has repeatedly **swum** in the polluted East River.

Shift in Point of View

- Even when we arrive ahead of time at the doctor's office, he makes **us** wait at least 15 minutes.

- If someone wants to play tennis, **he or she** should know how to serve.

- If one does not believe, **one** will not succeed.

Commas

- I did what I did to improve the system, not destroy it.

- Drinking coffee, scientists have discovered, may help prevent heart disease.

- I've decked out my laptop with a keyboard cover, pokemon stickers, and a transparent case.

- Our school's computer science club, which was founded in 2000, has prompted other schools to start their own.

- The panda is a/ warm, gentle/ animal that dines on bamboo shoots.

- The mailman dropped off the package, and I told my brother that his computer had arrived.

- As the plane took off, the flight attendants gave us emergency directions.

- Each year, only schools with good classroom sizes/ and a top test score average will receive funding.

- The public computers in the lab/ have been moved due to vandalism.

- Each of the students/ and teachers/ in the school will receive a handbook on proper conduct.

- I can't buy those new shoes/ if the price is too high.

Apostrophes

- **Tony's** hat is on the floor.

- **Louis's** scarf is 3 feet long.

- Both **players'** jerseys were soaked with sweat.

- The book has a cool picture on **its** cover.

- He is the actor **who's** most known for his role in *Batman*.

Dashes & Colons

- Consider the amount of paper that's wasted by unnecessary printing—a hundred thousand pages, three times as much as what our competitors use. (A colon also works.)

- The handbook lays out the most common mistakes when it comes to writing: lack of structure, having nothing to say, and repetitiveness. (A dash also works.)

- What you should remember from this whole ordeal **is that** there can be no progress without sacrifice.

- Cambridge is home to two of the best universities in the world: MIT and Harvard. (A dash also works.)

***You and Me* Errors**

- The girl scouts and **I** went out to sell cookies in the neighborhood.

- You are safe with the prison guards and **me**.

- After grabbing a drink, she plopped herself between the rest of the girls and **me**.

Idioms

- The Olympic athlete was capable **of** climbing Mt. Everest.

- The public was opposed **to** the war.

- The children were prohibited **from** playing outside at dark.

- Unless you comply **with** those food safety standards, we will shut you down.

Who vs. Whom

- The agency recruited overseas teachers **who** would be able to demonstrate a native fluency in English.

- Jane is the girl for **whom** I brought these gifts.

- The chaperones **whom** the students were assigned to made sure they walked in a single file.

Adverbs vs. Adjectives

- The **astonishingly** high height from which he fell only made his survival story more miraculous.

- The **rapidly** changing movements of the tides often catch some sea animals by surprise.

- You speak so **loudly** that I can't hear what you're saying.

Comparatives vs. Superlatives

- Between the lion and the tiger, the tiger is the **fiercer** and the **stronger**.

- China is not only the biggest of all the Asian countries but also the one with **the most** historical culture.

- Harry Potter and Frodo Baggins both rise to the challenges in their magical worlds, but I think Frodo has **more** courage.

31

Answers to the Exercises

Chapter 4: Prepositional Phrases

Exercise:

1. Hillary got ~~into the boat for the short trip to Haiti~~.

2. If you do business ~~with me~~, you'll never get the better end ~~of the deal~~.

3. We'll need to see the receipts ~~for the underwear~~ you bought ~~on Monday~~.

4. I drove ~~by my house~~ to check if the package ~~from Amazon~~ had arrived.

5. The eleven robbers broke ~~into the casino vault with their perfectly executed plan~~.

6. ~~Since the hypothesis of string theory~~, scientists have been back ~~at the drawing board~~.

7. Everything that man creates carries ~~within it~~ the seeds ~~of its own destruction~~.

8. Kelvin snuck ~~out the door during the school assembly~~.

9. ~~Within seconds of hearing about the trip to Antarctica~~, Charlotte packed shorts and sunglasses.

10. We found Teddy ~~in a broken elevator at a rundown hotel in Thailand~~.

Chapter 5: Relative Clauses

Exercise:

1. ~~Although it may better mankind~~, some critics of animal testing, ~~which is sometimes harmful to the animals~~, claim it is cruel and inhumane.

2. ~~After running the Boston marathon~~, Jack Kunis drank all the water ~~that was left in his bottle~~ and fell to his knees.

3. The lost ship and its treasure ~~that had fallen to the bottom of the ocean~~ were never found again.

4. Frank, ~~in addition to his cousins~~, suffers from a condition known as hyperthymestic syndrome, ~~which prevents one from ever forgetting anything~~.

5. ~~Starting at the age of 10~~, Mrs. Smith kept a daily diary, ~~which allowed her to recall the happy memories in life~~.

6. For years the chairman remained anonymous~~, referred to only by initials even within his inner circles~~.

7. Students ~~whose grades are low~~ will have to report to me, ~~the principal of the school~~.

8. Every detail about every day since 1976, ~~ranging from the time she got up to what she ate~~, has forever ingrained itself into her mind.

9. ~~Ever since it allowed internet games~~, ~~which were previously blocked~~, the library has been the place everybody wants to be nowadays.

10. ~~With such sadness occupying her thoughts~~, Erika, ~~a poor single mother of two~~, struggles to sleep at night, ~~even when the babies themselves are fast asleep~~.

11. Farmers ~~who want a good yield~~ should use fertilizers ~~that enrich the soil with nutrients~~.

12. ~~Having worked so hard with blood, sweat, and tears~~, I long for the day I can finally say the ACTs are over.

13. Culture shock, ~~in some cases~~, can be severe enough to trigger mental breakdowns.

14. Mastery of martial arts requires a dedication ~~that many do not have~~.

15. Mrs. Daughtry, ~~a 74-year old married housewife recently discharged from a local hospital after her first psychiatric admission~~, came to our facility for a second opinion, ~~one that she hoped would be different~~.

Chapter 6: Subject Verb Agreement

Exercise 1:

		To Be	To Go	To Have	To Win	To Kiss
Present Tense	He	is	goes	has	wins	kisses
	They	are	go	have	win	kiss
Past Tense	He	was	went	had	won	kissed
	They	were	went	had	won	kissed

Exercise 2:

1. **Participants** in the charity organization **were** angry when no one donated.

2. The **habit** of hugging your pillow while sleeping **indicates** that you miss someone.

3. Elderly **criminals** in Florida sometimes **lead** the police on chases at speeds of 10 to 15 mph.

4. **Bonnie and her boyfriend Clyde like** to jump into ponds to avoid the cops, often forgetting that they can't swim.

5. **Every** Bentley, Lamborghini, and Porsche **is** owned by Volkswagen.

6. **Propaganda** that's played off as the truth **has** been used throughout history to persuade the masses.

7. **Forcing** yourself to forget the pain someone else has caused you only **hurts** you more.

8. **One** of the skills I would like to learn **is** the ability to talk while inhaling through the nose.

9. **Some** of the superpowers I dream of having **include** summoning jack o' lanterns on people's lawns during Halloween and making people burst into the Gangnam style dance.

10. **Each** iPhone 5 **costs** Apple $168 and **costs** us $699.

11. **Each** of the three little pigs **was** afraid of the big bad wolf.

12. According to the phonebook, **the number** of Americans named Herp Derp **is** four.

13. **A good cook** rinses the dishes and **repeats** the same recipes to perfection.

14. Please let me know if **the group stumbles** upon or **manages** to find the train station.

15. **A number** of people **have** hyperthymesia, **a condition** that **allows** them to remember every detail of their lives. (*A number. . . have, a condition. . . allows*)

16. There **was** an awkward **silence** when Mike's date told him she hadn't showered in a month.

17. **A flock** of birds **and a bear have** been captured in the field.

18. There **are three types** of people in this world: those who can count and those who can't.

19. There **is** stashed below the frigid depths of the arctic a magnificent **treasure** that no one has ever been able to recover.

20. There **is** in the works of Emerson an underlying **tone** of quiet appreciation.

21. *Snow White and the Seven Dwarves* **was** purportedly based on cocaine; the seven dwarves were each side effects of the drug.

22. **Harry**, along with Ron and Hermione, **attends** Hogwarts School of Wizardry.

23. **Frodo**, as well as Merry and Pippin, **fights** to protect the one ring of power.

24. This picture **book** on the art of nudity in the modern age **is** a thought-provoking read.

25. The **extent** of our universe and those beyond constantly **amazes** me.

26. We found out that **his mother**, as well as his friends, **was** covering for Mike's crime.

27. **Aliens** from another planet **have** come here to kill us all.

28. The **pigs** you will be dissecting in this class **are** available as take-home dinners afterwards.

29. **Human brain cells, the universe, and the internet** all **have** similar structures.

30. **Each team** made up of one girl and one boy **has** to reenact a scene from Romeo and Juliet.

31. **Speaking** more than one language **makes** the brain more flexible and agile.

32. **Getting** to stuff my face silly with delicious food **is** the best part of being an obese food critic.

33. When **were the cowboy and the Indians** last here?

34. The class **bully** laughs at and then **interferes** with those trying to get work done.

35. **Brendan and Brianna** are out of money and **have** used up all possible guesses.

36. **Paris and Nicole** grew up rich and **were** sheltered all throughout life.

37. What **does** that **fact** have to do with anything we just talked about?

38. He sets his alarm but, when the morning comes, **fails** to wake up.

39. **Marcie and Michael** exercise everyday and, in doing so, **improve** their stamina.

40. **Alice**, in addition to a scarecrow, a tin man, and a lion, **tries** to find the Wizard of Oz.

41. **A jar** of hearts **is** on the counter.

42. **Several trucks and an oil tanker** near the highway exit **were** flipped on their sides.

43. **Dreams** within **a dream** that **is** spliced and diced up inside another dream **confuse** me. *(Dreams…confuse, a dream…is)*

44. **A herd** of cows **and** a slow moving **tortoise are** relaxing at the beach.

45. **The lines** for **the elevator** that normally **carries** just five passengers **were** reinstated because **the crowd** of fat commuters **was** too heavy for it. *(The lines…were, the elevator…carries, the crowd…was)*

46. **The diner** near **the dorms** which **house** the students **serves** breakfast all day. *(The diner…serves, the dorms…house)*

47. The widely recognized red **coloring** of stop signs everywhere **alerts** people who can't even read them to stop.

Exercise 3: The answers go in the format of *subject…verb.*

1. reference books… **are**

2. a stack… **sits**

3. case… **is**

4. the act… **is**

5. the notion… **misrepresents**

6. research and investigation… **play**

7. perfect grammar and well-crafted sentences… **do**

8. education… **encompasses**

9. education… **fosters**

10. attention… **rivals** (the key here is the singular *that*, which means the clause only applies to *attention* and not *dedication and attention*)

11. this dedication (to the craft) and attention (to detail)… **require**

12. authors… **have**

13. writers… **do**

14. answers… **are**

15. the belief… **persists**

Chapter 7: Run-ons

Exercise 1:

1. A caller from Memorial Park reported a man beating his head against a wall, he was heading to work.
⇑

2. A completely naked long-haired brunette in her 20s was pumping gas into a Hummer on the corner of Beachmont, no one got a good look at the vehicle's license plate.
⇑

3. In New York, the train system is difficult to learn, however, the food is fantastic and diverse.
⇑

4. When a man became so upset with the lack of parking enforcement in his town, he reported his own parking violation, and the police showed up to subdue him with a stun gun, apparently, he became
⇑
combative and screamed at the officers that they weren't doing their job.

5. There's a big chance that if you're 16 or older, you've already met the person you'll marry. *CORRECT*

6. Wanting to be sure that what he had been sold was real weed, Phillip Donahue approached two officers and asked them to test his pipe, as a result, he was arrested and charged with drug possession.
⇑

7. Jimmy hid in the dumpster when Mr. Clark, his boss, walked by, unfortunately, Mr. Clark had to throw
⇑
something away and saw him crouching there, forcing Jimmy to confess that he actually lived there.

8. Zoe likes to ace her tests but resents it when her classmates ask her how much she studied, sometimes
⇑
Zoe will just say that she didn't study at all when in fact she had stayed up all night.

9. At the time, discovering quantum physics looked like a waste of time and money, but it is now the foundation of all modern technology, thus, when people claim that math and science are of no relevance,
⇑
it drives Dr. Tyson into a deep rage.

10. Playing them day and night, Shawn and his video games were inseparable, however, once he got a
⇑
girlfriend, everything changed.

11. Despite his friends' tearful pleas for forgiveness, Jonathan maintained a deep grudge against everyone who had ever asked for a pencil and never returned it, an act he considered a crime against humanity.
CORRECT

12. Suddenly realizing the movie was too scary for her, Maya panicked and looked at her watch, there was
⇑
still 20 minutes left, enough time to still make her uneasy about what was to come.

13. The salesman, aware that he was going to lose a sale if he didn't make something up, claimed that the laptop could not be customizable and that the only options were in the store. *CORRECT*

14. As a young girl, Lindsay was praised as a talented and burgeoning actress, as an adult, she fell into the
⇑
dark world of sex, drugs, and alcohol and would never reclaim her former glory.

15. Omega-3 fish oil provides essential fatty acids for your nutritional health**,** furthermore, it soothes back
    pain and muscle aches.
    ⇑

16. Last Saturday, Peter Parker was bit by a spider**,** after that incident, he would never be the same again.
    ⇑

Exercise 2:

1. B	6. D	11. C
2. A	7. B	12. B
3. D	8. A	13. D
4. C	9. B	
5. C	10. C	

Chapter 8: Modifiers

Exercise 1:

1. Hunting for deer, Julian misfired his rifle which then burst into flames.
   While Julian was hunting for deer, his rifle misfired and burst into flames.

2. Having finished the ACT, I found the rest of life to be easy.

3. Having had no water for five days, we squeezed the steak and cheese sandwich for the grease that we
   could drink.

4. Active in community service and local affairs, Obama had a passion for politics that would eventually
   lead him to the presidency.

5. By blasting music at home, you will see that the neighbors will start to acquire your musical taste.

6. Because I majored in basket weaving, a lifetime of regret and despair awaits.

7. After catching a cold, I found that my lung surgery was the perfect cure.
   After I caught a cold, my lung surgery was the perfect cure.

8. While the talk show host was on air at the radio station, his microphone exploded.

9. As a young child growing up in Massachusetts, Mitt received airplanes as gifts from his father.

10. Hidden far from sunlight in the caves of Mars, an E.T. colony has been uncovered by scientists.
    Scientists have uncovered an E.T. colony, hidden far from sunlight in the caves of Mars.

11. Looking outside the window, Chris saw the march of marines as crowds cheered on either side.

12. Gordon Ramsay swore at the cook and dumped the fish that was overcooked and over-seasoned into the
    garbage.

13. Tiffany loved the soft feel of her teddy bear dressed in a cute outfit and filled with cotton.

14. Wearing a cloak and top hat, the magician dazzled and surprised the audience members.

15. We took pictures by the Christmas tree, which was decorated with colorful ornaments and stars.

16. After he missed an easy goal, the crowd booed the soccer player.
    After missing an easy goal, the soccer player was booed by the crowd.

17. Having forgotten about the homework assignment, he made comments on the book in class that were general statements that could apply to any book.
    Because he had forgotten about the homework assignment, his comments on the book in class were general statements that could apply to any book.

18. To get the best view of the movie, we reserved our seats in the front and center.

19. The scientist followed the deer prancing joyously from field to field.

20. Though skinny and awkward from the outset, Conan had a sense of humor that made him a television success.
    Though Conan was skinny and awkward from the outset, his sense of humor made him a television success.

21. The explorers avidly watched the red pandas climbing from tree to tree.

Exercise 2:

1. $\boxed{C}$ *Since the age of 10* is the modifer that must be placed next to *my daughter Cayla*.

2. $\boxed{B}$ Choices A, C, and D make it seem like Serena and Venus were watching something live, whereas it was Cayla who watched them.

3. $\boxed{A}$ Choice A is the only one that makes logical sense.

4. $\boxed{D}$ The modifier *as encouraging parents* needs to placed next to *we*.

5. $\boxed{B}$ The modifier *a simple sport* needs to be placed next to *tennis*. *The rules* themselves are not a sport.

6. $\boxed{C}$ The modifier *made and shaped from wood* needs to be placed next to *the first racquets*, not *players*. Choice C is much more concise than choice D.

7. $\boxed{D}$ The modifier *by improving the underlying technology* needs to be placed next to a person/people, namely *today's racquet creators*. After all, it's humans who improve the technology, not the racquets themselves.

8. $\boxed{D}$ The modifier *hitting the ball* must be placed next to *a player*.

9. $\boxed{B}$ It's a little confusing to see *squinting at the sky* describe *the tennis ball*. It should be placed at the start to modify a person, *she*.

10. $\boxed{B}$ The modifier *searching for one that was more patient* should be placed next to *we*.

11. 　$\boxed{D}$　Choices A and B make it sound like the teacher taught with spin and power. Choice C is an awkward placement because it interrupts the verb and object. It should be placed at the end to describe how Cayla serves the ball.

12. 　$\boxed{C}$　The modifier *growing in confidence* should be placed next to a person, *she.*

Chapter 9: Fragments

Exercise 1:

1. Tony's toys ~~which~~ were hidden in the cupboard so that nobody could get to them.

2. ~~When~~ I was given the opportunity to speak in front of the graduating class as if I were some celebrity or movie star.
   When I was given the opportunity to speak in front of the graduating class as if I were some celebrity or movie star, **I couldn't have felt more honored.**

3. **She dumped** him on the first date because he smelled so bad even though she knew he had just returned from a wrestling match.

4. It is very convenient that the grocery store I live next to **and** the surrounding malls and restaurants are open late at night.

5. In the middle of the night, ~~when~~ most people are sleeping while I sneak to the kitchen to eat.
   In the middle of the night, when most people are sleeping, ~~while~~ I sneak to the kitchen to eat.

6. Like the moment you realize your cereal is soggy because you left it in the milk too long, **the realization you're old comes quietly but swiftly.**

7. The butler who served the Wright family for several years ~~and~~ later became a successful businessman.

8. The tennis champion **waved** his racquet up towards a roaring crowd with his right hand and **lifted** the trophy with his left.

9. Even though Aaron fully believed that his actions, now the cause of much public controversy, were morally and ethically right, ~~but~~ the prosecutors would hear none of it.

10. The negative thoughts ~~that~~ were constantly on Floyd's mind as he got into the ring.
    The negative thoughts that were constantly on Floyd's mind as he got into the ring **made him even more nervous.**

11. **I was** disgusted by the lack of cleanliness in the men's bathroom yet curious about the sanitation in the ladies' room.

12. I wore the pants you bought me **and** the purple tie that the saleswoman picked out.

13. ~~As~~ They walked down the street, checked out the stores, and talked about life.
    As they walked down the street, checked out the stores, and talked about life, **they remembered how much they loved each other.**

14. ~~Although~~ Pandas are one of the most likable mammals but are one of the most rare.

Exercise 2:

1. C	5. B	9. B	13. B
2. C	6. C	10. D	14. D
3. A	7. B	11. B	15. C
4. D	8. B	12. D	

Chapter 10: Redundancy

Exercise 1:

1. In her biography ~~about her life~~, she writes about overcoming poverty and fear.

2. During high school, I sung in a trio ~~that consisted of three people~~.

3. Scratching the rash made it ~~more~~ worse than before.

4. ~~The reason why~~ Most people give up on New Year's resolutions ~~is~~ because they're too accustomed to old habits.
   The reason ~~why~~ most people give up on New Year's resolutions is **that** they're too accustomed to old habits.

5. The plagiarist ~~who copied the works of others~~ was banned indefinitely from the journalism industry.

6. There's a good chance that an earthquake ~~has the possibility of happening~~ **will happen** within the next week.

7. After her graduation speech, Zoe was thirsty ~~and needed to drink something~~.

8. Because James was an optimist ~~with a positive outlook on life~~, he faced his struggles with a smile on his face.

9. Seafood restaurants are becoming less and less expensive due to the abundance ~~and oversupply~~ of fish.
   Seafood restaurants are becoming less and less expensive due to the ~~abundance and~~ oversupply of fish.

10. ~~Her verbal statements in~~ Her conversation with me led me to believe that she was holding something from me.

11. The sisters reunited at the house where they grew up ~~as siblings~~ upon their father's death.

12. Building his own motorcycle, ~~which would belong to him,~~ Quentin looked forward to the day when he would be old enough to drive it.

13. My aunt ~~is a beginner who~~ just started learning about photography.

14. The president gave a strong message ~~that was quite powerful~~ to the world in his speech yesterday.

15. This year, the volcano came alive as if it were angry and the eruption lasted for days, ~~which numbered quite a few~~.

16. In 1742, Christopher Columbus set sail ~~and thereby rigged a boat~~ and charted a course towards India.

17. Since he quit his job, his savings have suffered~~, decreasing the balance in his bank account quite a bit~~.

18. When she walked into the room, he lost his concentration ~~and couldn't focus~~ on the task at hand.

Exercise 2:

1. ☐D *Famous for* means the same thing as what's underlined.

2. ☐B *Separation* means the same thing as *division*.

3. ☐C *Heir* implies *next in line* or *successive*.

4. ☐B *Died* is all that's needed. *Perished* and *fatally* both imply death.

5. ☐C *Recently* means the same thing as *a short time ago*.

6. ☐D *Father* implies that Henry was his son.

7. ☐B *King* implies that he ascended to the throne.

8. ☐D *Over the years* is the same thing as *throughout their time together*.

9. ☐C *Worried* and *troubled* mean the same thing.

10. ☐A *Sole* implies *only*, which is a word in all the answer choices except A.

11. ☐B *Declaring, announcement, proclaiming* all imply the same thing.

12. ☐B *Unswayed* means the same thing as *unconvinced*.

13. ☐D *His own hands* implies *on his own* or *by himself*.

14. ☐C *All he needed* means the same thing as *that would be sufficient, enough,* or *adequate*.

15. ☐C The exact year adds information here so it should be kept. However, *after that* and *subsequently* mean the same thing as *later*, which is found earlier in the sentence.

16. ☐D *Which led the way* offers nothing in the context of this sentence. The cause and effect relationship between Henry's actions and altering the future of his country is already clear.

17. ☐B If the number of years is going to be stated, there's no point in also saying that it was a *few* years.

Chapter 11: Parallelism

Exercise 1:

1. **Her beauty** and her charm help her get out of speeding tickets.

2. Visitors to my hometown in the middle of nowhere can experience rides on the bus, drinks at the tavern, and **meals** at the McDonald's.

3. Because of their amazing sense of smell, quick agility, and ~~they have~~ **fierceness** when protecting themselves, lions are the kings of the savannah.

4. My tasks today are to file for divorce, burn my house down, and ~~to~~ start all over.
   My tasks today are to file for divorce, **to** burn my house down, and to start all over.

5. By investing in nuclear energy, we can save the environment, jobs, and **money**.

6. In his free time, Wild Bill likes smoking Cuban cigars and **drinking** the finest red wine Martha's Vineyard has to offer.
   In his free time, Wild Bill likes **to smoke** Cuban cigars and to drink the finest red wine Martha's Vineyard has to offer.

7. Quickly and **silently**, Jesse and Walt snuck by the sleeping police officers and made off with a barrel of methylamine.

8. Inspired by the hard work of his immigrant father, Jeremy wanted to pay for college, find a job, and **buy** a new house.

9. According to Apple, Samsung's directors need to admit they violated Apple's patent, pay the fines, and ~~also needed is to~~ recall all their products.

10. Samsung's executives responded by completely rejecting Apple's ultimatum in court and **countersuing** Apple back for patent infringement.

11. The 300 men trained diligently, screamed fiercely into battle, and **fought valiantly**.

12. At the yard sale, Jimmy found dusty writings of Einstein, containers of fossils, and **boxes of Chinese opium**.

13. American immigrants took huge risks to leave their homelands and **search** for a better life elsewhere.

14. Come to the next party prepared to eat a lot, to dance a lot, and **to drink a lot**.

15. As soon as he graduated from high school, he packed all his belongings, rushed to the college campus, and **left** his parents behind.

Exercise 2:

1. B	5. B	9. B	13. A
2. C	6. A	10. D	14. D
3. D	7. C	11. B	15. D
4. A	8. B	12. C	

Chapter 12: Pronoun Reference

Exercise 1: Correct answers are bolded along with their references, if applicable.

1. When I looked up at **the stars**, I couldn't believe **they were** so many light-years away.

2. Although many people believe **the tiger** is fierce and ferocious, **it is** actually quite peaceful.

3. **Anyone** who misses **his or her** parents can just go home.

4. The toxic level of **water bottles** isn't apparent to most people because they assume **their** plastic content is harmless.

5. After searching the whole day for my brother's **shoes**, I told him I wasn't able to find **them**.

6. **Birds** must migrate south during the winter season because **they manage** to survive only in warmer climates.

7. Until technological advances enable **them** to consume less fuel for thrust and power, the possibility of **space rockets** to Mars will remain remote.

8. By the time **they** can be fixed up, cleaned, and upgraded, old **cell phones** will be completely irrelevant compared to newer ones.

9. The food that **the chefs** serve at the restaurant is absolutely delicious.

10. The secretary unplugged the keyboard from the computer and cleaned **the computer**.

11. Joey was required to go to a meeting but **the announcement** never stated the location.

12. Before **the state university** could open up a new program in astrophysics, **it** needed funding from alumni.

13. **The government** is so arrogant in **its** ability to solve problems that **it has** silenced the voice of the people.

14. The show *American Idol* has as **its** premiere judge a man who can't sing himself.

15. Elle told the teacher that **the teacher** had made a mistake.

16. My iPhone fell onto the glass plate, but thankfully **the phone** didn't break.

17. **Some spiders** can inject **themselves** with poison to enact revenge on their predators.

18. Anthony used to hang out all the time with Albert until **Albert** got the big promotion at work.

19. When **a person** dies, **his or her** sense of hearing is the last to go whereas touch and sight are the first.

20. **The city** of Boston, which weathered the American Revolution, regularly offers tours that honor **its** local heroes.

21. One of the unique features of **the red panda**, an exotic creature that lives in the eastern Himalayas, is **its** ringed tail, which is used as a blanket in the cold.

22. **The health department** should be able to handle the paperwork by **itself**.

23. My mom cooked some traditional Russian **dishes**, but I hate eating **them**.

24. I took my old computer to the store and luckily **the engineers** were able to fix it.

Exercise 2: If applicable, the relevant reference is in parentheses.

1. $\boxed{D}$ *They* needs to be defined.

2. $\boxed{B}$ (*Seattle Police Department*)

3. $\boxed{C}$ *It* needs to be defined.

4. $\boxed{C}$ *That* should be defined. That what?

5. $\boxed{B}$ (*the writing style*)

6. $\boxed{D}$ (*the characters*)

7. $\boxed{A}$ (*a movie*)

8. $\boxed{B}$ (*the script*)

9. $\boxed{C}$ (*actors*)

10. $\boxed{C}$ *Their* has no reference in the passage so we must define it.

11. $\boxed{A}$ (*book signings*)

12. $\boxed{B}$ There is no clear reference for *them*, so we have to define it.

13. $\boxed{A}$ (*any reader*)

Chapter 13: Tenses

Exercise 1:

1. Jay, with no care whatsoever, has repeatedly **swum** in the polluted East River.

2. Advocates of drug control have loudly and frequently **pointed** out the dangers to society.

3. Because we parted ways before the advent of Facebook, we have not **seen** one another since high school.

4. The soldiers have **begun** their march on Tehran.

5. Scientific studies have **shown** that it's possible for a human to grow a red panda tail.

6. My mom told me that my brother had **gone** to the park to play chess.

7. After the birds had **flown** south, the blizzard came and thrashed the trees in the forest.

8. The rooster's crow was a sign that the day had **begun.**

9. If you had told me that the deadline was tomorrow, I would **have** begun the calculations.

10. By the time the parents got home, the baby **had broken** the record player and was about to destroy the TV.

11. Had he won the lottery, he would **have** retired to a private beach in the south of France.

12. When Leonardo started the portrait, he did not know it would later **become** one of the most famous paintings in the world.

13. Tom knew that he should **have** kissed the girl, but he didn't have the courage.

14. Out of nowhere, China has **become** an economic superpower that other countries must depend on.

Exercise 2:

1. When Columbus and his crew discovered America in 1492, many Indian tribes **welcomed** them graciously.

2. The United States is considered the melting pot because its inhabitants **include** immigrants from all over the world.

3. Although the giant panda's diet consists primarily of bamboo, most other bears **hunt** for their food.

4. Tolkien's *Lord of the Rings* trilogy tells the tale of Frodo, a hobbit who **is** charged with the task of destroying the one ring of power.

5. She bought her dress at Wal-Mart yet it **impressed** everyone at the party.

6. Every year he wishes for an end to world hunger and **prays** for a cure for cancer.

7. Whereas astronomers focus on the stars to advance the frontier of science, astrologists **study** the constellations to predict whether bad things will happen today.

Exercise 3:

1. $\boxed{B}$ Past tense.

2. $\boxed{D}$ Present tense.

3. $\boxed{B}$ Present tense.

4. $\boxed{D}$ Past tense.

5. $\boxed{C}$ Past tense.

6. $\boxed{A}$ Present tense.

7. $\boxed{A}$ Past tense.

8. $\boxed{D}$ Past participle error.

9. $\boxed{A}$ Present tense.

10. $\boxed{B}$ Present tense.

11. $\boxed{D}$ Present tense.

12. $\boxed{B}$ Past tense.

13. $\boxed{D}$ Past tense.

14. $\boxed{D}$ Present tense.

15. $\boxed{C}$ Past tense.

16. $\boxed{D}$ Past tense.

17. $\boxed{B}$ Past (perfect) tense.

18. $\boxed{B}$ Past tense. *Called on* is the correct idiom here, meaning to demand that someone do something.

19. $\boxed{C}$ Past participle error.

20. $\boxed{D}$ Past tense.

Chapter 14: Point of View

Exercise:

1. The flight attendants demanded that we leave the plane even though **we** wanted to finish the movie.

2. Despite how hard salesmen try, sometimes **they** just can't get anyone **they** want to buy a house.

3. When you're married with your own kids, **your** life becomes infinitely more complicated.

4. Even when we arrive ahead of time at the doctor's office, he makes **us** wait at least 15 minutes.

5. Although I chose to become a math teacher, **I** sometimes wonder what it would've been like to have been born a panda.

6. One must not disregard **one's** moral compass when confronted with temptation.

7. In France, a tourist can spend a romantic night overlooking the Eiffel tower and **he or she** can also enjoy delicious coffee at all the cafes.

8. One is more likely to come back to this shop when **one is** treated with respect.

9. When I glanced into her eyes, **I** could see the tears she was holding back.

10. Registered voters will be notified of election time by a message to **their** email addresses.

11. To truly learn how computers work, we must take the time to study algorithms and how computers process them, regardless of whether **we find** it interesting.

Chapter 15: Commas

Exercise 1:

1. Gunpowder, which was invented in China during the Tang dynasty ‸, eventually spread to Europe through the Silk Road.

2. Jake had to answer quite a few boring ⁄ interview questions before he got the job offer.

3. Don and Marie, the architect who designed the building I live in ‸, went to the ball together.

4. I did what I did to improve the system ‸, not destroy it.

5. Drinking coffee ‸, scientists have discovered ‸, may help prevent heart disease.

6. I've decked out my laptop with a keyboard cover, pokemon stickers ‸, and a transparent case.

7. Our school's computer science club ‸, which was founded in 2000 ‸, has prompted other schools to start their own.

8. The company partnering with us is Amazon. *CORRECT*

9. When dawn came ‸, we woke up to prepare for Kanyadaan, the initial step in a traditional Indian wedding ceremony.

10. He typed up the essay that was due the next day and threw it in his backpack. *CORRECT*

11. Janice doodled on scrap paper while the teacher gave his lecture on trigonometry. *CORRECT*

12. Unfortunately ‸, Syed ran out of time before he could get to the last question.

13. Maine is known for its juicy lobster rolls and its friendly ‸, laid-back residents.

14. I sold my car to a dealer who stripped it for parts and shipped them to China ‸, where scrap metal fetches a high price.

15. Mario dodged blazing fireballs, turtles with hammers ‸, and venus fly traps to rescue Princess Peach.

16. Nevertheless ‸, the world's resources cannot sustain the current rate of population growth.

17. Homer's poem ⁄ *The Iliad* ⁄ recounts the rise and fall of the great Greek hero ⁄ Achilles.

18. The tigers slowly ⁄ and quietly crept up on the antelopes, but they still couldn't catch them.

19. Ron had mentioned ⁄ that the place on the corner had really good strawberry ice cream.

20. *Interpreter of Maladies*, the 2000 Pulitzer Prize winner, is the book Tom chose for his book report. *COR-RECT*

21. After the fumes were gone ‸, the cleaners rearranged the furniture.

22. The research suggests that the craters on Mars may contain ice, but evidence of life is far from conclusive. *CORRECT*

23. Jimmy's closest friend , Chris Hernandez , drove a 1998 Toyota Camry.
        ∧   ∧

24. Standing in front of the customers, Debbie announced/ discounts on all the clothing in the store.

25. Miyazaki's first film, *Lupin III*, was released in 1979. *CORRECT*

26. On clear nights, we could see the silver , shining stars in the sky.
                                            ∧

27. Circling the parking lot like a predator on the hunt , the driver anxiously waited for the next parking
                                                       ∧
    spot.

28. The rapid pace of technological development , however , has enabled more people to survive on less.
                                              ∧   ∧

29. The panda is a/ warm, gentle/ animal that dines on bamboo shoots.

30. To make the workplace more environmentally conscious, we put solar panels, recycling bins , and energy
                                                                                              ∧
    efficient dryers into place.

31. When Jacob stopped at the gas station, he realized that his wallet was back at home. *CORRECT*

32. Roger knew the ball wasn't going in as soon as he hit it , yet the fans shouted as if he had won the point.
                                                           ∧

33. If you put the eggs in the pan/ and stir them for a minute, the cake will be perfect.

34. Mutual respect and communication are the foundations of a good relationship , for better or worse.
                                                                              ∧

35. The chef picked up the carrots from the grocery store, chopped them up with his knife , and pushed them
                                                                                         ∧
    into the boiling pot of water.

36. The fan sitting in the fifth row on the right side of the stadium was dancing and screaming during every
    play. *CORRECT*

37. Pete had to stay at the dull, drawn-out/ play because his girlfriend was in it.

38. Polio was once a contagious , devastating disease that wiped out small towns.
                              ∧

39. The mailman dropped off the package , and I told my brother that his computer had arrived.
                                       ∧

40. As the plane took off , the flight attendants gave us emergency directions.
                        ∧

41. The boys finished their desserts and dashed out of the restaurant as soon as the waiter went back into
    the kitchen. *CORRECT*

Exercise 2: The applicable rule is shown next to the answer.

1. $\boxed{A}$ Use a comma before a FANBOYS conjunction when joining two independent clauses.

2. $\boxed{A}$ Use commas to set off transitions and intervening phrases. *Literally* is an intervening phrase.

3. $\boxed{B}$ Use commas to separate coordinate adjectives that describe the same noun.

4. $\boxed{B}$ Use commas to separate three or more items in a series.

5. $\boxed{C}$ There aren't two independent clauses so there's no need for a comma.

6. $\boxed{A}$ In general, there is no need for a comma before a prepositional phrase.

7. $\boxed{A}$ There aren't two independent clauses so there's no need for a comma.

8. $\boxed{A}$ Use commas to set off nonrestrictive/nonessential elements.

9. $\boxed{B}$ Use a comma after an introductory clause, phrase, or modifier.

10. $\boxed{B}$ Use commas to separate coordinate adjectives that describe the same noun. In this case, they are not coordinate adjectives.

11. $\boxed{C}$ Use commas to set off nonrestrictive/nonessential elements.

12. $\boxed{C}$ There aren't two independent clauses so there's no need for a comma.

13. $\boxed{D}$ No comma is necessary because the dependent clause *after the paper dries* is placed at the end.

14. $\boxed{A}$ Use a comma before a FANBOYS conjunction when joining two independent clauses.

15. $\boxed{B}$ Use commas to separate three or more items in a series.

Chapter 16: Comma Abuse

Exercise 1:

- Rule 1 – Don't separate the subject from the verb with a comma.
- Rule 2 – Don't use commas to separate compound elements that aren't independent clauses.
- Rule 3 – Don't use a comma after the introductory phrase of an inverted sentence.
- Rule 4 – Don't use a comma before a preposition (typically *at, for, in, of, on, to, with*).
- Rule 5 – Don't use a comma before an infinitive.

1. The train ran off the tracks that were twisted by the bandits, and tumbled down the cliff. *RULE 2*

2. Having a large stock of water and canned foods, is quite important, especially during the apocalypse. *RULE 1*

3. The public computers in the lab, have been moved due to vandalism. *RULE 1*

4. Each of the students, and teachers, in the school will receive a handbook on proper conduct. *RULE 2, RULE 3*

5. The bank told us that we would qualify for a credit card with a better interest rate, and greater rewards if we opened a savings account. *RULE 2*

6. A vast majority of the questionnaire, covers issues that are not relevant to what we're studying. *RULE 1*

7. Job placements were determined by test scores, calculated by the employer organization. *RESTRICTIVE ELEMENT*

8. Martin Luther King Jr. believed that all people have a right to freedom, and that everyone should be treated equally. *RULE 2*

9. The band members, at Newton High School, forgot to rehearse for their big concert. *RULE 4*

10. William broke through the glass window, and hopped over the fence, to get away from the police. *RULE 2, RULE 5*

11. All across China, where new housing projects accommodate the wealthy instead of the poor, protests are being staged at city government buildings. *CORRECT*

12. The professor will deduct points off your total score, unless you're able to turn in the essay today. *DEPENDENT CLAUSE AT THE END*

13. In the game of life, the people who work hard and hustle, will always succeed in spite of their circumstances. *RULE 1*

14. The roasted chicken was seasoned with a special mix of spices and cooked, to perfection. *RULE 4*

15. A senior at the big accounting firm PWC pleaded not guilty to forging the books, claiming that it was his coworkers who did it. *CORRECT*

16. Marjorie introduced the new students, to their dorm rooms for the year. *RULE 4*

17. The restaurant that two hours ago had a line out the door/ was now quiet and deserted. *RULE 1*

18. The movie theater, which was permeated by the smell of popcorn/ and illuminated by the motion picture, was 20 years old. *RULE 2*

19. Each year, only schools with good classroom sizes/ and a top test score average will receive funding. *RULE 2*

20. The books that were sitting on the shelf/ fell onto the floor below. *RULE 1*

21. The photographer rushed/ to the scene/ to get the best shot of the actors on the red carpet. *RULE 4, RULE 5*

22. Because he embraced failure instead of avoiding it, Chris quickly learned how to play the piano, speak Spanish, and solve the Rubik's Cube. *CORRECT*

23. Beneath the electric chair that Eric sat in/ was a knife that he used to cut himself free. *RULE 3*

24. The kids were swimming out to the outlying island/ when the great white shark approached. *DEPENDENT CLAUSE AT END*

25. Growing up in poverty, I often dreamed/ of the luxury/ that I was working towards. *RULE 4*

26. The mayor has not been able to repair his reputation/ since his dismissal from office. *DEPENDENT CLAUSE AT END*

27. Behind the dumpster/ were squirrels, mice, and Tom, foraging for food. *RULE 3*

28. Known for its noodle dishes, the restaurant down the street always has customers, most of whom are Asian. *CORRECT*

29. Donations poured in to help the victims of the crash/ and their families. *RULE 2*

30. Having had his arm in a cast for a month, Jacob found it difficult/ to type on his computer. *RULE 5*

31. Joshua Grossman, a professor at NYU, and his associate claim that their research is definitive and trustworthy. *CORRECT*

32. The greatest tennis players are the ones who have the courage/ to play the big points with no restraint. *RULE 5*

33. On the left wall of the living room/ hung five paintings and a poster. *RULE 3*

34. Joey sat in the waiting room/ until his wife got out of the doctor's office. *DEPENDENT CLAUSE AT END*

35. I can't buy those new shoes/ if the price is too high. *DEPENDENT CLAUSE AT END*

36. David wasn't able to play to the best of his ability/ because of the foot injury. *DEPENDENT CLAUSE AT END*

37. Novak Djokovic, one of the best tennis players/ of the modern era, is worshipped as a god in Serbia. *RULE 4*

38. It was my father who inspired me/ to pursue medicine as my course/ of study. *RULE 5, RULE 4*

Exercise 2:

- Rule 1 – Don't separate the subject from the verb with a comma.
- Rule 2 – Don't use commas to separate compound elements that aren't independent clauses.
- Rule 3 – Don't use a comma after the introductory phrase of an inverted sentence.
- Rule 4 – Don't use a comma before a preposition (typically *at, for, in, of, on, to, with*).
- Rule 5 – Don't use a comma before an infinitive.

1. $\boxed{A}$ Rule 4.

2. $\boxed{A}$ Rule 5.

3. $\boxed{B}$ Rule 4.

4. $\boxed{C}$ Rule 2.

5. $\boxed{A}$

6. $\boxed{A}$

7. $\boxed{B}$ Rule 4.

8. $\boxed{D}$ Rule 1.

9. $\boxed{A}$

10. $\boxed{C}$ Rule 2.

11. $\boxed{D}$ Rule 4.

12. $\boxed{A}$

13. $\boxed{C}$ Rule 2.

14. $\boxed{B}$ Dependent clause at the end.

15. $\boxed{B}$ Rule 4.

16. $\boxed{A}$

17. $\boxed{D}$ Rule 4.

18. $\boxed{A}$

19. $\boxed{B}$ Dependent clause at the end.

20. $\boxed{C}$ Rule 2.

Chapter 17: Apostrophes

Exercise:

1. B

2. D

3. B

4. A We know the plural *friends* is intended because of the *their* previously in the sentence.

5. B Yes, *whose* can be used for things.

6. A

7. C

8. B

9. C

10. D

11. A

12. C

13. D

14. C

15. B

16. B

17. B

18. A

19. B

20. A

Chapter 18: Word Choice

Exercise 1:

1. D	5. C	9. C	13. A
2. B	6. C	10. B	14. D
3. C	7. B	11. A	15. D
4. D	8. D	12. B	

Exercise 2:

1. C	5. B	9. C	13. A	17. D
2. A	6. B	10. B	14. B	
3. B	7. A	11. D	15. C	
4. A	8. D	12. C	16. B	

Chapter 19: Transitions

Exercise 1:

1. A	5. C	9. C	13. B
2. C	6. D	10. A	14. D
3. D	7. B	11. C	15. B
4. D	8. D	12. D	

Exercise 2:

1. D	5. B	9. A	13. C
2. B	6. C	10. D	14. B
3. D	7. D	11. A	15. D
4. A	8. B	12. C	

Chapter 20: Transitions II

Exercise 1:

1. $\boxed{B}$ The sentences following the underlined portion compare teenagers with older drivers (different age groups).

2. $\boxed{D}$ The chosen transition must describe *these failed attempts*.

3. $\boxed{A}$ A contrast between where the money is expected to come from and where it actually comes from needs to be expressed.

4. $\boxed{C}$ A link between the unknown purpose of the masks and staving off invaders is made only with choice C.

5. $\boxed{D}$ Choice D leads best into the next sentence, which mentions several sites (temples, sushi joints, mall).

6. $\boxed{B}$ From the context, the narrator watches other people on the train on a good day.

7. $\boxed{B}$ The chosen transition should reference *the long break*.

8. $\boxed{C}$ The chosen transition should clarify *Serena's winnings*.

9. $\boxed{A}$ The last sentence elaborates on the wide range of tasks a professor does. Choice A sets that up.

10. $\boxed{D}$ The narrator could not follow the doctor's advice. Choice D expresses why.

11. $\boxed{C}$ A connection must be made between the first paragraph (Boston's bustling economy) and the second (high cost of living). Choice C makes that connection.

12. $\boxed{D}$ The last phrase *loses composure when under pressure* means that pilots who can withstand the pressure are sought after.

13. $\boxed{B}$ From the last sentence, we can glean that the main benefit is that the desert approach is much less crowded.

14. $\boxed{D}$ The phrase *extreme pressures found at these depths* is a clear reference to the ocean.

15. $\boxed{C}$ The last sentence expresses an added reward for good work. Therefore, the transition must express what the standard reward is.

Exercise 2:

1. $\boxed{A}$ The chosen transition must define *these key metrics*.

2. $\boxed{B}$ The chosen transition should express how difficult card counting is to lead into the next sentence.

3. $\boxed{D}$ The chosen transition should express why Europe is upgrading their economic forecasts, *economic* being the key word.

4. $\boxed{A}$ The chosen transition needs to express the one vote restriction. The next sentence describes the consequences of voting more than once.

5. $\boxed{C}$ The chosen transition needs to express why decisions are left to the captain on the field.

6. $\boxed{D}$ To lead into the danger of a move somewhere else, the chosen transition needs to bring up that idea.

7. $\boxed{B}$ Because the last sentence boasts about price, the chosen transition should bring up price as the competitive advantage.

8. $\boxed{A}$ The chosen transition must clarify *the equipment*.

9. $\boxed{C}$ The chosen transition should express the risk of flying the BAC Concorde.

10. $\boxed{B}$ The chosen transition should make some reference to the findings in order to ease the build up to the next sentence.

11. $\boxed{C}$ The chosen transition needs to provide a reference for *these formations*.

12. $\boxed{B}$ The chosen transition should clarify parkour's *beginnings in the military*.

13. $\boxed{D}$ The chosen transition should specify what *another record* was.

14. $\boxed{C}$ The chosen transition should express the narrator's agreement with the philosophers since they have the same views.

15. $\boxed{C}$ Because the last sentence starts with *In his defense*, the chosen transition should offer a criticism of Mark Twain.

Chapter 21: Sentence Improvement

Exercise 1:

1. D	5. A	9. B	13. C
2. C	6. B	10. D	14. D
3. B	7. C	11. D	15. A
4. C	8. C	12. B	

Exercise 2:

1. B	5. C	9. C	13. D
2. A	6. D	10. B	14. B
3. C	7. A	11. D	15. D
4. B	8. D	12. C	

Chapter 22: Placement

Exercise 1:

1. $\boxed{B}$ Notice the pronoun *they* in sentence 6. For that pronoun to be defined by the context, sentence 6 should be placed after sentence 1 or sentence 2 so that *they* refers to *machines* (sentence 2 contains *they*, which also refers back to *machines*, so it's possible to continue from sentence 2). However, sentences 2 and 3 should stick together because they contrast with each other, *they usually win* vs. *intended to lose*. Furthermore, sentence 6 is a good supporting sentence for sentence 1.

2. $\boxed{A}$ It's only after both sentences 4 and 5 does Chloe confirm with certainty that Erik is gone.

3. $\boxed{D}$ The pronoun *it* in sentence 5 is best defined by sentence 3, *a weighty piece of machinery*. Sentence 4 talks about what happens if the machinery could be lifted, so it's logical it follows a statement that the machinery is too heavy to lift in the first place. So sentence 5 is best placed between sentences 3 and 4.

4. $\boxed{C}$ Sentence 5 needs to be placed right before sentence 3, which discusses pursuing the duke after he escaped the attack on his province.

5. $\boxed{A}$ Sentence 5 serves as a contrast to sentence 4, what we can't know vs. what we do know.

6. $\boxed{C}$ Sentence 1 should be placed after sentence 4, which defines *the city* as Los Angeles. Sentences 2, 3, and 4 need to stick together uninterrupted because they continue from the question posed in sentence 2.

7. [B] Sentence 5 should be placed right before sentence 3 so that it better defines *the renewed taste for coffee elsewhere.*

8. [B] Sentence 5 elaborates on sentence 1 and also provides a statement that Ramos can disagree with in sentence 2. Otherwise, it's a bit unclear what Ramos is disagreeing with.

9. [D] Sentence 5 should be placed right before sentence 4, so that *this vital physical clue* is defined as the *magnetized rock.*

10. [D] Notice that sentence 4 mentions *staying in the same place*, which is the only logical reference for *this lack of movement* in the given sentence.

11. [C] The given sentence logically follows after sentence 3, which talks about the rewards for delivering cargo the fastest. The given sentence also contains the word *merchants*, which is important to sentence 4, which makes a reference to *one such merchant.*

12. [A] Sentence 6 contains the pronoun *they*, which is in need of a clarifying reference. Sentence 5, which discusses *hydrocarbons*, provides that reference.

13. [A] The given sentence should be placed after sentence 1 because its purpose is to describe a *drug*, namely Chlorphenamine Maleate.

14. [D] Sentence 4 serves as a response to the question in sentence 8.

15. [B] The phrase *the project* references the tomb of Lorenzo brought up in sentence 2. Therefore, the given sentence should be placed after sentence 2. Note that sentences 3 and 4 must stick together since sentence 4 builds off of sentence 3.

Exercise 2:

1. [D] Sentence 5 follows up on *the dark side* mentioned in sentence 3. It also clarifies the statement that *the people have not surrendered so easily* in sentence 4. Otherwise, readers would be asking, "Surrendering to who?"

2. [C] Sentence 5 needs to be placed before sentence 3 to introduce Narcissus. Otherwise, sentence 3 comes off too abruptly.

3. [A] After sentence 1, readers are curious what the *sea creature* is. The given sentence answers that. It also transitions to the following sentences that talk about males and females. It would be odd to jump into those sentences without knowing what animal is being talked about.

4. [C] The given sentence describes one of Charles's childhood experiences. Since his childhood is brought up in sentence 4, the given sentence should be placed after that. It also serves as a reference for *those times* mentioned in sentence 5.

5. [B] Sentence 5 needs to be placed between sentences 1 and 2 to act as a transition between sugar and molasses.

6. [B] Sentence 2 talks about the rest of the world building faster ships. The given sentence is logically placed after that since it brings up the fall of British ships. The given sentence also serves as reference for sentence 3 by defining the pronoun *they.*

7. [A] Sentence 5 is the perfect topic sentence for this paragraph because it mentions what activity is being discussed—kettlebell training. If sentence 1 were left at the start, readers would be left scratching their heads.

8. [D] Sentence 3 brings up tree farming in general. It would awkward to place sentence 5 before that. Sentence 5 discusses Belen's famed trees, which is the perfect lead sentence for sentence 4, which talks about how Belen lost its fame for trees.

9. [A] Sentence 5 is a good conclusion sentence. It must come after the name *Louis Pasteur* is brought up and after *this process* is described.

10. [A] The given sentence should come before sentence 2, which contains the phrases *compared to the latest designs* and *those older models*. These phrases need to be clarified by the given sentence, which discusses *early versions* of the tank.

11. [C] The given sentence should be placed before sentence 4, which discusses *catching mice and other countryside rodents*.

12. [B] The given sentence should be inserted before sentence 3 since it would clarify what *both instruments* refers to. Also note that sentence 3 mentions *the pipe* brought up in the given sentence.

13. [C] Sentence 2 brings up *rock*. Sentence 3 mentions *these particles*. Sentence 5 should be placed in between to build off of sentence 2 and give a reference to *these particles* in sentence 3.

14. [B] Sentence 5 brings up *its unscientific character*, the *its* referring to *numerology* in sentence 1. Furthermore, sentence 5 should be placed before sentence 2 to define the time mentioned there, *around that time*.

15. [B] The given sentence should be placed before sentence 5 in order to define *this division process*.

Exercise 3:

1. [C] Paragraph 5, which starts out with a reference to Alexander, belongs after paragraph 3, which brings up Alexander at the end. Then paragraph 2's initial sentence is a good follow up to paragraph 5's ending discussion of *invasions over land*. Paragraph 2 discusses Hinduism, which leads into paragraph 4. Finally, paragraph 1 brings up *other religions*, which can only be brought up after the discussion of Hinduism.

2. [A] Paragraph 5, which describes what happens after the Medicis were exiled, belongs after paragraph 2, which takes place right before *the Medicis were expelled*. Paragraph 3, which states that *Michelangelo was eventually pardoned*, must follow paragraph 5, which states that *he was forced to go into hiding*. Paragraph 1 must come after paragraph 3 since it describes Michelangelo's later years, and paragraph 4 must come after that because it elaborates on Vittoria, who is introduced at the end of paragraph 1.

3. [D] Paragraph 3, which mentions *man's advances to the countryside*, must come after paragraph 5, which brings up *the onward expansion of farmland and urban developments...* at the end. Looking at the remaining paragraphs, paragraph 4 is really the only one that fits as a lead paragraph. Paragraph 5 provides an intentional contrast to the vibrant picture portrayed in paragraph 4, so paragraph 5 should follow paragraph 4. Paragraph 1 then builds off of paragraph 3's discussion of birds by bringing up bird varieties found on the ground. Finally, paragraph 2 wraps everything up—the topic sentence starts off by referencing previously mentioned *butterflies or flying birds*. It also has the best conclusion sentence.

4. $\boxed{D}$ Paragraph 1 should be placed before paragraph 5. The giveaway is the last sentence of paragraph 1, which describes new ways of discovering and extracting oil. This discussion leads perfectly into the topic of paragraph 5, which discusses how humans might create oil themselves. Furthermore, paragraph 1 mentions additional uses of oil, which builds off of the discussion in paragraph 4.

5. $\boxed{B}$ Paragraph 5 should be placed before paragraph 3. Paragraph 5 ends with a discussion of replicating waves in laboratory conditions, which is precisely what paragraph 3 begins to discuss. Paragraph 5 also follows naturally from paragraph 2, which talks about what we know about waves.

6. $\boxed{B}$ Paragraph 5 should be placed after paragraph 1, which builds suspense but does not specify exactly what ship is being discussed. Paragraph 5 relieves that suspense and informs the reader which ship it is—the *Cutty Sark*.

Chapter 23: Relevance & Purpose

Exercise 1:

1. A	6. C	11. D
2. C	7. B	12. D
3. C	8. C	13. D
4. D	9. C	14. C
5. A	10. C	

Exercise 2:

1. A	5. B	9. B
2. D	6. A	10. B
3. B	7. C	11. C
4. C	8. D	12. A

Exercise 3:

1. B	5. D	9. C
2. C	6. C	10. D
3. C	7. C	
4. A	8. A	

Chapter 24: Dashes & Colons

Exercise:

1. A	6. A	11. B	16. B
2. B	7. D	12. C	17. A
3. A	8. A	13. B	18. B
4. A	9. D	14. C	19. D
5. B	10. A	15. C	

Chapter 25: You and Me Errors

Exercise:

1. It's a good thing that the coach knows that you and **he** work well as a team.

2. Ron knows that **he** and his son must work together if the family business is to succeed.

3. Why is it that they always complain about you and **me**?

4. To meet the deadline, the President and **they** need to come to some sort of an agreement.

5. My sister says **she** and her friends rarely text message each other.

6. It's hard to get through the school day when the class bully considers my friends and **me** his source of lunch money.

7. The neighbors next door and **we** could not be any more different.

8. Her dogs and **she** got lost when they took a wrong turn in the forest.

9. To think that there's a special relationship between you and **me** is stupid indeed.

10. He can't stand how fast you and **I** talk.

11. After grabbing a drink, she plopped herself between the rest of the girls and **me**.

12. The girl scouts and **I** went out to sell cookies in the neighborhood.

13. You are safe with the prison guards and **me**.

14. The coach's extreme resentment towards the opposing team and **me** disturbed even his own players.

15. The secrets between **me** and her are starting to come to light as the investigation continues.

Chapter 26: Idioms

Exercise 1:

1. I don't care about your opinion **of** me.

2. Your ability **to get** the perfect cards has caught the attention of casino surveillance.

3. The Olympic athlete was capable **of** climbing Mt. Everest.

4. The public was opposed **to** the war.

5. The children were prohibited **from** playing outside at dark.

6. Unless you comply **with** those food safety standards, we will shut you down.

7. Those who don't abide **by** the rules are often the ones who successfully innovate.

8. China is becoming an economic hegemony **over** foreign rivals who dare to compete.

9. By taking good care of pandas, zoos have succeeded **in saving** pandas from extinction.

10. I hope you are aware **of** the raccoons that are living in your basement.

11. She has lived **on** Broome street for over fifty years.

12. After the pause, they resumed **playing** football until nightfall.

13. Paralyzed, Robert couldn't help but **watch** the thief steal the car.

14. He was inclined **to accept** the new job offer, but wanted to wait.

15. The young graduate yearned **for** the days when he didn't have to worry about the bills.

Exercise 2:

1. D	9. B
2. A	10. B
3. C	11. C
4. B	12. D
5. C	13. B
6. D	14. C
7. A	15. B
8. C	

Chapter 27: Who vs. Whom

Exercise:

1. The agency recruited overseas teachers **who** would be able to demonstrate a native fluency in English.

2. At Kim's birthday party were millionaires and celebrities, some of **whom** had flown in from New York to attend.

3. Julie's math teacher was a graduate student **who**, after completing his finance degree, decided to get into teaching instead.

4. The police officers, **who** were eating donuts at the time, didn't hear the cries for help.

5. The girl **whom** Dave was matched with was unimpressed by his sense of humor.

6. Anyone **who** has read the book will say that it's much better than the movie.

7. Reflecting on all her past accomplishments, the winner thanked everyone with **whom** she had been associated.

8. Can you tell the boys **who** are at the door to go away?

9. The girls with **whom** I'm going shopping need to borrow money.

10. I want to hire those chefs **who** cooked the perfect pasta at the restaurant we ate at last week.

Chapter 28: Adverbs vs. Adjectives

Exercise:

1. The **rapidly** changing movements of the tides often catch some sea animals by surprise.

2. He's been sent to therapy three times because he acts so **impulsively**.

3. He attributed the dramatic score improvement to his incessant studying. *CORRECT*

4. I am impressed by how **clean** your dog smells.

5. The Camry runs a lot more **efficiently** than the Hummer.

6. Please listen **closely** to the words I'm about to say to you.

7. Because he drove so **carefully**, cars behind him would get impatient.

8. He threw the baseball so **quickly** that his teammate couldn't react in time to catch it.

9. You need to get some rest because you look **awful** today.

10. The iPod is the most **cleverly** designed music player to date.

11. The waiter acted so **graciously** in serving our table that we left him a huge tip.

12. The plane flew **directly** from New York to Seoul.

13. The **astonishingly** high height from which he fell only made his survival story more miraculous.

14. After I finished my final exams, I felt less **uneasy** about my grades.

15. Grammar usually comes so **naturally** to us that we don't think about it in conversation.

16. My dog walks so incredibly **awkwardly** that I no longer have the patience to take him out everyday.

Chapter 29: Comparatives vs. Superlatives

Exercise:

1. Harry Potter and Frodo Baggins both rise to the challenges in their magical worlds, but I think Frodo has **more** courage.

2. Of all the essays I've read, this one has the **best** chance of impressing admissions.

3. The raspberry pie is my favorite **among** the four of them.

4. China is not only the biggest of all the Asian countries but also the one with **the most** historical culture.

5. Of the two main types of books out there, Jose finds non-fiction to be **more** enlightening.

6. Because they're so smart and diligent, it's hard to tell which of the two frontrunners is **more** likely to be valedictorian.

7. There are no secrets **between** the the president and vice president.

32

Practice Test 1

45 Minutes—75 Questions

PASSAGE I:

A Bird Feeder in Winter

I live in a little cottage in the woods. The bird feeders, which hang from my front porch, attracts a wide array of forest birds from all different varieties. The hummingbirds of summer are some of my favorites among all the birds, with their iridescent green feathers, their whirring flight, and their harsh tweets. But I've had a harder time with the perching birds. Every time I would put out seed for them, and squirrels would take over the feeder and enjoy the food.

1. **A.** NO CHANGE
   B. attract
   C. attracting
   D. as an attraction for

2. **A.** NO CHANGE
   B. from differing varieties.
   C. from various differences.
   D. OMIT the underlined portion.

3. **A.** NO CHANGE
   B. of all the birds,
   C. of them all,
   D. OMIT the underlined portion.

4. **A.** NO CHANGE
   B. them; squirrels
   C. them, squirrels
   D. squirrels

5. The writer would like to suggest the squirrels have quite the appetite for the narrator's bird seed. Given that all the choices are true, which one best accomplishes the writer's goal?

   A. NO CHANGE
   B. eat.
   C. have a meal.
   D. devour every last kernel.

My family tried every deterrent, including rubbing Vaseline on the pole, throwing rocks at them, and to

   6

hang the feeder from a long string. Nothing seemed

   6

to work. [7]

This past winter, however, my mother-in-law

              8

sent us a squirrel-proof bird feeder. It has a wire cage around it that only small perching birds can fit through. The squirrels lost interest in our win-

  9

ter food emporium, and in their place descended a flurry of chirping, fluttering, and pecking, sending us to our bird identification guide as we watched from the living room windows.

6. **A.** NO CHANGE
    B. we hung
    C. hanging
    D. trying to hang

7. The writer is considering deleting the preceding sentence. Should the writer make this deletion?

    A. Yes, because it expresses a negative attitude that contradicts the tone of the rest of the paragraph.
    B. Yes, because it distracts the reader from the paragraph's focus on birds.
    C. No, because it foreshadows the narrator's eventual problems with the wildlife around his cottage.
    D. No, because it informs the reader of a result that is relevant to the narrator's efforts described in the paragraph.

8. **A.** NO CHANGE
    B. winter however,
    C. winter; however,
    D. winter, however

9. Which of the following alternatives to the underlined portion would NOT be acceptable?

    A. go
    B. get
    C. transfer
    D. fly

The little chickadees with their black caps most easily fit through the caged walls of the feeder. Nuthatches having larger bodies and longer beaks, [10] would drive them away, but they tentatively pecked at the seeds, keeping an eye out for bigger or more [11] aggressive birds. Though not the biggest, the sparrows certainly seemed to be some of the more assertive birds, scaring away most others when they arrived. With their short sharp beaks and striped [12] caps, we saw them hop around like military offi- [13] cers giving orders to issue commands. They puffed [14] their feathers out, making themselves look even bigger and more intimidating. The undisputed kings of the feeder, however, were the red cardinal and the tufted titmouse, with its crested heads and com- [15] manding calls. [15]

My favorite days were the snow days. We threw seeds onto the porch for the junco bird—coalblack, rotund, and poorly adapted to perching on the sides of feeders. We watched them peck about as their more colorful cousins flitted to and from the feeder above.

10. **A.** NO CHANGE
     B. Nuthatches that have
     C. Nuthatches, which have
     D. Nuthatches having had

11. **A.** NO CHANGE
     B. most
     C. many
     D. many more

12. **A.** NO CHANGE
     B. short, sharp
     C. short, sharp,
     D. sharply short

13. **A.** NO CHANGE
     B. they hopped
     C. we saw them hopping
     D. hopping

14. **A.** NO CHANGE
     B. giving orders.
     C. giving orders issuing commands.
     D. giving orders by issuing commands.

15. At this point, the writer would like to indicate that the tufted titmouse is a vicious and dangerous bird. Given that all of the choices are true, which one best accomplishes the writer's goal?

     A. NO CHANGE
     B. which pierces the skulls of other birds to claim its food.
     C. which is a fierce competitor despite its small size.
     D. a wild bird that is always on the move.

PASSAGE II:

Bach in the House

There is nothing more relaxing than listening to classical music. My favorite composer is Johann Sebastian Bach. I love to dim the lights to a lower
₁₆
brightness and lay back while I take of his mu-
₁₆   ₁₇
sic's beauty. At other times I use the music as back-
₁₇
ground noise while doing housework.

Bach's music is timeless. Even though he cre-
₁₈
ated his compositions, in the early 1700's, his music
₁₈
is still enjoyed today by many people all over the world. He had many mentors, one of whom was his
₁₉
older brother. I was surprised in learning that when
₂₀
he was a child, Johann stole work from his older brother and other classmates. It makes me wonder,
₂₁
why those young men didn't reach the level of fame
₂₁
as he did. If he stole their work, they must of been
₂₂
very talented. How much of his work is really his own and how much is a compilation of the stuff he stole?

16. **A.** NO CHANGE
    B. to a less bright level
    C. so that it's darker
    D. OMIT the underlined portion.

17. **A.** NO CHANGE
    B. take of the beauty in his music.
    C. take in the beauty of his music.
    D. take in the music of his beauty.

18. **A.** NO CHANGE
    B. He created his compositions in
    C. Having created his compositions in
    D. Even though he created his compositions in

19. **A.** NO CHANGE
    B. one of who
    C. who
    D. one

20. **A.** NO CHANGE
    B. to learn
    C. of learning
    D. learning

21. **A.** NO CHANGE
    B. wonder why
    C. wonder: why
    D. wonder why,

22. **A.** NO CHANGE
    B. must have been
    C. had been
    D. have been

[1] Bach was an important influence for other famous composers like Mozart and Beethoven. [2] He defined the baroque style and wrote extensively for the church organ. [3] He not only had a great talent for playing and composing, but also he was the reason behind a wide range of classical music that came afterwards. [4] Because of his impact, he is considered one of the founding fathers of classical music. 26

23. A. NO CHANGE
    B. the reason for
    C. the inspiration of
    D. inspired

24. Which of the following alternatives to the underlined portion would NOT be acceptable?
    A. NO CHANGE
    B. followed.
    C. later emerged.
    D. eventually established.

25. A. NO CHANGE
    B. father's of
    C. fathers' of
    D. father of

26. Upon reviewing this paragraph and realizing that some information has been left out, the writer composes the following sentence:

    Examples include the works of Brahms and Mendelssohn, who once said, "Study Bach and you will find everything."

    This sentence should most logically be placed after Sentence:
    A. 1.
    B. 2.
    C. 3.
    D. 4.

One day, I hope to be a composer as influ-
___
27
ential as Bach. When I have Bach playing in the
___   ___
27   28
background, I can let my mind drift away in the
melody and forget about the displeasure of cleaning my room or washing the dishes. Cleaning the
bathroom is my least favorite chore. 29 Even when
I'm painting or writing an essay, my work turns out
to be much more creative and interesting after I've
listened to one of Bach's violin concertos. In fact,
everything I do seems to go much smoothly when
___
30
I have Bach keeping me company and washing all
my worries away.

27. Given that all the choices are true, which one
    most effectively introduces this paragraph?
    A. NO CHANGE
    B. Bach's most famous composition is called
       "Air on the G String."
    C. Listening to Bach energizes me—not to
       compose music, but to do other things.
    D. It's hard to appreciate classical music
       without knowing about the composer's
       life.

28. Which of the following alternatives to the un-
    derlined portion would NOT be acceptable?
    A. With Bach
    B. I have Bach
    C. While Bach is
    D. Once Bach is

29. The writer is considering deleting the preced-
    ing sentence. Should the sentence be kept or
    deleted?
    A. Kept, because it provides another exam-
       ple of a chore that the narrator does not
       like to do.
    B. Kept, because it emphasizes how much
       work the narrator has to do around the
       house.
    C. Deleted, because it distracts from the fo-
       cus of the essay.
    D. Deleted, because it discusses a chore that
       is not as significant as those previously
       mentioned.

30. A. NO CHANGE
    B. smoother
    C. more smoother
    D. smooth

PASSAGE III:

Pablo Picasso

[1]

Pablo Picasso was born in 1881 in Málaga, Spain. He started showing talent as an artist at a very young age. It is rumored that his first words were "piz piz," in an attempt to say *lapiz*, which means "colored pencil." By about the age of ten, he
_____
            31
began dedication to all of his free time to drawing
       _____
              32
pictures.

[2]

Picasso was a poor student. He spent much of his school days in the calaboose, a room sent to chil-
                                        _____
                                            33
dren for misbehaving. The youngster loved being
_____
       33
sent there because it gave him more time for art. He would hide a sketch pad and a few colored pencils underneath his shirt so that he could draw scenes from his imagination the entire time he was there.

[34]

[3]

When Pablo was 14 years old, he and his family moved to Barcelona. The lad immediately enrolled in the prestigious School of Fine Art. Although
                                                _____
                                                   35
students had to be much older to be admitted, Pi-
_____
                    35
casso's extraordinary entrance exam impressed the elders so much, that they made an exception to the
          _____
             36
rule.

31. Which of the following alternatives to the underlined portion would NOT be acceptable?
    A. Around the age of ten,
    B. Approximately at the age of ten,
    C. Like the age of ten,
    D. Roughly at the age of ten,

32. A. NO CHANGE
    B. to dedicate
    C. dedication of
    D. dedicating to

33. A. NO CHANGE
    B. for misbehaving that children were sent to.
    C. for children who were sent to misbehave.
    D. children were sent to for misbehaving.

34. If the writer were to delete the preceding sentence, the paragraph would primarily lose:
    A. details that reinforce Picasso's passion for art.
    B. information that emphasizes Picasso's mischievous personality.
    C. a description of what most artists did during childhood.
    D. a transition to the next paragraph.

35. Which of the following alternatives to the underlined portion would NOT be acceptable?
    A. Although admitted students were much older,
    B. Although students were required to be much older for admission,
    C. Although the school admitted only students who were older,
    D. Although admitting only students who were older,

36. A. NO CHANGE
    B. much that
    C. much—that
    D. much; that

[4]

You would have thought Pablo would be a happy camper learning about what he loved most, but no. [37] Even though he was allowed to draw and paint, he soon found the strictness of the school and the structure of their curriculum stifling. He
                                    ——
                                    38
skipped classes and spent his days roaming around
                        ————
                        39
the city, sketching everything he saw.

[5]

Two years later Picasso moved to Madrid to study at the Royal Academy of San Fernando, how-
                                            ——————————
                                            40
ever, he found that the classroom was still no place
————
40
for him. Once again, he began missing classes to ex-plore the city. He sketched beggars, gypsies, prosti-tutes, and anyone else he saw along his travels and sold them for food.
    ————
    41

[6]

Picasso returned to Barcelona in 1899. This time he met up with a bizarre group of artists and intel-
                                            —————
                                            42
lectuals, and they all hung out at a quaint café called
——————————
42
the *Four Cats*. Picasso found great inspiration in the odd collection of anarchists and radicals who, after
                                    ————————————
                                    43
a long day, stopped by to casually chat with each
——————————
43
other.

37. The writer is considering deleting the preceding sentence. Should the writer make this deletion?

   A. Yes, because it contradicts a statement made earlier in the essay.
   B. Yes, because it is inconsistent with the style and tone of the essay.
   C. No, because it provides a transition between what the reader might expect and what actually happened.
   D. No, because it reinforces Pablo Picasso's attitude towards school.

38. A. NO CHANGE
    B. its
    C. its'
    D. it's

39. A. NO CHANGE
    B. spending
    C. spends
    D. has spent

40. A. NO CHANGE
    B. Fernando. However,
    C. Fernando, therefore,
    D. Fernando. Therefore,

41. A. NO CHANGE
    B. it
    C. these
    D. those sketches

42. Which of the following alternatives to the underlined portion would NOT be acceptable?

    A. NO CHANGE
    B. intellectuals they
    C. intellectuals; they
    D. intellectuals. They

43. A. NO CHANGE
    B. radicals, after a long day, who
    C. radicals who after a long day,
    D. radicals, who after a long day,

[7]

Picasso passed through several artistic phases in his career before breaking into Cubism. ☐44

His first real breakthrough came in 1907 when he painted *Les Demoiselles d'Avignon*, an eerie rendition of four naked prostitutes that is considered by experts to be the beginning of Cubism.

44. At this point, the writer is considering adding the following phrase to the preceding sentence (putting a comma after "Cubism"):

an art style characterized by fractured objects and geometry forms

Should the writer make this addition?

A. Yes, because it helps define a term that may be unfamiliar to the reader.
B. Yes, because it gives readers a sense of the art that was considered popular during Picasso's life.
C. No, because it distracts the reader from the main focus on the essay.
D. No, because it is not necessary to understanding the essay as a whole.

Question 45 asks about the preceding passage as a whole.

45. For the sake of the logic and coherence of this essay, Paragraph 7 should be placed:

A. where it is now.
B. after Paragraph 3.
C. after Paragraph 4.
D. after Paragraph 5.

PASSAGE IV:

The Disappearing Panda

The Giant Panda is the rarest breed of bears in the world, yet they are one of the most well-known. <u>they are</u>₄₆ With a diet consisting mostly of bamboo trees and a home high in the western mountains of China, these bears <u>don't bother anyone. They don't have any nat-</u>₄₇ ural predators, so why are they disappearing from the face of the Earth?

Extinction is a natural process that happens over the course of hundreds of thousands of years, sometimes millions of years. [48] The rapid decline in the panda population is evidence that the two main <u>causes are;</u>₄₉ hunting and habitat loss. Only a few pandas <u>fall down</u>₅₀ to poachers each year, but many are accidentally killed by hunters of other animals. Furthermore, human developments increasingly invade their <u>forests,</u>₅₁ the natural habitat of the panda gets smaller and smaller, as does the supply of bamboo.

46. A. NO CHANGE
     B. it is
     C. one is
     D. which are

47. Which of the following choices is most consistent with the style and tone of the essay?
     A. NO CHANGE
     B. aren't annoying at all.
     C. are harmless.
     D. keep it to themselves.

48. The writer is considering deleting the preceding sentence. Should this sentence be kept or deleted?
     A. Kept, because it helps provide a contrast that supports a later point.
     B. Kept, because it clarifies a term that may confuse readers.
     C. Deleted, because it is not relevant to the topic of the paragraph.
     D. Deleted, because it does not answer the question posed in the preceding paragraph.

49. A. NO CHANGE
     B. causes are
     C. causes, are
     D. causes—are

50. A. NO CHANGE
     B. fall over
     C. fall in
     D. fall victim

51. A. NO CHANGE
     B. forests, but
     C. forests, and so
     D. forests

The good news is that humans are now work-
52
ing very hard to protect the panda bears and their

home in the magnificent forests of the Yangtze

Basin. They've established systems to track existing

pandas and to look after their numbers. Therefore,
53   54
these efforts must be coupled with stricter laws if

extinction is to be prevented.

Pandas are important to these forests and the

survival of other wildlife. As they forage for food,
55
they spread the seeds of the vegetation, many types
56
flourishing in their environment, and foster its con-
56
tinued growth. The plants then support a variety

of other wildlife such as multi-colored pheasants,

dwarf blue sheep, and the golden monkey.

Pandas are also an important part of the Chi-

nese economy. As the national symbol of China,

the panda, along with its habitat, draw millions of
57
tourists to the area every year. [58] But this activity

is also part of the problem. With the increased traf-

fic, more roads and railways are created, slicing up

the beautiful forests and preventing the bears from

finding suitable mates.

52. Which choice fits most specifically with the in-
formation in this sentence?
   A. NO CHANGE
   B. nature lovers
   C. tree huggers
   D. conservationists

53. A. NO CHANGE
   B. for looking
   C. looking
   D. to be looking

54. A. NO CHANGE
   B. For example,
   C. Still,
   D. As a result,

55. A. NO CHANGE
   B. living wildlife.
   C. undomesticated wildlife.
   D. incredible wildlife.

56. A. NO CHANGE
   B. vegetation, which grows in the hotter cli-
      mates,
   C. vegetation, a mix of plants and trees not
      found in Europe,
   D. vegetation

57. A. NO CHANGE
   B. draws
   C. drew
   D. drawing

58. The writer is considering deleting the following phrase from the preceding sentence (and
revising the capitalization accordingly):

As the national symbol of China,

Should this phrase be kept or deleted?
   A. Kept, because it helps explain why pan-
      das only live in China.
   B. Kept, because it helps explain the
      panda's appeal.
   C. Deleted, because it digresses from the
      main focus on the paragraph.
   D. Deleted, because it overstates the
      panda's popularity in China.

The bears isolated from each other often die
<u>59</u>
without reproducing. Zoologists have had some success with mating bears in captivity on a small scale, but the real answer is controlling development in their habitat so that the panda bear can live and breed as nature intended. As it stands now, the
<u>60</u>
Giant Panda bear could be extinct in as little as three generations.

59. **A.** NO CHANGE
     B. bears, isolated from each other,
     C. bears; isolated from each other,
     D. bears isolated from each other,

60. Which of the following alternatives to the underlined portion would NOT be acceptable?

     A. In the current situation,
     B. If nothing changes,
     C. Under present conditions,
     D. At any moment now,

PASSAGE V:

Bumba-meu-boi

Bumba-meu-boi, a Portuguese word that
<u>that</u>
means hit-the-bull,ăis a traditional Brazilian folk
61
festival involving dance, music, and theater. The act

revolves around a bull, which represents happiness,

celebration, luck, life, and fantasy. Usually, it has the

same name <u>of</u> the city or neighborhood in which it is
62
being used. <u>An artifact made</u> with very nice cloth,
63
bright colors, and intricate illustrations, the bull is

the <u>central</u> festival symbol, but it's only one part of
64
the cultural story.

61. Which of the following alternatives to the underlined portion would be the MOST acceptable?

    A. that has the meaning of
    B. means
    C. meaning
    D. meant

62.   **A.** NO CHANGE
    B. as
    C. after
    D. from

63.   **A.** NO CHANGE
    B. Making an artifact
    C. It is an artifact made
    D. The artifact is made

64. Which of the following alternatives to the underlined portion would be the LEAST acceptable?

    A. NO CHANGE
    B. main
    C. most important
    D. middle

The tradition had arose from the social structure and economic forces in the Brazilian northeast
during the colonial period. Under a system of slav-
ery, the region grew cattle to support themselves.
Bumba-meu-boi tells the story of Chico, a slave who
is much loved by the local community, and his preg-
nant wife, Catirina. A soon-to-be father Chico constantly worries, about herself and the child. In order to satisfy his wife's pregnancy craving for ox
tongue, a delicacy, he kills the best ox on the farm.
Upon realizing that the ox is dead, the owner hunts
Chico down and sentences him to death. When the
owner returns to the farm, however, he discovers
the ox is magically reviving shamans and healers.
The owner has no choice but to pardon Chico, and
the community rejoices. As with many old tales,
there are different versions told in different commu-
nities.

65. **A.** NO CHANGE
    B. arose
    C. arised
    D. had came

66. **A.** NO CHANGE
    B. its self.
    C. itself.
    D. them.

67. **A.** NO CHANGE
    B. (Do NOT begin new paragraph) A soon-to-be father, Chico constantly worries
    C. (Begin new paragraph) A soon-to-be father, Chico constantly worries,
    D. (Begin new paragraph) A soon-to-be father, Chico constantly worries

68. **A.** NO CHANGE
    B. she and the child.
    C. her and the child.
    D. the child and herself.

69. Which of the following alternatives to the underlined portion would NOT be acceptable?

    A. While he realizes
    B. Once he realizes
    C. As soon as he realizes
    D. After he realizes

70. **A.** NO CHANGE
    B. a magical revival by the ox of shamans and healers.
    C. the reviving of shamans and healers by the magical ox.
    D. the ox is magically revived by shamans and healers.

71. Given that all of the choices are true, which one best illustrates the story's significance in Brazilian culture?

    A. NO CHANGE
    B. This story has taught generations of Brazilians about right and wrong, forgiveness, and family.
    C. Everyone in Brazil looks forward to a retelling of this story every year.
    D. This narrative is told countless times in schools all across Brazil.

In a typical performance, we can expect that
72
beautiful women dress in colorful clothing and put

on elaborate makeup. Performers in bull costumes

charge the streets as crowds circle around them.

Several groups perform pieces of traditional Brazil-
73
ian music: the orchestra, the Zabumba (drums), and

the Pindare (special instruments like pandeiros and

rattles). Street food available at these gatherings

include barbecued meat, fried pastries, and cheese
74
bread. Local vendors begin by setting up stalls

made of straw and by their preparing of food weeks
75
in advance. One of the most intriguing aspects of

the festival is: that it typically takes place outside

of churches. The event starts on June 13th and lasts

until Saint Peter's day, June 29th.

72. **A.** NO CHANGE
    B. it's expected to see
    C. one can expect
    D. OMIT the underlined portion.

73. At this point, the writer would like to reinforce the idea that Bumba-meu-boi is an exciting outdoor party. Which of the following choices best accomplishes that goal?
    A. NO CHANGE
    B. play songs from
    C. enliven the atmosphere with
    D. produce great

74. **A.** NO CHANGE
    B. includes
    C. including
    D. had included

75. **A.** NO CHANGE
    B. by preparing food
    C. by their preparing food
    D. preparing of food

Answers to Practice Test 1

Score your test using the Score Calculator at http://thecollegepanda.com

1. [B] Subject verb agreement. The verb *attract* agrees with the subject *bird feeders*.

2. [D] Redundancy. The underlined portion means the same thing as *a wide array of forest birds*.

3. [D] Redundancy. It's clear from the context that the author is talking about *forest birds*.

4. [C] The first part of the sentence (*Every time...*) is a dependent clause, which needs to be followed by an independent clause. In that case, there is no need for a semicolon or a conjunction, so **A** and **B** are out. **D** blends both the clauses in a weird way (*squirrels* can't be used for both the independent clause and the dependent clause).

5. [D] Not only is the verb *devour* more lively, but *every last kernel* shows the full specific extent of the squirrels' appetite.

6. [C] Parallelism with the *ing*'s.

7. [D] The narrator's efforts refer to all the deterrents they tried. The result is that none of them worked.

8. [A] Transitional words like *however* should be set off with commas when interrupting a sentence.

9. [C] Although *transfer* can mean to go from one place to another, it's never used to say that something *went through* something else. For example, you would never say, "He transferred through the tunnel."

10. [C] The comma after *beaks* needs another comma to pair with it. Only **C** provides that comma.

11. [A] The word *bigger* signals that the writer intends to use the comparative, not the superlative.

12. [B] The two adjectives *short* and *sharp* are coordinate adjectives that need a comma between them.

13. [B] Modifier error. The modifier *With their short, sharp beaks and striped caps* cannot be used to describe people (*we*), but birds (*they*).

14. [B] Redundancy. Giving orders is the same as issuing commands.

15. [B] Answer **B** is the one that clearly and specifically shows how vicious the bird is. All the other choices either miss the point or tell rather than show.

16. [D] Redundancy. *Dim* means the same thing as the phrases in the wrong answer choices.

17. [C] The correct expression is *take in*, which means to fully absorb or appreciate something. And it doesn't make sense to say *the music of his beauty*, which sounds like his beauty produces music, so the answer is not **D**.

18. [D] No need for a comma before the prepositional phrase *in the early 1700's*.

19. ☐A☐ *Whom* is correct because it follows the preposition *of*. Answer **C** doesn't work because *mentors* is plural whereas *his older brother* is just one person. **D** doesn't work because it produces a run-on.

20. ☐B☐ Answer **B** is the correct idiom. We need an infinitive after *surprised*.

21. ☐B☐ No comma is necessary.

22. ☐B☐ The phrase *must of been* doesn't exist. It just sounds like the correct phrase, which is *must have been*.

23. ☐D☐ Parallelism. *He not only **had**. . . , but also **inspired**. . . .*

24. ☐D☐ The word *established* is only correct if it has the helping verb *was: was eventually established*. Otherwise, it sounds like classical music established something, which is not the intended meaning.

25. ☐A☐ No apostrophe is needed because *fathers* is not possessing anything.

26. ☐C☐ The given sentence gives examples of the *wide range of classical music that came afterwards* (Sentence 3). Note that we wouldn't place it after Sentence 1, which specifically mentions Mozart and Beethoven, NOT Brahms or Mendelssohn.

27. ☐C☐ The paragraph brings up some of the narrator's activities—cleaning his room, washing dishes, painting, writing essays—that are made easier by Bach's music in the background.

28. ☐B☐ Answer **B** produces a run-on sentence.

29. ☐C☐ Although the narrator brings up chores he has to do, it's important to relate that back to the main focus (Bach's music) and not drift off. The fact that cleaning the bathroom is the narrator's least favorite chore has nothing to do with Bach.

30. ☐B☐ *Smoothly* is an adverb, which doesn't belong here. We need a simple comparative. *More smoother* is redundant with both the *more* and the *-er* ending.

31. ☐C☐ The word *like* makes it sound like Picasso is being compared to an age. A nonsensical comparison.

32. ☐B☐ The correct phrasing is to say either *began dedicating* or *began to dedicate*. However, answer **D** adds the awkward preposition *to*.

33. ☐D☐ The incorrect answer choices all change the meaning to something ridiculous. For example, answer **B** makes it sound like the room's purpose was for misbehaving.

34. ☐A☐ Although the reader can extrapolate that Picasso was a mischievous child, the primary point is that he had a passion for art, which is indicated explicitly in the second sentence of the paragraph.

35. ☐D☐ Answer **D** produces a modifier error.

36. ☐B☐ A comma is almost never needed before the word *that*. In this case, *so much that* should not be interrupted by any punctuation.

37. ☐B☐ The given sentence is way too conversational, especially the *happy camper* and the *but no*.

38. ☐B☐ Possessive pronoun that needs to refer to *school*, which is singular.

39. |A| The sentence is in the past tense, so the main verbs should be kept in the past tense.

40. |B| Choices **A** and **C** are run-ons because transitions words cannot act as conjunctions. The new sentence should start with the correct transition, which is *however*.

41. |D| The pronoun *them* has no clear reference in the sentence—what's *them*?—so we must define it.

42. |B| Choice **B** produces a run-on.

43. |A| Remember that commas are used to separate intervening phrases, but the sentence should still make sense when those intervening phrases are taken out. Here, the intervening phrase is *after a long day*. If we take that out, we get . . . *radicals who stopped by to casually chat . . .*, which is grammatically fine. If you repeat this process with answer **D**, you'll see that the remaining sentence is grammatically incorrect. Answer **C** is wrong because the comma isn't paired up. Answer **A** is wrong because it separates the *who* from the noun it's supposed to modify, *radicals*. In fact, it makes it seem like *day* is a person.

44. |A| The given phrase helps the reader understand what *Cubism* is. It's especially important because it's the focus of the paragraph.

45. |A| Paragraph 7 brings up the year 1907. Paragraph 6 brings up 1899. Based on chronological order, Paragraph 7 should stay where it is now.

46. |B| *The Giant Panda* is singular, so we need to refer to it with *it*.

47. |C| The incorrect answer choices are all too informal in tone.

48. |A| The slow process of extinction should be placed side by side with the rapid decline of the panda to make the narrator's point that there must be human factors at play: hunting and habitat loss.

49. |B| Don't separate the subject and verb with unnecessary punctuation.

50. |D| The narrator would like to say that pandas die from poachers who hunt them, meaning pandas *fall victim* to poachers.

51. |C| The run-on needs to be corrected with the correct conjunction: *and* followed by *so* to signal cause and effect.

52. |D| *Conservationists* is the most specific word and fits perfectly within the context of protecting nature and animals.

53. |A| Parallelism. **to track** . . . *and* **to look** . . .

54. |C| The narrator is saying that despite the current efforts, more must be done. The correct transition here is *still*.

55. |A| The incorrect answer choices are unnecessarily wordy.

56. |D| The incorrect answer choices add information that is irrelevant to the focus of the essay.

57. |B| The subject *the panda* is singular so we need the singular verb *draws*. Don't be fooled by the comma phrase *along with its habitat*. It is separated off by commas and does not count towards the subject.

58. $\boxed{B}$ The fact that the panda is the national symbol of China can help explain why it's such a well-known attraction.

59. $\boxed{B}$ The phrase *isolated from each other* is an intervening phrase that should be set off by a pair of commas.

60. $\boxed{D}$ *At any moment now* makes it sound like the Giant Panda's impending extinction is not yet a real possibility.

61. $\boxed{C}$ Choice **A** is unnecessarily wordy. Choice **B** inappropriately puts another main verb in the sentence. Choice **D** is in the wrong tense.

62. $\boxed{B}$ The correct phrasing is *same...as*, as in *this is the same as that*. Therefore, the correct preposition is *as*.

63. $\boxed{A}$ Choices **C** and **D** produce run-ons. Choice **B** produces a modifer that makes it sound like the bull is making an artifact.

64. $\boxed{D}$ Choice **D** has a different meaning than the other choices.

65. $\boxed{B}$ The past participle form of *arise* is *had arisen*, not *had arose*, and *arised* is not a word. Similarly, the past participle form of *come* is *had come*, not *had came*. Answer **B** is simple past and is the only one that's grammatically correct.

66. $\boxed{C}$ The pronoun *itself* refers to *the region*, which is singular.

67. $\boxed{B}$ A new paragraph should not be started because the previous sentence introduces the story, which we're now in the middle of.

68. $\boxed{C}$ The objective pronoun case is needed here to refer to the wife and child.

69. $\boxed{A}$ Answer **A** makes it sound like the owner hunts Chico down while he realizes that the ox is dead, but the two obviously cannot occur at the same time.

70. $\boxed{D}$ The incorrect answer choices all have ridiculous meanings in the context of the story. For example, answer **A** makes it sound like the dead ox is reviving shamans and healers when it should be the other way around.

71. $\boxed{B}$ Choice **B** is the most specific and shows how the story has impacted Brazil. The other choices just suggest how popular the story is.

72. $\boxed{D}$ The extra phrase is not necessary and makes the sentence awkward.

73. $\boxed{C}$ The incorrect choices are very generic and don't suggest a festive vibe.

74. $\boxed{B}$ Subject verb agreement. The singular subject *street food* should be paired with the singular verb *includes*.

75. $\boxed{B}$ Parallelism. ***By setting up stalls...and by preparing food...***

33

Practice Test 2

45 Minutes—75 Questions

PASSAGE I:

Sushi

An ancient emperor once enjoyed a special dessert so much that he kept it a royal secret until Marco Polo, who was the first European to record his travels in China and took the dessert to Italy.

<u>1</u>

That delicious dessert was ice cream. This fact may come as a surprise since many people think Chinese

<u>2</u>

food tends to be associated with chop suey rather than the creators of the ice cream. What's ironic is

<u>3</u>

that chop suey didn't even originate in China, but in Chinese restaurants in America that wanted to cater to Western tastes.

1. **A.** NO CHANGE
   B. China, took
   C. China, taking
   D. China, and had taken

2. **A.** NO CHANGE
   B. the common misconception is that
   C. it's widely known that
   D. OMIT the underlined portion.

3. **A.** NO CHANGE
   B. making ice cream.
   C. the invention of ice cream.
   D. ice cream.

Just as ice cream was invented in one place be-
<u>   </u>
                    4
fore <u>their rise</u> in popularity elsewhere, the sushi that
        5

Japan is famous for was first created in Southeast

Asia and then spread to Southern China before it

was introduced in Japan. The original type of sushi,

called "nigiri," <u>are</u> typically made by hand. <u>Some-</u>
                  6   7

<u>one</u> takes a small amount of vinegared rice and
 7

presses <u>these</u> into a round shape. Sliced raw fish
          8

is then placed on top. ⑨ Tuna is the most widely

used fish for sushi among the Japanese, but other

kinds of seafood—salmon, lobster, eel, octopus, and

squid—are also much appreciated. Despite sushi's

<u>simplicity, but</u> it usually takes more than a year
           10

to learn how to make sushi with the proper tech-

nique.

4. **A.** NO CHANGE
    B. Though
    C. While
    D. Similarly,

5. **A.** NO CHANGE
    B. it's
    C. its
    D. OMIT the underlined portion.

6. **A.** NO CHANGE
    B. is
    C. being
    D. was

7. Which choice fits most specifically with the in-
    formation in this sentence?

    A. NO CHANGE
    B. The cook
    C. The kitchen worker
    D. Whoever's making it

8. **A.** NO CHANGE
    B. them
    C. it
    D. OMIT the underlined portion.

9. At this point, the writer is considering adding
    the following true statement:

    Raw fish is an acquired taste and may take a
    while to get used to.

    Should the writer make this addition here?

    A. Yes, because it explains why not all peo-
        ple enjoy sushi.
    B. Yes, because it encourages readers to
        keep eating sushi.
    C. No, because the focus of paragraph is
        more about making sushi than eating it.
    D. No, because it contradicts sushi's popu-
        larity, which is mentioned previously in
        the essay.

10. **A.** NO CHANGE
    B. simplicity,
    C. simplicity, and
    D. simplicity in that

In Japan, there are several different types of sushi restaurants competing with each other. Of
<u>11</u>
course, there's the convenient take-out sushi available at most fast food places. Then there are the sushi bar restaurants where diners are served by a chef at the bar or a waiter at a table. *Kaiten* sushi is a restaurant in which a revolving conveyer <u>belt that</u>
<u>12</u>
<u>goes round and round, allows</u> a customer to select
<u>12</u>
<u>their</u> own food. There are even restaurants where
<u>13</u>
one can fish for <u>your</u> own meal. The prices of sushi
<u>14</u>
<u>is</u> different depending on the quality of the fish and
<u>15</u>
the experience of the restaurant.

11. Which of the following alternatives to the underlined portion would NOT be acceptable?

    A. that compete
    B. in competition
    C. to be competitors
    D. that are competing

12.   A. NO CHANGE
    B. belt allows
    C. belt, allows
    D. belt that spins allows

13.   A. NO CHANGE
    B. there
    C. our
    D. his or her

14.   A. NO CHANGE
    B. one's
    C. his or her
    D. their

15.   A. NO CHANGE
    B. are
    C. were
    D. had been

PASSAGE II:

Dubai

The city of Dubai, located on the southeast coast of Persian Gulf in the United Arab Emirates, has turned up as one of the globally prominent cities
<u>16</u>
in the world and heavily influences significant issues <u>important</u> in the Arab world.   Regarded as
<u>17</u>
the Las Vegas of the Middle East, the city brings in tourists looking for fun, cultural attractions, and luxury. 18

Dubai's economy <u>flew into the sky</u> with the
<u>19</u>
discovery of oil, which has brought in higher and higher revenues <u>at an increasing rate</u> since 1960.
<u>20</u>
This continued boom has fostered the growth of businesses, skyscrapers, roads, and parks. Recently, however, oil reserves have been depleting <u>rapidly,</u>
<u>21</u>
thus there has been <u>a development of an interest in</u>
<u>21</u>   <u>22</u>
other areas such as tourism, real estate, financial services, and airlines.

16. **A.** NO CHANGE
    B. emerged
    C. unfolded
    D. appeared

17. **A.** NO CHANGE
    B. that have impact
    C. of great consequence
    D. OMIT the underlined portion.

18. The writer is considering deleting the following phrase from the preceding sentence (and revising the capitalization accordingly):

    Regarded as the Las Vegas of the Middle East,

    If this phrase were deleted, the sentence would primarily lose:

    A. a comparison that describes Dubai in a frame of reference that may be more familiar to readers.
    B. information that explains Dubai's high standard of living.
    C. details that clarify where Dubai is located.
    D. support for the point that the West has greatly influenced the city of Dubai.

19. Which of the following choices is most consistent with the style and tone of the essay?

    A. NO CHANGE
    B. ran wild
    C. took off
    D. went crazy

20. **A.** NO CHANGE
    B. at a fast pace
    C. quite quickly
    D. OMIT the underlined portion.

21. **A.** NO CHANGE
    B. rapidly, thus,
    C. rapidly; thus,
    D. rapidly thus

22. **A.** NO CHANGE
    B. an interest in developing
    C. an interesting developing of
    D. an interested development of

Retail has become one the prime strategies of the government to ensure a constant flow of cash into the emirates. With more than 70 shopping centers, the biggest source of local jobs, the city has made retail shopping the biggest attraction to tourists. Luxury brands and local boutiques eager to capitalize on the demand, have opened multiple locations that feature the very latest offerings. Among the most popular items to shop for are designer handbags, jewelry, and shoes.

Another main attraction is the architecture. Architectural innovation and a boom in the construction industry has enabled Dubai to build some of the tallest buildings in the world. The greatest display of the city's technological capability is the Burj Khalifa, or the Khalifa Tower. The tower reflects an Islamic style of architecture and accounts for being the tallest building of the world.

23. Given that all of the choices are true, which one provides the most relevant information at this point in the essay?
   A. NO CHANGE
   B. many of which I've bought souvenirs from,
   C. which are a great way to get out of the heat,
   D. hundreds of stalls and stores at each one,

24. A. NO CHANGE
   B. boutiques,
   C. boutiques that are
   D. boutiques which,

25. A. NO CHANGE
   B. for are:
   C. are for
   D. are for,

26. A. NO CHANGE
   B. stands as
   C. rises to be
   D. measures for

One of the most recent endeavours is the city's Miracle Garden, which covers more than 72,000 square meters. The garden holds 45 million flowers and employs technology to reuse water through
27

the means of drip irrigation.
27

The airline industry has also surfaced as a fast growing sector. The International Airport in Dubai is now the fifth most busiest airport in the world.
28

29 Airlines such as Emirates and Flydubai offer a variety of flights to thousands of passengers every day. Given how the city has grown so quickly, it
30

will be exciting to see what the city looks like in a few years.

27.   A.   NO CHANGE
      B.   drip irrigation technology to reuse water.
      C.   reusable water by technology in drip irrigation.
      D.   drip irrigation to reuse water by technology.

28.   A.   NO CHANGE
      B.   most busier
      C.   busiest
      D.   busy

29.   Upon reviewing this paragraph, the writer considers deleting the preceding sentence. If the writer were to delete the sentence, the paragraph would primarily lose:

      A.   evidence supporting a previous statement.
      B.   a comment on the service of various airports.
      C.   an indication of Dubai's diverse population.
      D.   a detail that helps the reader visualize Dubai's airport.

30.   A.   NO CHANGE
      B.   in leaps and bounds,
      C.   at warp speed,
      D.   on the fast-track,

PASSAGE III:

Mark Twain

Samuel L. Clemens's pen name was Mark
Twain, using which the famous author wrote numerous novels and essays. Two of his most prominent classics in English literature are "The Adventures of Tom Sawyer" and "The Adventures of
Huckleberry Finn." His writings contain reflec-
tions on life in America and society's truths and
hypocrisies. His unique voice made him one of
the most illustrious literary icons in American history.

Sam grew up in a town by the Mississippi River
called Hannibal. The sudden demise of his father
who worked in a variety of jobs but never earned
enough for a comfortable lifestyle, left Samuel with
a tough childhood as a kid. His family didn't have
a safe place to live or a stable income. His town
was plagued by violence and suffering. In a way,
his mother was a fun loving and peaceful housewife who tried her best to provide for her kids. The
struggles that young Samuel faced had a great impact on his eventual career path.

31. **A.** NO CHANGE
    B. Clemens'
    C. Clemens, whose
    D. Clemens

32. **A.** NO CHANGE
    B. under which
    C. from which
    D. to which

33. **A.** NO CHANGE
    B. to
    C. at
    D. in

34. **A.** NO CHANGE
    B. father whom
    C. father, who
    D. father,

35. **A.** NO CHANGE
    B. when he was young.
    C. growing up.
    D. OMIT the underlined portion (ending the
    sentence with a period).

36. **A.** NO CHANGE
    B. Despite the circumstances,
    C. As a consequence,
    D. For example,

37. Which of the following alternatives to the un-
    derlined portion would NOT be acceptable?

    A. pitched into
    B. played a large role in
    C. were a major factor in
    D. were instrumental in

Sam continued schooling until he found a job

38

at 12 years old. He began working at Hannibal

Courier as an apprentice for a very nominal amount

of money. Soon after, he was editing and writing

occasional articles at the Hannibal Western Union

newspaper, which was owned by his brother. 39

There, he honed his writing skills and developed a

humorous take on the issues of the day.

38. The writer would like to indicate that Sam had no choice but to earn a living at an early age. Which of the following choices best accomplishes that goal?

  A. NO CHANGE
  B. went to work
  C. looked for employment
  D. was forced to find a source of income

39. The writer is considering deleting the following phrase from the preceding sentence (revising the capitalization accordingly):

at the Hannibal Western Union newspaper, which was owned by his brother

Should this phrase be kept or deleted?

  A. Kept, because it provides information regarding the "There" referred to in the next sentence.
  B. Kept, because it supports the point that Twain received help in starting his career.
  C. Deleted, because it distracts from the focus of the essay.
  D. Deleted, because this level of detail is not necessary for an overview of someone's life.

[1] At the time, it was impossible for a writer
<u>to become wealthy.</u> [2] In California, he created
40
<u>compositions in many different formats,</u> establish-
41
ing himself as one of the best story tellers in the nation. [3] <u>Writing</u> in a unique style of narration that
42
was friendly, funny, and yet satirical, Mark Twain's
stories gained a loyal following that <u>brought up</u>
43
his work with others. [4] His first major success
was the publication of "Jim Smiley and His Jumping Frog." [5] In 1869, "Innocents Abroad," Twain's
novel about the Mediterranean, was released to crit-
ical acclaim. [6] A year later, he married with Olivia
Langdon, the daughter of a rich coal merchant in
New York. [7] Concerned about status and the ris-
ing influence the East Coast had on the country, they
moved to Buffalo and had four children. 44

40. Given that all of the choices are true, which
of the following would most effectively introduce the main focus of this paragraph?
   A. NO CHANGE
   B. He learned a lot from the classic literature
   he read.
   C. Other writers criticized him for his un-
   structured prose and informal tone.
   D. Moving to the West marked the next part
   of his career.

41. Which choice provides the most specific and
precise information?
   A. NO CHANGE
   B. a variety of written works,
   C. diverse pieces of non-fiction,
   D. editorials, news stories, and sketches,

42. A. NO CHANGE
   B. Written
   C. By writing
   D. Having written

43. At this point, the writer would like to con-
vey how passionate Mark Twain's readers
were about his work. Which of the following
choices best accomplishes that goal?
   A. NO CHANGE
   B. discussed
   C. read through
   D. couldn't help but share

44. Upon reviewing this paragraph and realizing
that some information has been left out, the
writer composes the following sentence:

The tale about life in a mining camp made
it into newspapers and magazines all across
America.

This sentence should most logically be placed
after Sentence:
   A. 2.
   B. 3.
   C. 4.
   D. 5.

Question 45 asks about the preceding passage as a
whole.

45. Suppose the writer's goal had been to write an
essay on the commonalities of great American
authors and their work. Would this essay ful-
fill that goal?
   A. Yes, because the essay discusses Mark
   Twain's influence on future writers.
   B. Yes, because the essay describes Mark
   Twain's work, much of which is a com-
   mentary on American society.
   C. No, because the essay focuses only on
   Mark Twain and not any other authors.
   D. No, because the essay mentions only
   the differences between Mark Twain and
   other authors.

PASSAGE IV:

The Black Bear on the Porch

[1]

One spring morning my family awoke to find teeth marks and a hole bitten out of the side of a large, plastic tool bin on our porch. That same morning, our neighbors in the house across the street reported that his bird feeders had been man-
46
gled and said that it must have been a bear. We were new to the area and had no idea what to think.

[2]

My wife realized that she had stored a bag of bird seed in the damaged bin, which must have at-tracted the hungry bear. 47 The lid was secured with a lock, so it couldn't open it, and that it had bit-
48
ten a hole in the side. We didn't worry to much be-
49
cause the lock had held—the hole it had made was
50
only the size of a fist. We figure it would focus on
51
easier snacks in the future.

46. **A.** NO CHANGE
    B. street, reported
    C. street; reported
    D. street reported:

47. At this point, the writer is considering adding the following true statement:

    As omnivores, bears have a diet that consists of meat, vegetation, nuts, and insects.

    Should the writer make this addition here?

    A. Yes, because it elaborates on why the bear was drawn to the narrator's porch.
    B. Yes, because it supports the point that bears are able to eat a wide range of foods.
    C. No, because it provides information that the narrator's wife did not know at the time.
    D. No, because it distracts from the narrator's account.

48. **A.** NO CHANGE
    B. that why
    C. thats why
    D. that's why

49. **A.** NO CHANGE
    B. too much
    C. too many
    D. much too

50. Which of the following alternatives to the underlined portion would NOT be acceptable?

    A. held; the hole
    B. held, the hole
    C. held. The hole
    D. held, and the hole

51. **A.** NO CHANGE
    B. were figuring
    C. have figured
    D. figured

[3]

[1] That night, I had some friends over. [2] We were eating in the dining room when we heard a loud bump on the porch. [3] We zipped on over to the window and, sure enough, a black ball of fur $\underline{}$ 52
hovered over the tool bin. [4] It was a big one, conceivably a male recently awakened from hibernation, ravenous in its hunger for food. [5] Startled, the bear hurried back down the steps and into the woods. 55
53
54

52. **A.** NO CHANGE
    B. moved really quickly
    C. rushed
    D. made a mad dash

53. Which of the following alternatives to the underlined portion would NOT be acceptable?

    A. perhaps
    B. coincidentally
    C. possibly
    D. maybe

54. **A.** NO CHANGE
    B. ravenous
    C. hungrily ravenous
    D. ravenous and hungry

55. Upon reviewing this paragraph and realizing that some information has been left out, the writer composes the following sentence:

    One of my friends opened the door and barked like an angry dog.

    This sentence should most logically be placed after Sentence:

    A. 2.
    B. 3.
    C. 4.
    D. 5.

[4]

But the bear wasn't finished with us. Before I went to bed that night, I moved my gas grill in front of the steps, the bear had used to access the
<u>56</u>   <u>57</u>
porch. I didn't think to block the stairs on the other side. In the middle of the night, I awoke to a loud crash. Scanning the scene outside, the grill was
<u>58</u>
still in place, but a huge gap in the railings testified
<u>58</u>
to another hasty escape. Apparently, the bear had clambered up the other stairway this time but had gotten spooked again after finding its' earlier escape
<u>59</u>
route blocked.

[5]

After that incident, we kept our bird seed inside. That was the last we saw of our furry friend, but the tool bin still bears the scars of that encounter.

56. **A.** NO CHANGE
    B. steps the bear
    C. steps; the bear
    D. steps, for the bear

57. **A.** NO CHANGE
    B. access and get through to
    C. gain complete access to
    D. access and enter

58. **A.** NO CHANGE
    B. Scanning the scene outside, still in place was the grill,
    C. I scanned the scene outside to see the grill was still in place,
    D. The grill still in place, I scanned the scene outside,

59. **A.** NO CHANGE
    B. it's
    C. their
    D. its

Question 60 asks about the preceding passage as a whole.

---

60. Upon reviewing this essay and finding some information has been left out, the writer composes the following sentence incorporating that information:

We went back to investigate, checking the grill, chairs, and bins that had been displaced.

This sentence would most logically be placed after the last sentence in Paragraph:

    A. 1
    B. 2
    C. 3
    D. 4

PASSAGE V:

Chinese New Year

Chinese New Year is the biggest occasion in China. Some travel for a week across the country to arrive home, spending a few days with family before they must return for work. It's a time for family reunions, gatherings, fireworks, and plates of delicious meat; fresh from the market.

One of the biggest events is the lantern festival, which features the dragon dance as the highlight of the event. The paper lanterns that fill the streets are decorated with birds, flowers, and with Chinese characters, to commemorate the occasion.

Each new year celebrates a different animal in Chinese culture. The twelve animal signs constituting the Chinese zodiac, are much different than the horoscope signs of the Western world. The biggest difference is that instead of one sign for all the people born in the same month, each zodiac sign encompasses people born in the same year. In addition, 1988 was the year of the dragon. Since the Chinese calender works differently than our calender, it can be difficult for people born in January or February to figure out exactly which sign they were born under.

61. Which of the following alternatives to the underlined portion would NOT be acceptable?
   - **A.** home and spend
   - **B.** home, only to spend
   - **C.** home. They spend
   - **D.** home. Spending

62. **A.** NO CHANGE
   - **B.** plates, of delicious meat,
   - **C.** plates, of delicious meat
   - **D.** plates of delicious meat

63. Given that all of the choices are true, which one provides the most relevant information at this point in the essay?
   - **A.** NO CHANGE
   - **B.** the one I most look forward to.
   - **C.** which should be experienced at least once in your lifetime.
   - **D.** a stunning exhibition that celebrates the end of darkness with the invention of man-made light.

64. **A.** NO CHANGE
   - **B.** Chinese characters
   - **C.** Chinese characters,
   - **D.** with Chinese characters

65. **A.** NO CHANGE
   - **B.** signs, constituting the Chinese zodiac,
   - **C.** signs, constituting the Chinese zodiac
   - **D.** signs constituting the Chinese zodiac

66. **A.** NO CHANGE
   - **B.** On the other hand,
   - **C.** For instance,
   - **D.** Similarly,

[1] Born under the sign of the sheep, I am always on the lookout for floats or lanterns with my sign whenever I attend Chinese New Year celebrations. [67] [2] People born as sheep are considered to be compassionate and caring. [3] They don't just befriend people; they develop deep connections with
<u>68</u>
them. [4] I often wish I were a dragon. [5] The dragon is not just a sign of the zodiac, but also one of the most <u>famously recognized</u> symbols in Chinese
<u>69</u>
culture. [6] In many Chinese New Year <u>celebrations,</u>
<u>70</u>
<u>held across North America,</u> the final dragon dance
<u>70</u>
<u>that comes last</u> is held on a weekend so more people
<u>71</u>
can attend. [72]

67. The writer is considering deleting the following phrase from the preceding sentence (revising the capitalization accordingly):

Born under the sign of the sheep,

Should this phrase be kept or deleted?

   A. Kept, because it gives a sense of the narrator's personality.
   B. Kept, because it helps to explain why the narrator discusses the sheep zodiac sign later in the paragraph.
   C. Deleted, because it misleads readers into thinking Chinese New Year is mainly about animal signs.
   D. Deleted, because it repeats information mentioned previously in the essay.

68. Which of the following alternatives to the underlined portions would NOT be acceptable?

   A. people; instead, they
   B. people—they
   C. people. They
   D. people they

69. A. NO CHANGE
     B. recognizably famous
     C. famous recognition
     D. recognized

70. A. NO CHANGE
     B. celebrations held
     C. celebrations held,
     D. celebrations,

71. A. NO CHANGE
     B. at the end
     C. that closes the event
     D. OMIT the underlined portion.

72. At this point, the writer wants to add several sentences to the preceding paragraph but wants to split it into two shorter paragraphs first so that each one has a clear focus. The new paragraph should begin with Sentence:

   A. 3.
   B. 4.
   C. 5.
   D. 6.

The dragon typically consists of two parts: a menacing head with wide-open eyes, fiery face paint, and glaring teeth, and a long silk cloth lined with red and yellow scales. [73] Traditionally, it is held up by dancing young men who shake up and down one part of the dragon from beneath the body, making it look like the dragon is alive and floating through the air. It is a remarkable sight to see. I hope to experience a traditional Chinese New Year celebration in China some day, but until then I will happily attend the North American version every year.

73. The writer is considering deleting the preceding sentence. If it were deleted, the essay would primarily lose:

    A. details that help the reader picture the festival dragon.
    B. information that explains why the dragon is such a popular attraction.
    C. a description that supports the narrator's desire to be a dragon.
    D. a portrayal that is accurate only outside of China.

74. The best placement for the underlined portion would be:

    A. where it is now.
    B. after the word *dancing*.
    C. after the word *part*.
    D. after the word *dragon*.

75. Given that all the choices are true, which one most specifically and vividly describes the dragon dance?

    A. NO CHANGE
    B. The dragon moves down each street so that everyone can see.
    C. Firecrackers pop on either side as the dragon prances through the crowd to the beat of the drums.
    D. The spectators get even more excited as the colorful dragon draws near.

Answers to Practice Test 2

Score your test using the Score Calculator at http://thecollegepanda.com

1. [B] The *who* clause after *Marco Polo* must be set off with a pair of commas and what remains if that clause is taken out must still be a sentence.

2. [D] The incorrect answer choices present phrases that are redundant.

3. [D] The comparison must make sense: **chop suey** *rather than* **ice cream**. Compare food with food.

4. [A] The sentence draws a comparison between what happened with ice cream and how sushi became famous in Japan. The correct transition is *just as*.

5. [C] The singular pronoun *its* refers to the singular noun *ice cream*.

6. [B] The singular subject *original type* needs a singular verb, *is*.

7. [B] The most specific choice that fits is *cook*.

8. [C] Because *vinegared rice* is a singular noun, we need a singular pronoun to refer to it.

9. [C] Nowhere in the paragraph is eating sushi ever brought up.

10. [B] We're not connecting two independent clauses so there is no need for a conjunction. Choice **D** produces a long sentence fragment.

11. [C] Choice **C** is awkward and makes it sound like restaurants are opened for the sole purpose of competing with other ones.

12. [B] Choices **A** and **D** have redundant words since the belt is already described as a *revolving* one. Choice **C** has an unnecessary comma—don't separate the subject (*belt*) and verb (*allows*) of a clause with a comma.

13. [D] The pronoun must refer to the singular noun *customer*. Remember that *his or her* is a singular pronoun.

14. [B] The phrase *one can fish* establishes that the sentence is from *one*'s point of view. We must keep that point of view consistent.

15. [B] The plural subject *prices* must be paired with the plural verb *are*. Furthermore, the sentence is in present tense.

16. [B] No easy explanation. Choice **B** is the one that most naturally fits.

17. [D] The incorrect answer choices are repetitive because the sentence already mentions that the issues were *significant*.

18. [A] The phrase compares *Dubai* with *Las Vegas* to help the reader understand Dubai as a city in the context of the Middle East.

19. $\boxed{C}$ The incorrect choices are too informal.

20. $\boxed{D}$ The incorrect choices are repetitive because they offer phrases that mean the same as *higher and higher.*

21. $\boxed{C}$ The word *thus* cannot act as a conjunction. Therefore, a semicolon is needed to start a new independent clause.

22. $\boxed{B}$ Choice **B** is the most natural phrasing. Choice **D**, for example, makes it sound like *development* is *interested* in something, as if *development* were a person.

23. $\boxed{D}$ The sentence emphasizes how big shopping is in Dubai. The choice that supports that point is **D**.

24. $\boxed{B}$ A comma is necessary to pair up with the comma later on in the sentence. Choice **D** produces a sentence fragment (remove the intervening comma phrase starting with *eager* to see this more clearly).

25. $\boxed{A}$ *Shop for* is the idiomatic phrase—you shop **for** something. That's why the *for* should come before *are.* No colon is necessary after the main verb. Remember that a colon must be preceded by an independent clause.

26. $\boxed{B}$ Choice **B** is the most natural phrasing.

27. $\boxed{B}$ The incorrect answer choices are too wordy.

28. $\boxed{C}$ We just need a superlative here. *Most busiest* is redundant because *most* serves the same function as the *-est* ending.

29. $\boxed{A}$ The sentence under consideration adds to the point that Dubai's airline industry is a fast growing sector.

30. $\boxed{A}$ The incorrect answer choices are too informal.

31. $\boxed{A}$ Add an apostrophe-*s* after everything that's singular and possessive.

32. $\boxed{B}$ You write novels *under* a certain name.

33. $\boxed{A}$ The preposition *on* is idiomatically correct.

34. $\boxed{C}$ A comma is necessary to pair up with the comma that closes the clause later on in the sentence.

35. $\boxed{D}$ The wrong answer choices are repetitive because *childhood* already implies that Mark Twain was a kid at the time.

36. $\boxed{B}$ Previous sentences state what a tough upbringing Mark Twain had. His mother, however, wasn't weighed down by her surroundings. The correct transition is *Despite those circumstances.*

37. $\boxed{A}$ Answer **A** is too informal.

38. $\boxed{D}$ The key word is *forced.* That's what makes answer **D** the correct one.

39. $\boxed{A}$ Without the given phrase, we wouldn't know what place *there* refers to in the next sentence.

40. [D] The previous paragraphs talk about Mark Twain's early career in Hannibal, which is by the Mississippi River. This paragraph shifts to California. Therefore, the correct choice is **D**.

41. [D] Choice **D** lists out exactly the types of things he wrote. Therefore, it's the most specific.

42. [B] We're dealing with a modifier that describes *Mark Twain's stories*. The only way to setup this modifier so that it makes sense is to start it with *written*. The other choices make it sound like the stories themselves did some writing.

43. [D] Choice **D** makes it sound like they were so passionate, they had no choice but to share his work.

44. [C] The given sentence describes a book. Therefore, it should be placed after Sentence 4, which brings up "Jim Smiley and His Jumping Frog." Note that it shouldn't be placed after Sentence 5 because "Innocents Abroad" is already described as a novel about the Mediterranean.

45. [C] You can't write about commonalities between authors if only one author is brought up.

46. [A] No need for punctuation to interrupt the main verb *reported*.

47. [D] A sentence about a bear's diet is excessive here. Keep the focus on the story.

48. [D] Answer **A** doesn't give us the independent clause we're expecting after the comma. We need an apostrophe for the contraction of *that is*.

49. [B] The correct word is *too*. As a side note, we use *much* when we're dealing with something we can't count and *many* when we're dealing with something that we can.

50. [B] Answer **B** produces a run-on.

51. [D] The story is told in the past tense.

52. [C] The incorrect choices are too informal or wordy/stale (as in the case of **B**).

53. [B] Choice **B** does not express the same meaning as the other choices.

54. [B] *Ravenous* means very hungry, so it's redundant to use both words in the same phrase.

55. [C] In the story, it only makes sense that the given sentence is placed before Sentence 5, which starts off with the bear being startled. Startled by what? The given sentence answers that. Before Sentence 5 = After Sentence 4. Furthermore, the bear must be introduced before the friend barks like an angry dog. Otherwise, there's no reason for the friend to do that.

56. [B] In choices **C** and **D**, an independent clause isn't produced such that a semicolon or a conjunction would be required. Because *the bear had used to access the porch* describes *steps* in a restrictive way, a comma is not needed in between.

57. [A] The incorrect answers are all repetitive and wordy. For example, *get through to* means the same thing as *access*.

58. [C] Answers **A** and **B** suffer from modifier errors. Answer **D** puts the components in an illogical order. The narrator must scan the scene outside before he sees that the grill is still in place.

59. [D] The correct possessive pronoun referring to the singular *bear* is *its*.

60. [A] In the first paragraph, the narrator and his wife are trying to figure out what happened on the porch. In the second paragraph, the wife has a realization. The given sentence fits best between paragraphs 1 and 2 because it makes the *investigation* more explicit.

61. [D] Answer **D** produces a sentence fragment starting with *Spending*.

62. [D] No need for commas to set off prepositional phrases in this case.

63. [D] The most relevant piece of information would describe what the lantern festival is. Answer **D** is the one that does that.

64. [B] Parallelism. No need to repeat the *with* at the start of the series. If it were to be repeated, every element in the series should have it (*with birds, with flowers, and with Chinese characters*).

65. [D] No need to separate *constituting the Chinese zodiac* off with commas since it describes the *animal signs* in a restrictive way.

66. [C] Read the previous sentence. Now, the sentence containing the transition is providing an example of one animal sign pertaining to an entire year.

67. [B] If the phrase were left out, the reader might be confused about why the sign of the sheep is abruptly brought up later on.

68. [D] Answer **D** produces a run-on.

69. [D] The meanings of *famous* and *recognized* overlap so there is no need to have both words in the same phrase.

70. [B] The phrase *held across North America* describes *celebrations* in a restrictive way, so there is no need to set it off with commas in choice **A**. Nor is there a need to separate a prepositional phrase off with a comma as in choices **C** and **D**. The comma after *America* is necessary to separate the independent clause from the leading non-essential portion of the sentence (*In many Chinese New Year celebrations held across North America*).

71. [D] The word *final* is all that's necessary. The incorrect answer choices just repeat the same meaning.

72. [B] The paragraph abruptly shifts to the sign of the dragon at Sentence 4, which is where the paragraph break should happen.

73. [A] The sentence's purpose is to describe the dragon in great detail.

74. [D] Answer **A** is awkward because it interrupts the verb and direct object, *shake* and what they're shaking. Answer **B** is not the best placement because *men* is already being described by *dancing* and *young*. Adding *up and down* overloads those adjectives. It's the equivalent of saying *dancing slowly young men*. Doesn't sound natural. Answer **C** is not a good placement because it interrupts two words that go together: *part* and *of*. The phrase *up and down of the dragon* would be awkward. The answer is **D** because it's natural sounding and it doesn't split up any words that typically follow one another.

75. [C] Answer **C** offers the most detail and vivid description.

34

Practice Test 3

45 Minutes—75 Questions

PASSAGE I:

Attack of the Yellow Jackets

We were playing pirates in the backyard when an unexpected enemy attacked. We had built a clubhouse <u>at the edge of the woods</u> in the lower
₁
branches of a magnolia tree and were pretending it was a ship we were attacking. <u>James and my-</u>
₂
<u>self</u> climbed the ladder of 2' x 4' <u>scraps nailed</u> to the
₂   ₃
trunk and then threw a knotted rope over the other side for Teddy to climb, just as real pirates <u>would of</u>
₄
<u>done.</u>
₄

1. The best placement for the underlined portion would be:
   - A. where it is now.
   - B. after the word *built*.
   - C. after the word *branches*.
   - D. after the word *tree*.

2. A. NO CHANGE
   B. James and me
   C. James and I
   D. James and mine

3. A. NO CHANGE
   B. scraps, nailed
   C. scraps nailed,
   D. scraps: nailed

4. A. NO CHANGE
   B. will have done.
   C. would have done.
   D. would have did.

261

Everything was going fine until Teddy's foot slipped into a hole in the side of the tree just as he was <u>close</u> to climb onto the "ship." None of
₅
us had noticed the little yellow-and-black-striped wasps that had been buzzing around that hole. It turns <u>out that: yellow jackets</u> like to build their pa-
₆
pery nests in the <u>kinds of</u> places kids play in—in
₇
holes in the lawn, under thick bushes, and inside hollow trees like this magnolia.

We were leaning over the <u>edge: pulling</u> the rope
₈
when it happened. The swarm looked like a dusty cloud <u>revolving</u> around Teddy's leg. We froze, and
₉
the buzzing filled our ears. Then we screamed, flailed our arms, and half fell, half climbed out of the tree. We <u>shot</u> across the yard and leapt onto the front
₁₀
porch. Unfortunately, when yellow jackets swarm, <u>they lock onto their targets and pursue them,</u> at-
₁₁
tracted by the frantic motion. Our attackers followed us <u>in our direction</u> all the way home, darting
₁₂
towards us viciously as we tried to escape.

5. **A.** NO CHANGE
   B. almost
   C. nearly
   D. about

6. **A.** NO CHANGE
   B. out that yellow jackets
   C. out that yellow jackets,
   D. out, that yellow jackets

7. Which of the following alternatives to the underlined portion would NOT be acceptable?
   A. types of
   B. various
   C. forms of
   D. sorts of

8. **A.** NO CHANGE
   B. edge, pulling
   C. edge. Pulling
   D. edge we pulled

9. At this point, the writer would like to convey that the swarm attack was fast and unexpected. Which of the following choices best accomplishes that goal?
   A. NO CHANGE
   B. hovering
   C. exploding
   D. moving

10. At this point, the writer would like to convey a sense of fear and urgency. Which of the following choices is LEAST effective in accomplishing that goal?
    A. NO CHANGE
    B. proceeded
    C. dashed
    D. fled

11. **A.** NO CHANGE
    B. it locks onto their targets and pursues them,
    C. it locks onto its target and pursues them,
    D. they lock onto its target and pursue it,

12. **A.** NO CHANGE
    B. along the same way
    C. towards our house
    D. OMIT the underlined portion.

Inside, the stings continued as we each found at least five of the little demons attached to our clothes. <u>Obviously,</u> others were perched on our bare arms
13
and legs and repeatedly jabbing their stingers into our skin. Yellow jackets, unlike bees, do not die after stinging their victims. Once we'd killed all the invaders, my mom <u>attending</u> our wounds. The sting
14
count was eight for James, ten for me, and thirteen for Teddy. The next day, we <u>continued to nurse our</u>
15
<u>wounds with ice and skin ointment.</u>
15

13. A. NO CHANGE
    B. After all,
    C. Even worse,
    D. Fortunately,

14. A. NO CHANGE
    B. attended with
    C. attended to
    D. attended along

15. Given all of the following choices are true, which choice would best tie the conclusion of this essay to its opening paragraph?

    A. NO CHANGE
    B. bragged to our friends about the encounter we had survived.
    C. were pirates again, this time armed with wasp spray instead of cutlasses.
    D. made sure to look outside for yellow jackets before we stepped outside.

PASSAGE II:

Fixing Up an Old House

My first house which was a Victorian built in
_____
16
1904, had its own unique charm. I loved its sturdi-

ness and the way it hearkened back to another cen-

tury. It was tall and narrow with awnings above

the windows, a heavy, solid bannister that curved
_____
17
down the stairs, and even a stained glass window

inside! Next door was its duplicate clone, a house
_____
18
built in 1908 using the same blueprint.

[1] The house was in good shape overall, but

when you own a house that's more than one hun-
_____
19
dred years old is going to require some repairs. [2]

Over time, paint dries out and starts to crack and
_____
20
peel, which lets in moisture and causes wood to rot.
_____
21
[3] Inside the house, pipes eventually deteriorate as

well, causing damaging leaks. [4] At some point,

the foundation settles, leaving cracks in the walls.

22

16. **A.** NO CHANGE
    B. house was
    C. house,
    D. house

17. **A.** NO CHANGE
    B. heavy solid
    C. heavy solid,
    D. heavy, solid,

18. **A.** NO CHANGE
    B. twin,
    C. look-alike copy,
    D. double replica,

19. **A.** NO CHANGE
    B. when owning a house
    C. because a house
    D. a house

20. **A.** NO CHANGE
    B. start
    C. started
    D. had started

21. Which of the following alternatives to the underlined portion would NOT be acceptable?
    A. peel; this
    B. peel this
    C. peel. This
    D. peel, a condition that

22. The writer is considering removing the phrases "Over time" from sentence 2, "eventually" from sentence 3, and "At some point" from sentence 4 (revising capitalization and punctuation accordingly). If the writer were to make these deletions, the paragraph would primarily lose:
    A. an emphasis on how exhausting fixing an aging house can be.
    B. the sense that a gradual process is taking place.
    C. details that point to the difficulty of knowing when a house will need repairs.
    D. information that helps establish the time and place of the narrative.

My favorite repair involved one of the windows. I noticed a soft fissure under some peeling paint in one corner. Gravity draws water down onto window sills, and if the paint has any cracks in it, the water will just sit there and cause even more damage, rather than dripping down or evaporating. [23] I had hoped I could have fixed it with
24
some caulk and paint, but the wood was too soft. As I dug out the rotting wood, the gaping hole grew and grew. I began to wonder where I'd find a piece
25
of wood to replace the window sill, which in the old days would have been built with a thicker and broader piece of wood than the ones found in stores today. At my local home improvement store, a 2' x 4' is really a 1.5' x 3.5', and this thinner quality applies to all sizes of wood. [26]

23. At this point, the writer is considering deleting the preceding sentence. If it were deleted, the paragraph would primarily lose:

   A. scientific research on the properties of certain elements.
   B. an important suggestion that the narrator lives in a rainy town.
   C. an illustration that allows the reader to visualize what the narrator's window looked like.
   D. details that elaborate on why the window needed to be repaired.

24. At this point, the writer would like to express that the narrator wanted to do the minimal amount of work possible. Which of the following choices best accomplishes that goal?

   A. NO CHANGE
   B. patched it
   C. gotten by
   D. finished up

25. A. NO CHANGE
   B. wonder: where
   C. wonder, where
   D. wonder; where

26. The writer is considering deleting the preceding sentence. If it were deleted, the essay would primarily lose:

   A. information that explains why wood is cut differently than it was in the past.
   B. a description of the wood that the narrator needed.
   C. an example that helps the reader understand a generalization.
   D. an opinion regarding the practices of false advertising.

Having looked for so long, I almost gave up
<u>27</u>
and placed a custom order for the wood. My neigh-
27

bor had renovated his house previously and had an

old door step <u>that</u> was exactly the right thickness
28
and even had an angled edge that matched the edge

of my window sill. (The angle helps water flow off

the sill properly.) All I had to do was remove the old

piece, cut the new one to the right width and shape,

and stick it in place. It was almost as if the neigh-

boring house had become a <u>bodyguard.</u>
29

27. Given that all of the following choices are true, which one would most effectively introduce the topic of this paragraph?
  A. NO CHANGE
  B. I called up every hardware store in the state to see what was available.
  C. I typically run into my neighbor when he's out walking the dog in the morning.
  D. After quite the search, the house next door came to the rescue.

28. A. NO CHANGE
  B. and which
  C. and
  D. OMIT the underlined portion.

29. Which choice fits most specifically with the information in this paragraph?
  A. NO CHANGE
  B. an organ donor.
  C. a manager.
  D. a doctor.

Question 30 asks about the preceding passage as a whole.

30. Suppose the writer's goal had been to write an essay on how to fix up old Victorian houses. Would this essay fulfill that goal?

  A. Yes, because the essay discusses the struggles the narrator faced in repairing his own Victorian.
  B. Yes, because the essay describes some characteristics of Victorian houses.
  C. No, because the essay focuses on one problem that was particular to the narrator's house.
  D. No, because the essay mentions that Victorians are too difficult to fix alone.

PASSAGE III:

Clippers

Not far down the river Thames, a few miles from the capital of London, in a specially built dry dock, <u>rests</u> one of the last ships from a bye-gone
31
maritime era. Considered the most famous clipper of all time, she is named after the witch in the <u>poem
32
Tam-o-Shanter</u> Robert Burn's gothic tale of drunken
32
Scots and haunted churches.

The ship is the *Cutty Sark*. Take one glance at her smooth, flowing lines and her towering masts, bedecked with bleached white canvas, <u>it is obvi-
33
ous</u> why she is regarded as a thoroughbred of the seas.

Like the other clipper ships of that era, she was <u>exceeded in being fast.</u> The main use was to quickly
34
transport goods <u>from place to place</u> in and out of
35
the country. ☐36 These ships stole the imagination of a thrilled nation <u>and</u> marvelled at their record-
37
breaking speeds.

31. A. NO CHANGE
    B. rest
    C. resting
    D. takes a rest

32. A. NO CHANGE
    B. poem, *Tam-o-Shanter*
    C. poem *Tam-o-Shanter*;
    D. poem *Tam-o-Shanter*,

33. A. NO CHANGE
    B. which is
    C. and it's
    D. and its

34. A. NO CHANGE
    B. exceeding fast.
    C. exceededly fast.
    D. exceedingly fast.

35. A. NO CHANGE
    B. to different areas
    C. from one location to another
    D. OMIT the underlined portion.

36. At this point, the writer is considering adding the following true statement:

    Built to lightweight standards, clippers take their name from their ability to "clip" days off the journey time taken by lesser vessels.

    Should the writer make this addition here?

    A. Yes, because it supports the point that clippers were amazingly fast ships at the time.
    B. Yes, because it clarifies a possible point of confusion.
    C. No, because it repeats information found previously in the passage.
    D. No, because it abruptly shifts the focus of the paragraph.

37. A. NO CHANGE
    B. that
    C. which,
    D. who

Clippers developed out of a maritime "arms-race" of sorts, in what was a unique set of economic
 <u>   </u>
                          38
circumstances at the time. Tea was quickly replacing <u>beer as,</u> the national drink of England, and the
      <u>   </u>
          39
tea came mostly from China. Buyers were desperate to be the first to try a new variety of tea arriving in port from overseas, and so the ships that could deliver their cargo the fastest could charge the highest prices.   40   <u>Merchants's</u> investments were increasingly put towards building the sleekest ships to compete with one another.

38. A. NO CHANGE
     B. were
     C. is
     D. OMIT the underlined portion.

39. A. NO CHANGE
     B. beer, as
     C. beer as
     D. beer with

40. Which of the following phrases from the preceding sentence is LEAST necessary and could therefore be deleted?

     A. to be the first
     B. a new variety of
     C. from overseas
     D. the fastest

41. A. NO CHANGE
     B. Merchant's
     C. Merchants'
     D. Merchants

268

When the British government repealed the
<u>42</u>
British Navigation Acts and previously inaccessible
<u>42</u>
tracts of the global marketplace opened up to foreign traders. Suddenly, merchants in the United States and all over Europe were free to compete with British businessmen on level <u>terms; they</u> wasted no
<u>43</u>
time in building even faster ships to capitalize <u>off of</u>
<u>44</u>
the situation. Soon, the ships of Great Britain were no longer the envy of the world. They were still admired, but their aura of invincibility had gone. The golden age of the British vessel was over; the new age of the steam ship was just around the corner.

45

42. **A.** NO CHANGE
    B. government, repealed the British Navigation Acts
    C. government, repealed the British Navigation Acts,
    D. government repealed the British Navigation Acts,

43. Which of the following alternatives to the underlined portion would NOT be acceptable?

    A. terms. They
    B. terms, and they
    C. terms and
    D. terms, they

44. **A.** NO CHANGE
    B. on
    C. in
    D. from

45. The writer is considering deleting the following clause from the preceding sentence (revising punctuation accordingly):

    the new age of the steam ship was just around the corner

    If this clause were deleted, the essay would primarily lose:

    A. information that gives a sense of the length of time British ships dominated the seas.
    B. an indication of what overthrew the clipper ships of Britain.
    C. a metaphor for the economic downfall of Britain and the rise of the United States.
    D. nothing at all; this information is irrelevant to the essay.

PASSAGE IV:

The Cycle of Life

Summer is a time for long country walks, picnics, and ball games in the open meadow. But if you stop, listen, and look a little closer, you'll realize you are not <u>alone by yourself.</u> The fields are buzzing
<u>   </u>
             46
with the natural world—honeybees gathering nectar for winter reserves, butterflies mating and <u>pos-</u>
                                                    47
<u>sibly lay</u> eggs, caterpillars crawling out for the first
47
time. The cycle of life continues every day.

But life is fragile for <u>creatures</u> everywhere, and
                        48
many species face the continual threat of extinction. The swallowtail butterfly uses <u>its</u> cunning camou-
                                    49
flage to hide from predators, but predators aren't the only <u>danger; the</u> onward expansion of farmland
              50
and urban developments are destroying breeding sites, and the loss of this native breed is a very real <u>deal.</u>
51

46. **A.** NO CHANGE
    B. alone.
    C. alone as one.
    D. unaccompanied alone.

47. **A.** NO CHANGE
    B. to lay
    C. laying
    D. they might lay

48. Which of the following choices fits most specifically with the first two paragraphs of the essay?
    A. NO CHANGE
    B. bees
    C. insects
    D. small animals

49. **A.** NO CHANGE
    B. they're
    C. their
    D. it's

50. **A.** NO CHANGE
    B. danger, the
    C. danger the
    D. danger while

51. **A.** NO CHANGE
    B. chance.
    C. likelihood.
    D. possibility.

Bird life flourishes, in both the meadows, and
52
the towns, the creatures having adapted more suc-

cessfully to the spread of man's advances into the

countryside. Sparrows are abundant around the

sprawling farmsteads, and as you're lucky, you
53
might just spot the Italian variety with its white

cheeks and distinctive beak. Those with keen ears

might also hear the skylark, its high-pitched song

soaring over the trees, whose leaves are colorful in
54
autumn.
54

52. **A.** NO CHANGE
    B. flourishes in, both the meadows,
    C. flourishes in both the meadows,
    D. flourishes in both the meadows

53. **A.** NO CHANGE
    B. if
    C. whether
    D. as if

54. **A.** NO CHANGE
    B. trees with multi-colored autumn leaves.
    C. the colorful leaves of autumn trees.
    D. trees.

Many bird varieties can be found on the ground too. The quail is known to hide in dense foliage but <u>can be harried out of the meadow grass to be seen</u>
₅₅
dancing over the low brush in little bursts of <u>short</u>
₅₆
<u>time intervals of intense flying.</u> This game bird can
₅₆
<u>be distinguished as a consequence of</u> its sandy color
₅₇
and its "quik-ik-ik" call.

If the butterflies or the flying birds prove too elusive for you, <u>then, keep your eyes peeled,</u> for an-
₅₈
other meadow resident—the humble spider. Look for glistening webs in the morning dew or the frantic shimmering of its captured prey. [59] If you wait long enough, you might glimpse the gruesome spectacle of the spider immobilizing an unfortunate <u>fly, plunging</u> its poisoned fangs into the insect's
₆₀
body. You'll realize nature is beautiful, but also cruel. It's that cycle of life again, continuing on its merry way.

55. Which of the following alternatives to the underlined portion would NOT be acceptable?

   A. Known to hide in dense foliage, the quail can

   B. The quail, known to hide in dense foliage, but can

   C. The quail, which hides in dense foliage, can

   D. The quail, which is known to hide in dense foliage, can

56.   A. NO CHANGE
     B. intensity of flight.
     C. flying in brief intensity.
     D. intense flying.

57.   A. NO CHANGE
     B. set apart as a result of
     C. identified by
     D. recognized by way of

58.   A. NO CHANGE
     B. then keep your eyes peeled
     C. then keep your eyes peeled,
     D. then, keep your eyes, peeled

59. At this point, the writer is considering deleting the following phrase from the preceding sentence (ending the sentence with a period):

in the morning dew or the frantic shimmering of its captured prey

If this phrase were deleted, the essay would primarily lose:

   A. a sense of how dangerous the spider can be.

   B. details that help the reader spot the spider.

   C. information that distracts from the focus of the paragraph.

   D. an indication of where the narrator is located.

60. Which of the following alternatives to the underlined portion would NOT be acceptable?

   A. fly so it can plunge
   B. fly to plunge
   C. fly and plunging
   D. fly that plunges

PASSAGE V:

Michelangelo

Upon completing the Sistine Chapel, Michelangelo underwent a period of great despair. Florence of that time was enmeshed in political rivalries, and despite Michelangelo's desire to work independently on the burial chamber of Pope Julius II, he himself <u>got swept up</u> in the affairs and machi-

61

nations of state. After Julius died in <u>1513 and</u>

62

<u>Rome</u> fell to Charles V, and Pope Clement VII, who

62

succeeded Julius, was locked away, and Michelangelo's patrons, the Medicis, were expelled from Florence.

Florence once again reverted to a republic, but instead of following the Medicis into exile, <u>he re-</u>

63

<u>mained where Michelangelo was.</u> <u>A quiet and shy</u>

63   64

<u>person,</u> he soon changed his mind and went to

64

Venice but returned to Florence again not long after. <u>Sadly for Michelangelo,</u> the political situation

65

had changed in Florence; the republic had fallen, Pope Clement VII and the Medicis had returned to power, and Michelangelo was forced to go into hiding.

61. At this point, the writer would like to reinforce the idea that Michelangelo didn't intend to get involved in political issues. Which of the following choices best accomplishes that goal?

  A. NO CHANGE
  B. meddled
  C. took part
  D. played a role

62. A. NO CHANGE
  B. 1513, Rome
  C. 1513 Rome
  D. 1513: Rome

63. A. NO CHANGE
  B. he was where Michelangelo remained.
  C. Michelangelo was where he remained.
  D. Michelangelo remained where he was.

64. Given that all of the choices are true, which one is most consistent with the information that follows in this sentence?

  A. NO CHANGE
  B. Impulsive as always,
  C. Finding inspiration everywhere,
  D. Never accepting work below his standards,

65. A. NO CHANGE
  B. Michelangelo, who was sad
  C. Sadder than Michelangelo,
  D. Michelangelo, sad

Because of his reputation as a great artist, Michelangelo was eventually pardoning and re-suming work for the Medicis. During this period, he spent time in the craft of the tomb of Lorenzo de Medici. He would never finish the project during his lifetime, but scholars still acknowledge it as one of their finest pieces ever. His sculpture of Lorenzo seeks to capture the inner personality of the dark, pensive, and brooding man. Indeed, Lorenzo's nickname, "The Thoughtful One," wasn't given to him with no justification being there.

66. **A.** NO CHANGE
    B. pardoned and resuming working
    C. pardoned and resumed to work
    D. pardoned and resumed work

67. **A.** NO CHANGE
    B. crafting
    C. for craft—
    D. to be crafting

68. **A.** NO CHANGE
    B. lifetime, and
    C. lifetime because
    D. lifetime, so

69. **A.** NO CHANGE
    B. its
    C. his
    D. those

70. **A.** NO CHANGE
    B. seeking to capture
    C. seeks to capturing
    D. capturing

71. **A.** NO CHANGE
    B. without them having a reason.
    C. for no reason.
    D. on an absent basis.

Later, in 1534, when Michelangelo was nearly 60 years old, Paul III became Pope, he traveled to Rome and began working on arguably his most famous painting, *The Last Judgment*. During this time, he met Vittoria Colonna, whom he held feelings for even after her death.

Vittoria had a great impact on Michelangelo. [74] This was reflected in his choice of subject matter for two of his last pieces–the *Crucifixion of St. Peter* and the *Conversion of St. Paul*. Michelangelo depicts Paul as an old and suffering man, perhaps, suggesting his own state of mind during that time.

72. **A.** NO CHANGE
B. old; Paul III
C. old and Paul III
D. old, Paul III, who

73. **A.** NO CHANGE
B. who
C. to which
D. as

74. At this point, the writer is considering adding the following true statement:

She inspired him to grow a deep and renewed interest in the divine.

Should the writer make this addition here?

A. Yes, because it provides a summary of the life of Michelangelo's wife.
B. Yes, because it develops a previous statement in more detail.
C. No, because it shifts the focus of the paragraph.
D. No, because the essay does not say whether Michelangelo was religious or not.

75. **A.** NO CHANGE
B. man perhaps,
C. man perhaps
D. man, perhaps

Answers to Practice Test 3

Score your test using the Score Calculator at http://thecollegepanda.com

1. $\boxed{D}$ To make this sentence the clearest it can be, place the underlined portion after *tree* so that the tree is *at the edge of the woods.* Currently, it may sound like *the woods* are *in the lower branches of a magnolia tree.* Obviously, most people wouldn't try to read it that way, but we're looking for the clearest and best placement.

2. $\boxed{C}$ We need the subjective case since we're dealing with the subject: *James and I.*

3. $\boxed{A}$ The phrase *nailed to the trunk* restrictively describes *scraps* so there is no need for commas (or any other punctuation).

4. $\boxed{C}$ The phrase *would of done* is nonsensical. It just sounds like the correct answer, *would have done.* Answer **B** is in the wrong tense.

5. $\boxed{D}$ The incorrect answer choices are unidiomatic and unnatural. For example, **A** would only work if it read *close to climbing....*

6. $\boxed{B}$ An independent clause must precede a colon. Very rarely does a comma ever precede the word *that.*

7. $\boxed{C}$ Answer **C** is just unnatural sounding and unidiomatic.

8. $\boxed{B}$ No need for a colon in the case where we have a describing phrase at the end. Answer **C** produces a sentence fragment. Answer **D** produces a run-on.

9. $\boxed{C}$ Of the choices, only **C** has the connotation of being fast and unexpected.

10. $\boxed{B}$ Of the choices, only **B**, *proceeded,* has the connotation of moving slowly and deliberately, which is the opposite of what the narrator intends to express.

11. $\boxed{A}$ This is a question of pronoun case. Because *yellow jackets* is plural, all pronouns should be plural.

12. $\boxed{D}$ Redundancy. The phrases *followed us* and *all the way home* are enough.

13. $\boxed{C}$ The sentence only expresses more pain and suffering. Because it adds on to the situation described in the previous sentence, the correct transition is *even worse.*

14. $\boxed{C}$ Answer **A** is a sentence fragment. *Attended to* is the correct idiom.

15. $\boxed{C}$ The opening paragraph discusses the game of pirates being played. Answer **C** is the only one that makes that reference.

16. $\boxed{C}$ A comma is needed to pair up with the one later on.

17. $\boxed{A}$ Coordinate adjectives require a comma between them.

18. $\boxed{B}$ Answer **B** is the only one that's not redundant.

19. ☐D☐ Answers **B** and **C** produce long sentence fragments. Answer **A** is too wordy and introduces a shift in point of view that's not necessary.

20. ☐A☐ The singular subject *paint* requires the singular verb *starts*. Furthermore, we're in the present tense, so **C** and **D** are out.

21. ☐B☐ Answer **B** produces a run-on sentence.

22. ☐B☐ All the phrases the writer is considering removing are timing words that imply a wait.

23. ☐D☐ The information adds a sense of urgency and makes explicit the damage that will happen if the window is left unfixed.

24. ☐C☐ Choice **C**, *gotten by*, has the connotation of just squeezing by with the bare minimum.

25. ☐A☐ No punctuation is necessary. The colon is not introducing a list or building up to a dramatic phrase. We're not connecting two independent clauses so there's no need for a semicolon. A comma is unnecessary because we're not introducing an intervening phrase.

26. ☐C☐ This sentence is one example of the generalization the narrator describes in the previous sentence— pieces of wood used to be sold thicker and broader.

27. ☐D☐ The best lead into the second sentence of this paragraph, which describes borrowing from the neighbor's house, is **D**.

28. ☐A☐ The phrase *exactly the right thickness* describes the *old door step* so we must use *that* to make that relationship.

29. ☐B☐ The narrator borrowed something from the neighbor's house, making the neighbor's house most like an organ donor.

30. ☐C☐ The narrator discusses only one repair and it's never mentioned whether the problem he fixed is specific to Victorian houses.

31. ☐A☐ The singular subject *one (of the last ships)* needs the singular verb *rests*. Answer **C** results in a sentence fragment.

32. ☐D☐ Following *Tam-o-Shanter* is a noun phrase that describes the poem. These phrases need to be set off with commas. Note that *Tam-o-Shanter* itself does not need to be set off with commas because it restrictively modifies *the poem*.

33. ☐C☐ We need the conjunction *and* to prevent a run-on. We need an apostrophe for the contraction of *it is*.

34. ☐D☐ Because *exceedingly* is an adverb (modifying the adjective *fast*), the *-ly* ending is necessary. By the way, *exceedingly* means extremely or especially. In choice **C**, *exceededly* is not a word.

35. ☐D☐ All the wrong answer choices repeat the meaning of *transport*.

36. ☐A☐ The entire focus of the paragraph is how fast the clippers ships were. The given statement furthers that point, so it should be added.

37. $\boxed{B}$ Using *and* makes it sound like the ships marvelled at themselves, which doesn't make sense. Answer **A** is out. Answer **C** puts the comma in the wrong place. It should go before the *which*. Answer **D** inappropriately uses *who* to modify *nation*, which isn't a person.

38. $\boxed{A}$ The subject of the verb in question is *a unique set*, which is singular. Therefore, the singular verb *was* is needed.

39. $\boxed{C}$ We're not dealing with clauses or intervening phrases. A comma is unnecessary.

40. $\boxed{C}$ *From overseas* is the LEAST necessary because *arriving in port* conveys the same meaning. Furthermore, removing it doesn't change the meaning of the sentence, whereas removing the other answer choices does.

41. $\boxed{C}$ Use the *s'* when dealing with a plural noun possessive.

42. $\boxed{D}$ Answer **A** is a long sentence fragment. Answers **B** and **C** interrupt the subject and verb with a comma. Answer **D** appropriately separates independent clause from dependent clause.

43. $\boxed{D}$ Choice **D** produces a run-on.

44. $\boxed{B}$ *Capitalize on* is the correct idiom.

45. $\boxed{B}$ Until this point, the reader has no idea what faster ships caused the decline of the clippers, something that is definitely relevant to the essay. The given clause gives the reader that information.

46. $\boxed{B}$ The wrong answer choices are redundant. For example, *alone* means the same thing as *by yourself*.

47. $\boxed{C}$ Parallelism. **mating** and **laying** *eggs*.

48. $\boxed{C}$ The first two paragraphs talk solely about insects, so that's the most specific choice.

49. $\boxed{A}$ Because *the swallowtail butterfly* is singular, the pronoun must also be singular (and possessive).

50. $\boxed{A}$ Choices **B** and **C** produce run-ons. Choice **D**'s use of *while* does not make sense in the sentence.

51. $\boxed{D}$ The wrong answer choices are all unidiomatic. For example, you don't say *is a chance*; you say *has a chance*.

52. $\boxed{D}$ No need to set off the prepositional phrase with commas.

53. $\boxed{B}$ The correct word here is *if*. The other choices don't produce the same meaning.

54. $\boxed{D}$ The wrong answer choices all give unnecessary and irrelevant information. The paragraph is about birds, not how colorful the leaves are in autumn.

55. $\boxed{B}$ Answer **B** uses the conjunction *but* when it is not called for.

56. $\boxed{D}$ Answer **A** is redundant because *little bursts* imply *short time intervals*. Answers **B** and **C** are awkward and unnecessarily wordy.

57. $\boxed{C}$ The wrong answer choices are unnecessarily wordy.

58. [B] The underlined portion is a dependent clause, not an intervening phrase. No comma is necessary besides the one after *you*.

59. [B] The given phrase provides specific details on where (*morning dew*) and what to look for (*shimmering of its captured prey*).

60. [D] Choice **D** changes the meaning of the sentence. It makes it sound like the fly is plunging its poisoned fangs into the insect's body, when it's actually the spider that does so.

61. [A] *Got swept up* is the only passive answer choice. The others are all active.

62. [B] Answer **A** produces an extremely long run-on (see if you can follow it through). Answer **C** does not provide the necessary comma to separate the initial dependent clause from the independent one. Answer **D** uses a colon, which requires an independent clause to precede it.

63. [D] Answer **D** correctly places *Michelangelo* next to the initial modifier and is in the active voice.

64. [B] The sentence discusses Michelangelo changing his mind and moving back and forth. The word to describe this behavior would be *impulsive*.

65. [A] Choices **B** and **D** produce sentence fragments. Choice **C** is a nonsensical modifier that changes the intended meaning.

66. [D] Choice **D** is parallel and uses the correct idiom (*resumed work*, not *resumed to work*).

67. [B] Choice **B** is the correct idiom. You spend time *doing* something.

68. [A] Only choice **A** uses the correct conjunction *but* to express the contrast between the two clauses.

69. [C] We're talking about Michelangelo's sculptures, not the scholars', so we have to use *his* to refer to Michelangelo.

70. [A] Choices **B** and **D** produce sentence fragments. Choice **C** does not use the correct idiom.

71. [C] The incorrect answer choices are all wordy and awkward.

72. [C] Answer **A** produces a run-on. Answer **D** produces an awkward blend of run-on/fragment. Answer **B** uses a semicolon when two independent clauses aren't being joined together (the part before the semicolon is a dependent clause).

73. [A] The preposition *for* is the key to this question. You can read it as *Vittoria Colonna,* **for whom** *he held feelings*.... After a preposition, we use *whom*.

74. [B] The additional sentence expresses *how* Vittoria impacted Michelangelo, so it develops the previous sentence.

75. [D] In this case, *perhaps* is not an intervening word like *however* might be. Instead, it modifies the suggestion, so we don't need to set it off with commas as in choice **A**. Choice **B** places *perhaps* on the wrong side of the comma, altering the meaning to suggest that perhaps Michelangelo depicted Paul as an old and suffering man, when that part is a fact. Choice **C** lacks the comma to separate the additional description from the main independent clause. The lack of a comma makes it sound like the suffering man in the painting is suggesting his own state of mind, when the writer intends to say that about Michelangelo.

Thank You!

Thank you for purchasing and reading this book. If you enjoyed it, I ask that you please leave a review on amazon. It really helps support my work. I read all of them.

If you haven't already, make sure to sign up for The College Panda newsletter at http://thecollegepanda.com

You'll also receive exclusive tips and tricks, updates, college admissions advice, inspirational stories, and resources that go far beyond the useless College Board information packets. This information is not found on the blog or anywhere else.

Don't miss out on tips that could make the difference on the SAT and in college admissions. Sign up now.

Made in the USA
Coppell, TX
19 June 2022